NEXT GOAL WINS!

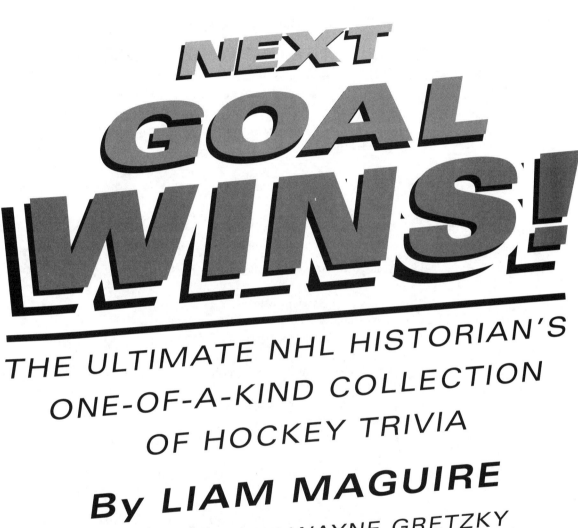

NEXT GOAL WINS!

THE ULTIMATE NHL HISTORIAN'S ONE-OF-A-KIND COLLECTION OF HOCKEY TRIVIA

By LIAM MAGUIRE

FOREWORD BY WAYNE GRETZKY

RANDOM
HOUSE
CANADA

PUBLISHED BY RANDOM HOUSE CANADA

 Published in 2012 by Random House Canada, a division of Random House of Canada Limited, Toronto. Originally published in Canada by Random House Canada in 2001. Distributed in Canada by Random House of Canada Limited.

www.randomhouse.ca

Library and Archives Canada Cataloguing in Publication

Maguire, Liam
Next goal wins! : the ultimate NHL historian's one-of-a-kind collection
of hockey legends, facts and stats / Liam Maguire.

Issued also in electronic format.

ISBN 978-0-307-36340-4

1. Hockey—Miscellanea. 2. National Hockey League—Miscellanea. I. Title.

GV847.M1855 2012 796.962 C2012-902119-9

Text and cover design by Andrew Roberts

Cover images: (Bossy and Dryden) Mecca/Hockey Hall of Fame;
(Gretzky) Steve Babineau/NHLI via Getty Images

Printed and bound in the United States of America

10 9 8 7 6 5 4 3 2 1

To my mother, Sarah Maguire, for her incredible love, patience and understanding as I follow the game of hockey through life; to my children, Rory and Shanna Maguire—where they go, I go; and to the memory of my father, Noel Patrick (Pat) Maguire: until our next pint, Dad, God bless

ACKNOWLEDGMENTS

On December 4, 1995, my father passed away. It was one of the most emotional nights of my life. That day was also the first time I met Paul Henderson. My father had been fighting cancer, and things were not going well. As a family, we knew that the end was near. However, I was scheduled to appear on *Pamela Wallin Live* with Carl Brewer and Paul Henderson. It would be my first opportunity to meet Paul, and if you've read the last chapter in this book you'll know what that must have meant to me. I agonized over what to do, but my mother, Sarah Maguire, convinced me to go. She said that's what Dad would have wanted. So I travelled down to Toronto and headed to the studio. I was scheduled to go on the show in the last block at 9:40 p.m.

In the early days of my trivia travels, I would quite often give a quick call home moments before the show started to let my folks know I had arrived and was okay. I looked at my watch at 9:31 p.m., said a prayer for my father and told him that I was soon going to meet a true Canadian hero. Moments later I was called out and I finally got to shake Paul Henderson's hand. Later that evening, I found out that my dad had passed away at 9:31 p.m. Although this book is dedicated to my family and my father, I just want to thank him again—and Paul Henderson—for being my heroes. Two men who never, ever gave up.

To my brothers and their families, Jennifer and Mike Maguire, Kiera and Mariah Maguire, Sean and Patrick Maguire, thank you all for your support, especially Spike with his timely help financially. You are always there to get that last round and then some, brother, and it's always been very much appreciated.

I would also like to thank Craig Pyette of Random House of Canada who took on this project with me late in the game. He's done an outstanding job pulling the copy out of me, as well as editing and overseeing the process, despite the fact that we were well into the third period. Thank you to the entire team at Random House who helped in this project.

On May 10, 11 and 12, 2012, I had occasion to work with Wayne Gretzky in Fort McMurray, Alberta, at a fundraiser for Keyano College. It was another in a long line of incredible opportunities for me, and born out of that were some extremely kind words from Number 99 about yours truly, which he put together for our foreword, and for that I am extremely grateful.

Finally, I'd really like to acknowledge three people who went the extra mile to help me during the rough few years after my separation. Rock Villeneuve, Ken Craig and Rodd Brown, your help to me was immeasurable. A huge thanks for your friendship and your support over the years. God willing, we've got a few miles of road to go yet. Next goal wins, fellas. Gidday.

And finally to all those people who have asked me questions over the years, to the fans of the game and the players, thank you. Let's make 2012 a hockey trivia odyssey!

CONTENTS

FOREWORD

I owe most of what I've enjoyed in life to the sport of hockey. Having had the chance to win the Stanley Cup, play for my country and compete with and against some of the greatest athletes in the world is something I will always cherish.

Equally important have been the fans, and as you can imagine, I've met many. I had the chance to formally meet Liam Maguire at a function in Fort McMurray, Alberta, in May of 2012. Liam and I were able to sit down a couple of times and talk hockey. It was one thing for him to enlighten me on how many times Jean Beliveau has his name on the Stanley Cup or how many assists Tom Barrasso had in his career or who was drafted by Philadelphia ahead of Bobby Clarke; it was another thing entirely when we discussed the minutiae of my career, such as historical data surrounding my first NHL goal, the 1851 connection, who was the goalie of record the night I scored my 500th career goal and who served the delay-of-game penalty on December 30, 1981, the night I scored my 50th in my 39th game.

Liam took a hobby, turned it into an obsession and then made a career out of it. For that I commend him. His passion for hockey and knowledge of it, specifically regarding the NHL, are second to none. All of that comes through in *Next Goal Wins!*, a must-read for fans of all ages. It shares the trivia, statistics and history of the sport as seen through his keen eyes and mind, and the result is a very comprehensive look at our game and a great read.

And by the way, the answers to those questions I mention above can be found in these pages. Enjoy!

Wayne Gretzky

INTRODUCTION

INSIDE THE WORLD OF HOCKEY trivia with Liam Maguire: To say the least, it's an unusual world. The years have flown by. It seems like only yesterday that I'd get on the school bus on a Monday morning, bound for St. Leonard's or St. Pius in the Ottawa area. Waiting patiently in the back would be Phil Byrne, ready to drill me on all the teams' leading scorers and who had accomplished what over the weekend in the NHL.

On another day at St. Pius, in Mr. Duggan's science class, I spent the better part of the 40 minutes memorizing the Hart Trophy winners from the 1930s. That's when Brian Leroux, without question the smartest kid I ever knew, taught me my first memory tip.

"The 1930s are easy, Liam. Only two cities won the Hart Trophy in that decade: Montreal and Boston. Eddie Shore was a four-time winner—1933, 1935, 1936 and 1938. Toe Blake won in 1939 for Montreal, Babe Siebert in 1937, Aurel Joliat in 1934, Howie Morenz in 1932 and 1931 and Nels Stewart in 1930 with the Montreal Maroons. Two cities, three teams, easy." This, of course, from a kid who, in high school, would ace algebra and calculus exams. And I'm not kidding, he would get 100 percent on them.

Later that year, Brian and four others were a part of a night that changed my life forever.

In September 1975, Brian, Rob Drapeau, Paul Horscroft, Chris Traynor, Andrew Marquis and I attended an exhibition game between Montreal and Chicago at the Ottawa Civic Centre. To find out who was in the lineup you had to purchase a media guide for two bucks. Nice little scam. We all bought one. I took that little booklet home that night and read it from cover to cover well into the night. Names like the aforementioned Toe Blake, Dickie Moore, Elmer Lach, Bill Durnan, George Hainsworth and many others were documented throughout, along with the current players, and there was loads of statistical information and trivia. The next day at lunch we had a little trivia contest. I happened to have retained the most, probably because I'd been reading until two in the morning, and the seed was sown.

Over the next six years, I developed an insatiable appetite for reading everything hockey related, specifically on the NHL. I took one of my many Montreal Canadiens sweaters and had the words "NHL Trivia Expert" silk-screened on the back.

Once I reached drinking age—and maybe once or twice before—my buddies and I would go into the watering holes around Ottawa, and after a couple of pints, I'd take my jacket off so patrons could read this bold statement. Inevitably the questions would soon be flying and another great hockey night would be in full swing.

This routine would alter drastically after May 21, 1981. By now I was an employee of Rideau Township, working at the Manotick Arena. I was a rink attendant—drove the Zamboni, mopped up, played lots of hockey and of course read NHL stats every single day. One day, after flooding the rink, I was lying on top of the Zamboni and listening to a call-in show on radio station CFRA. Hal Anthony was the host. He was using both phone lines to run a trivia contest, and some of the questions were hockey oriented. It was late in the show. I phoned in, and cleaned the plate of hockey questions. So he asked me to throw one out to the public for the last few minutes of the show. I asked, "What was the first year the Montreal Canadiens won the Cup?"

Although there were a number of other questions still unanswered from other subjects, the last dozen or so callers all tried to answer mine. They would guess 1914, and I'd say, "No, that was the Toronto Blueshirts." They'd guess 1917, and I'd say, "No, that was the Seattle Metropolitans." And so on. Finally, Mr. Anthony asked if I had a book in front of me and I told him I didn't. The show ended and that was that.

A couple of weeks later he ran the same type of show. I phoned in again. He asked me to contact him after the show and I did, at which point he asked me if I'd come in and be a studio guest. The date of my first appearance was May 21, 1981. I did a two-hour call-in show, my first one, and I missed seven questions in two hours.

That was 31 years ago.

Since that time I've done several thousand radio and television appearances, banquets, dinners—you name it, I've probably talked hockey trivia on it. I've been on *Hockey Night in Canada* and every national radio and TV station, been featured in countless newspaper and Internet articles, blogs and columns. All because of hockey trivia.

I've had the good fortune to emcee and perform my hockey trivia gig in every province in Canada. When I was growing up, my favourite player was Yvan Cournoyer. I speak at his golf tournament every summer. I also do Bobby Orr's in his hometown of Parry Sound. I've emceed countless Team Canada '72 Alumni events, I've worked with Bobby Hull and Don Cherry, and in May 2012, in Fort McMurray, Alberta, I did my first official gig with Wayne Gretzky. I've been very fortunate indeed.

The book you are about to read is a culmination of what makes Liam Maguire tick with regard to hockey trivia. What I do in my gigs and my personal appearances is try to give the audience the rest of the story. There's so much more behind every record, every statistic, every name and every team.

Here's an example: Wayne Gretzky scored his 500th career goal on November 22, 1986, against Vancouver, and it was into an empty net. You can find out that much in a lot of places. What you won't find is that Troy Gamble was the goalie of record for Vancouver, and that this was the only game he would play all year in the NHL.

Here's another: Rocket Richard scored his first NHL goal on November 8, 1942, and 10 years later to the day, November 8, 1952, he became the NHL's career goal-scoring leader. Gordie Howe broke the Rocket's record 11 years later almost to the day, on November 10, 1963, and it was scored shorthanded. The Red Wing in the box was serving a major penalty, the only one of his career.

He was also the first player in the NHL from Newfoundland. His name was Alex Faulkner.

Bobby Orr set the single-season goal-scoring record for a defenceman in 1969. The previous mark was 20 goals. Orr scored number 21 on his 21st birthday, March 20, 1969. The time of the goal was 19:59—one second to play in the game.

Wayne Gretzky scored his first NHL goal on October 14, 1979. The time was 18:51. Ten years later, almost to the day, on October 15, 1989, he passed Gordie Howe for career points with a goal against his former team, the Oilers. The number of career points he now had? It's 1,851.

Isn't that wild? And these coincidences happen all the time. This is what I do. I take you into the twilight zone of hockey trivia.

What you'll also get in this book is a little bit of editorial content. The year 2012 is the 40th anniversary of the Summit Series, and in the final chapter of this book I weigh in on a great travesty: the exclusion of Paul Henderson from the Hockey Hall of Fame. It was the single most important goal scored in the most defining series of hockey played in the history of the sport—and this man can't get the proper acknowledgment afforded his peers, despite a long, successful pro hockey career surrounding those 28 days in September 1972 that will stand the test of time. I look forward to any feedback on my comments or any of my questions and historical content.

On January 5, 2012, I launched a new company called Liam Maguire's Ultimate Hockey. Our goal is to become the go-to hockey portal online, and with that in mind we set out to do an exclusive interview to help launch our site. We sat down with a man who had not had a camera in front of him in more than 20 years, Alan Eagleson. If you're interested in seeing that interview, please go to www.liamaguiresultimatehockey.com and join our site. It's free, and we welcome all hockey fans.

We've all heard or used the expression, "Don't burn that bridge." Well, I've blown many bridges to kingdom come. Despite those setbacks, and through all the good times and bad, I always fall back on hockey trivia. On this subject, I take no back seat. So sit back, snap a cap and enjoy.

Liam Maguire
liam@liammaguiresultimatehockey.com

KEVIN LOWE was responsible for a number of firsts in the Edmonton Oilers' NHL history. He was their first draft choice, selected 21st overall from the Quebec Remparts. He scored their first NHL goal, on October 10, 1979, at 9:49 of the first period against Chicago Black Hawks goaltender Tony Esposito. It was the Oilers' first power-play goal. Lowe also received the team's first fighting major, taking on Chicago's Grant Mulvey in the third period of their 4–2 loss. He would win six Stanley Cups during his nineteen NHL seasons.

Denis Brodeur/NHLI via Getty Images

THIRTY TEAMS, THIRTY QUESTIONS

DURING MANY OF MY TRIVIA nights, I'm asked to throw some questions to the audience, and quite often they will request a question slanted toward a specific team. The list below contains some of my best questions pertaining to the 30 teams currently in the NHL, as well as some of the players and personnel who have been associated with them. I've arranged the teams in alphabetical order.

ANAHEIM DUCKS

What former Anaheim captain wore number 19 for Detroit before Steve Yzerman?

Randy Ladouceur. Originally signed as a free agent by Detroit, Ladouceur spent parts of five seasons in Motown before being dealt to Hartford in 1987. He was claimed by Anaheim in the 1993 expansion draft and served as captain of the Ducks in 1994–95 and 1995–96. He took over the "C" from original Ducks captain Troy Loney, who had been traded to the New York Islanders for Tom Kurvers in the summer of '94. Ladouceur retired in 1996, and Paul Kariya became the captain.

Ladouceur wore number 19 in Detroit during his rookie season, 1982–83. When Steve Yzerman became a Red Wing the next year, Ladouceur surrendered the number to him and switched to number 29. He wore that number for the rest of his tenure in Detroit and kept it during his years in Hartford and Anaheim.

BOSTON BRUINS

The 1977–78 Boston Bruins hold the NHL record for the most 20-goal scorers in one season: 11. The previous record was 10, held by two teams, the 1970–71 Boston Bruins and the 1974–75 Montreal Canadiens. The St. Louis Blues also had ten 20-goal scorers in 1980–81. What Bruins player became the record-setting 11th man, and what were the unusual circumstances surrounding his 20th goal?

The date was April 8, 1978. The Bruins were playing Toronto at Maple Leaf Gardens and they led 2–1 late in the game. Toronto coach Roger Neilson pulled goalie Mike Palmateer for an extra attacker. Bruins coach Don Cherry was fully aware that he had 10 players with 20 goals and an 11th, Bob Miller, with 19. (The players who had already broken the barrier were Peter McNab, with 41; Terry O'Reilly, 29; Bobby Schmautz and Stan Jonathan, 27; Jean Ratelle and Rick Middleton, 25; Wayne Cashman, 24; Gregg

Sheppard, with 23; Brad Park, 21; and Don Marcotte, with an even 20.)

Bob Miller scored his 20th goal into the empty Leafs net. Not an uncommon event, except that the face-off originated in the Leafs' end. Normally a coach would put his goalie back in the net prior to a draw in his team's end, but Neilson chose not to. The net stayed empty, Boston won the draw and Miller found himself with the puck—and an empty net to shoot at. You'll never get a better chance to set an NHL record. The time of the goal was 19:54 and it was assisted by Sheppard and Schmautz.

Boston lost its last game of the season the next night, 5–2 to the Islanders. Brad Park added his 22nd of the season and John Wensink popped his 16th. Wensink would have been next in line to break the 20-goal mark—however, to expect the man known as "the Animal" to score four more goals in that game would have been a bit much.

BUFFALO SABRES

Three Sabres set a rather dubious record during the 1991–92 season. Who were the players, and what was the record?

The players were Rob Ray, Gord Donnelly and Brad May. Does that give you a hint? The Buffalo Sabres are the only team in NHL history to have three players accumulate more than 300 penalty minutes each in one season. Ray was the high man with 354. Donnelly's total of 316 included 11 minutes picked up as a Winnipeg Jet. He was traded to Buffalo on October 11, 1991, and amassed a total of 305 the rest of the way with the Sabres. Brad May's total of 309 was the most impressive of the bunch, given that he was a rookie in the NHL. He fell only 11 minutes short of the rookie record set the previous season by Mike Peluso of Chicago.

CALGARY FLAMES

What Calgary player was awarded the goal when Edmonton's Steve Smith shot the puck off Grant Fuhr and into his own net during the 1986 division finals?

Perry Berezan. Berezan played nine pro seasons, including 31 career NHL playoff games in which he scored a total of four goals. None was bigger than the game- and series-winning goal against Edmonton on April 30, 1986.

With 15 minutes to play in the seventh and deciding game, Berezan rifled the puck around the boards and into the Edmonton zone. In an attempt to pass the puck over to his defence partner, Don Jackson, Smith inadvertently banked the puck off the back of goalie Grant Fuhr's skate and into his own net. He immediately collapsed to the ice in disbelief while the Flames celebrated. A short while later, it was determined that Berezan had been the last Flame to touch the puck, so he was awarded the unassisted goal. It was his only goal that playoff year. Calgary would advance to the Cup finals, where they lost to Montreal in five games.

CAROLINA HURRICANES

The Carolina Hurricanes are one of nine teams to win the Stanley Cup in the past nine seasons of NHL competition. Additionally, they are one of five teams to make at least two finals in the past ten seasons. How many players were in both of Carolina's runs to the finals, of 2002 and 2006?

Nine players won the Cup with the Hurricanes in 2006 after being with the team during the spring of 2002, when they lost the final to Detroit. They are Rod Brind'Amour, Erik Cole, Brett Hedican, Aaron Ward, Kevyn Adams, Craig Adams, Glen Wesley, Josef Vasicek and Niclas Wallin.

CHICAGO BLACKHAWKS

One of the great quirks related to NHL history is the nickname of the Chicago Blackhawks. For 60 years people had been spelling it "Black Hawks" with abandon. In 1986, someone in the front office discovered that the name had been spelled "Blackhawks" in their 1926 franchise charter. It's been that way ever since. In this book any reference to the Blackhawks prior to 1986 is spelled "Black Hawks."

Chicago owns one of the most inauspicious records in NHL history, involving shutouts. What is it?

During the 1928–29 season, the Chicago Black Hawks were shut out in eight consecutive games and a total of 20 times over the course of the season. Both are records. The streak started on February 7, 1929, with a 1–0 loss to the New York Americans. The next seven games went as follows: 1–0, three nights later in a rematch against the Americans; 1–0 to the Montreal Canadiens on February 14; 3–0 to Boston on February 17; 3–0 to the Ottawa Senators on February 21; a scoreless draw with the Detroit Cougars on February 24; a 3–0 loss to Detroit two nights later; and another 0–0 tie, this time with the New York Rangers, on February 28. The Hawks finally scored a goal on March 2, 1929, when they beat the Montreal Maroons 2–1.

The Hawks also set the all-time futility mark for goal scoring in a regular season. Their offence mustered only 33 goals in the 44-game schedule. The leading scorer for the Hawks that season amassed 13 points, including 11 goals. His name? Vic Ripley—believe it or not!

COLORADO AVALANCHE

Including their years as the Quebec Nordiques, this franchise has had four 50-goal scorers in the NHL: Jacques Richard, Michel Goulet, Joe Sakic, and Milan Hejduk. Sakic and Hejduk both reached the plateau as members of the Avalanche. The night he scored his 50th, April 1, 1996, Sakic joined an eclectic club among the 80 NHL players who have had 50-goal seasons to date. What does Sakic have in common with six other 50-goal scorers?

Joe Sakic is one of seven players whose 50th goal has been scored into an empty net. Reggie Leach of Philadelphia was the first, in 1980. Wayne Gretzky was the second, in 1981. Gretzky's was his fifth goal of the night—this was the game in which he shattered Rocket Richard and Mike Bossy's 50-in-50 record by scoring goal number 50 in his 39th game.

It would be 10 years before the next empty-net 50th goal was scored by Boston's Cam Neely in 1991. Next came Pavel Bure with Vancouver in 1994, then Sakic and Keith Tkachuk of Winnipeg, both of them in 1996. Anaheim's Teemu Selanne did it in 1997, and Pavel Bure pulled it off a second time in 2000, when he was with Florida.

COLUMBUS BLUE JACKETS

For the first time in NHL history, a rookie scored two penalty-shot goals. The first-year player was a member of the Columbus Blue Jackets. Who is he?

David Vyborny. Vyborny was born in Jihlava, in the Czech Republic. Originally an Edmonton Oiler draft pick in 1993, Vyborny was signed by the Columbus Blue Jackets as a free agent on June 8, 2000. At the age of 25, Vyborny made it under the wire as far as qualifying as a rookie in the NHL. His penalty-shot goals were recorded on October 15, 2000, against Robbie Tallas of the Chicago Blackhawks and March 19, 2001, against Tomas Vokoun of the Nashville Predators.

The last rookie to be awarded two penalty shots in one season was Pavel Bure in 1991–92—he scored on one of them.

Also of note in the Columbus Blue Jackets' inaugural year, goaltender Ron Tugnutt recorded 22 wins, breaking Cesare Maniago's mark of 21 set in 1967–68 with the Minnesota North Stars.

DALLAS STARS

Derian Hatcher became the Dallas Stars' captain during the 1994–95 season. At that time he and his brother Kevin joined a very exclusive group. What was it?

With Derian's appointment as the captain of the Stars in February 1995 he joined his brother Kevin as one of only six brother combinations to have worn the "C" in NHL history.

The Sutters lead the way, of course. Four of the six brothers wore the "C" at one point: Brian in St. Louis, Darryl in Chicago, Brent with the New York Islanders and Ron with Philadelphia. Then there were the Cleghorns (Sprague with Montreal and Odie with the Pittsburgh Pirates), the Richards (Maurice and Henri both led the Montreal Canadiens) and the Dineens (Kevin with the Philadelphia Flyers and Hartford Whalers, his brother Gord with the Ottawa Senators). Derian Hatcher's older brother Kevin was the captain of the Washington Capitals for about a season and a half. Most recently we've had the Koivus—Saku, who captained the Montreal Canadiens for ten years, including the lockout season of 2004-05, and his brother Mikko, who first wore the "C" in 2008 for the Minnesota Wild.

DETROIT RED WINGS

Paul Coffey scored 14 goals for the Detroit Red Wings in 1995–96. His 13th goal that season held great significance for the Red Wings and the NHL. What was the historical significance of that goal?

It was the game-winning goal in the Wings' 5–3 win over the Chicago Blackhawks on April 12, 1996. It was Detroit's 61st victory of the season, breaking the record of 60 set by the Montreal Canadiens in 1976–77: a standard that was thought to be insurmountable. Coffey's goal, scored in the second period, was his second of the game, and it was scored shorthanded. Bob Errey and Kris Draper assisted.

Two nights later, in the last game of the regular season, the Wings beat Dallas 5–1, and their record was 62–13–7 for 131 points: one shy of Montreal's record total in 1976–77. In terms of points, it was a quantum leap ahead of Detroit's performance in any other season. In the playoffs, they went down to defeat in the Western Conference finals against Colorado.

Oddly enough, in 1996–97, Detroit would drop 37 points in the standings, to 94, yet win the Stanley Cup that had eluded them in their record-setting year. The 1990s were a strange decade for the NHL. You can blame parity, free agency, injuries to key players, or a lack of commitment on the part of some teams to survive four gruelling rounds of the playoffs. In any event, 15 different teams made the finals between 1990 and 1999. Only twice did the regular-season champion win the Cup. Eleven teams had 100 or more points in the regular season, only to lose in the first round of playoffs.

In the next ten years of Cup play, 1999–2000 through 2009–10, the number of teams to make the final was 14. Three of the Cup winners were President's Trophy winners: Colorado in 2001, Detroit in 2002 and the Red Wings again in 2008. Interestingly, since 2002–03, the NHL has extended a very unique distinction, nine different Cup winners in the past nine years of competition:

Los Angeles in 2012, Boston in 2011, Chicago in 2010, Pittsburgh in 2009, Detroit in 2008, Anaheim in 2007, Carolina in 2006, Tampa Bay in 2004 and New Jersey in 2003.

The previous Stanley Cup record for single-time Cup winners in consecutive years was six, occurring twice in back-to-back groups of seasons, 1925–30 and 1931–36: Victoria Cougars, Montreal Maroons, Ottawa Senators, New York Rangers, Boston Bruins, and Montreal Canadiens; then Montreal Canadiens, Toronto Maple Leafs, New York Rangers, Chicago Black Hawks, Montreal Maroons, and Detroit Red Wings.

EDMONTON OILERS

A team's draft history can provide a treasure chest of trivia. The Oilers' draft record illustrates this better than most. For instance, who was their first-ever NHL draft pick, selected in 1979? What Scottish-born player did they select in 1981? Which of their first-round selections of the 1980s did not score a goal in his draft year? Who became an Oilers captain after being drafted 188th overall? In what year did they draft the first-ever player born in Brazil? In what year did they draft the first player born, raised and trained in Scotland? What first-round pick of the 1990s went on to score a Stanley Cup–winning goal? And, finally, in what year did the Oilers draft the first Swiss-born player to be selected in the first round?

Kevin Lowe, the Oilers' third GM, was their first-ever draft selection in 1979. He scored Edmonton's first NHL goal against Chicago on October 10, 1979. It was also the first power-play goal in franchise history. Brett Callighen and Wayne Gretzky assisted. Lowe also was in Edmonton's first fight, against Grant Mulvey, in the same game.

Steve Smith, born in Glasgow, Scotland, was their fifth pick, 111th overall, in 1981. Smith played on three Cup winners in Edmonton, scored the infamous goal into his own net in 1986 against Calgary, and would captain those same Flames later in his career, which ended in December 2000 due to injuries.

Jeff Beukeboom, selected 19th overall in 1983, was the first Oiler taken in a first round who had not scored a goal in his draft year. Beukeboom more than made up for that statistic. He would win a gold medal with Team Canada at the 1985 World Junior Championships, and in that same year he played in the Memorial Cup tournament for the Sault Ste. Marie Greyhounds. Beukeboom would win a total of four Stanley Cup championships in his career, three in Edmonton and his last with the New York Rangers in 1994. He retired after receiving a severe concussion in 1999.

Kelly Buchberger, drafted 188th overall in 1985, became the Oilers' ninth captain in 1995. He also was the first captain of the Atlanta Thrashers, scored the first goal in Thrashers history—in a 4–1 loss to the New Jersey Devils on October 2, 1999—and drew Atlanta's first fighting major after taking on the Devils' Lyle Odelein. Odelein would become the first-ever captain of the Columbus Blue Jackets in 2000–01. At the time of this writing, Buchberger is the third-lowest draft choice ever to become an NHL team captain. Dave Taylor was selected 210th overall in 1975 by the Los Angeles Kings, and he wore the "C" for them for four years. Dan Frawley was captain of the Pittsburgh Penguins in 1987–88, prior to Mario Lemieux. He had been chosen 204th overall in 1980 by Chicago.

Contrary to reports, Robyn Regehr, a defenceman who began his NHL career with the Calgary Flames in 1999–2000, was not the first NHL player born in Brazil. That honour belongs to goalie Mike Greenlay, drafted 189th by the Edmonton Oilers in 1986. Greenlay was born in Vitoria, Brazil. He played in the 1989 Memorial

Cup finals with the Saskatoon Blades, made the tournament's all-star team and was voted top goaltender in the tournament. Greenlay had a seven-year pro career, including two games with the Edmonton Oilers in 1989–90 and a Turner Cup championship with the Atlanta Knights of the International League in 1994.

With their last pick in 1986, Edmonton selected Tony Hand, the first player born, raised and trained in Scotland to be drafted in the NHL. Hand was a star in the British league for many years, but he couldn't crack the Edmonton lineup.

Jason Arnott, the Oilers' first selection in 1993, scored the Cup-winning goal for New Jersey in game six of the 2000 finals against Dallas. Arnott became a Devil on January 4, 1998, in a four-player deal. In 1997, the Oilers once again made history on draft day when they chose Michael Riesen, born in Oberbalm, Switzerland, with their first pick. Riesen was the first player from that country to be drafted in the first round. In 1976, the St. Louis Blues selected the first-ever Swiss-born player, a centre named Jacques Soguel, with the 121st pick overall.

Additionally, the Oilers joined exclusive company by securing a first overall selection for the third year in a row. Taylor Hall and Ryan Nugent-Hopkins, picks for 2010 and 2011 respectively, will be joined by Nail Yakupov on what Oiler fans are hoping will be a playoff contender in 2012–13 and beyond. Interestingly, the only other team to draft number one in three straight years, the Quebec Nordiques in 1989, 1990 and 1991, did not have any of those players on its Colorado Avalanche Cup-winning roster of 1996. Quebec moved to Colorado at the beginning of the 1995–96 season, and by then had traded Eric Lindros, Mats Sundin and Owen Nolan, all of whom went on at some point to play in Toronto.

FLORIDA PANTHERS

Who were the Florida Panthers playing the night the "rat craze" started, and what team were they playing against on the final night that the little varmints—most plastic, some real—rained down on Florida's ice during the 1996 playoffs?

On October 8, 1995, the Panthers were playing their first home game of the season against the Calgary Flames, having lost their season opener on the road, 4–0 against the defending Cup champion New Jersey Devils. Prior to the game, a rat made its way into the Florida dressing room. Scott Mellanby grabbed a stick and shot it across the room. It hit a wall and died. Mellanby went out and scored two goals that night, leading Florida to a 4–3 win. The feat prompted his teammates to call it a "rat trick." Once the media got hold of the story, a craze was born, and soon dozens of rats were thrown onto the ice at the Miami Arena every time a Panther scored a goal. It became quite the wild scene.

The Panthers rode the craze, and their neutral-zone trap, all the way to the 1996 Stanley Cup finals. By then it was no longer dozens but hundreds of plastic rats—and, unfortunately, still the odd real one—that cascaded from the stands for every goal. The rat mania came to an end after the game on June 10, 1996, a game four triple-overtime 1-0 shutout by the Colorado Avanlanche that completed their four game sweep of the series. During the off-season, the NHL passed a rule stating that any objects thrown on the ice that caused a delay could result in the home team being assessed a minor penalty for delay of game. For the record, the last night the critters were tossed was on June 8, during game three, a 3–2 loss to the Avalanche. Rob Niedermayer scored the final Florida goal in that game.

With the Panther success in the 2011–12 season, fans revived the "rat tossing"—celebrating each home victory by throwing plastic rats onto the ice. On April 15, 2012, the Panthers beat the New Jersey Devils 4–2 for their first playoff victory since 1997. To celebrate, the fans threw plastic rats on the ice. After game five of the series, workers at the Bank Atlantic Center collected hundreds of rats and brought them to the Pantherland gift shop for resale.

The Panthers organization alleged that some Devils fans were purchasing rats and throwing them on the ice in the hope of causing the delay-of-game penalty instituted due to this celebration in 1996–97. As a result, the sale of plastic rats was discontinued. It's unknown as of this writing if it will rain rats again in the 2012–13 season.

LOS ANGELES KINGS

One of the greatest player combinations in NHL history was the Los Angeles Kings' Triple Crown Line. Who played on that line, and what feat were they the first to accomplish?

Marcel Dionne, Dave Taylor and Charlie Simmer were the trio known as the Triple Crown Line. (In those days, the Kings' sweaters had their big crown logo on the front, hence the name of the line.) It was the first forward line in NHL history on which all three members accumulated at least 100 points in the same season.

L.A. coach Bob Berry was the one who put the threesome together during the 1978–79 season. On January 12, 1979, Simmer was recalled from Springfield of the American Hockey League and inserted on Dionne and Taylor's left wing. It was a perfect fit: Dionne was the set-up man who could also score, Simmer was the sniper and Taylor was the one who dug the puck out of the corners. In the following season, 1979–80, Dionne won the scoring crown over Wayne Gretzky. Both players had ended up with 137 points, but Dionne had scored two more goals during the season, 53 to Gretzky's 51, and so he was given the Art Ross Trophy. Dionne's linemates were also productive. Although he broke his leg late in the season, Simmer tied for the league lead in goal scoring with 56 in only 64 games. He shared the distinction with Danny Gare of the Buffalo Sabres, who appeared in 76 games, and Blaine Stoughton of the Hartford Whalers, who played in all 80. Simmer added 45 assists for 101 total points. Taylor amassed 90 points despite missing 19 games.

In 1980–81, the trio made history. Dionne led the way with 135 points, Taylor had 112—still an L.A. record for right wingers—and Simmer picked up 105. Despite their consistent scoring punch, the Kings were unable to mount any type of charge in the post-season, and they bowed out in the first round. The line stayed together until early in the 1984–85 season, when Simmer was dealt to Boston for a first-round draft pick.

MINNESOTA WILD

The same NHL club holds the record for the longest undefeated streak on home ice by an expansion team and the highest attendance by an expansion team. What team is it?

The Minnesota Wild. The Wild went 5–0–4–0 in the 2000–01 season, setting a record of nine straight home games without a loss. Their attendance record was set on March 28, 2001, with their 39th straight regular-season sellout. The Wild would sell out the two remaining home games for a combined attendance over the season of 754,472 fans and an average of 18,402.

Minnesota also set a new mark with 13 shorthanded goals, the most ever by an expansion team, and three penalty shots, tying the existing record held, coincidentally, by the Minnesota North Stars and the Washington Capitals.

MONTREAL CANADIENS

Montreal goaltender George Hainsworth holds the NHL record for most shutouts in one season: 22, set in 1928–29. How many times did the Canadiens win in those 22 games?

Your initial reaction would naturally be to suggest that they won all of them. Especially if you were studying the Habs' record that year and noticed that, coincidentally, they had 22 wins that season. But chances are you'd take a second to consider that one or two of Hainsworth's shutouts might have come in scoreless draws. That's the right line of thinking. Hainsworth and the Canadiens were involved in six 0–0 ties—incredibly, one short of the NHL record for one team: the Ottawa Senators were involved in seven scoreless ties in 1927–28. That means the Habs' record when Hainsworth chalked up a shutout was 16–0–6.

The Canadiens finished first overall that year, but they were swept in a best-of-five first-round series against the eventual Cup champions, the Boston Bruins. Ironically, Montreal was shut out in the first two games of the series by identical 1–0 scores.

Hainsworth won his third straight Vezina Trophy that year. In fact, he had won it in each of the first three years it was awarded. The trophy was presented to the league in 1926–27 to honour Georges Vezina, who passed away during the start of the 1925–26 season. One other note about Hainsworth: he was one of seven goalies to be a captain in the NHL. The others were John Ross Roach with the Toronto St. Pats, Roy Worters with the New York Americans, Alex Connell with the Ottawa Senators, Charlie Gardiner with the Chicago Black Hawks, Bill Durnan with the Montreal Canadiens and Roberto Luongo with the Vancouver Canucks. Luongo couldn't actually wear the "C," so Willie Mitchell was acting captain on the ice, and Henrik Sedin took the ceremonial face-offs required during the 2008–09 and 2009–10 seasons.

NASHVILLE PREDATORS

What former Louisiana Ice Gators rookie of the year became a part of Nashville history during the 1999–2000 season?

Rob Valicevic, who became the first Nashville Predator to score a hat trick in the regular season. The date was November 10, 1999, when Nashville beat the Chicago Blackhawks, 4–2. Valicevic scored all three of his goals in the first period. Twelve two-goal games had been recorded by Predators players in the club's first season. Valicevic's hat trick came in the 14th game of year two.

I've always loved players who battle their way up from the minors to make it in The Show. In 1996, the Louisiana Ice Gators—who play in the East Coast league, two steps below the NHL—named Valicevic their top rookie. A year later he was with the Houston Aeros of the International League, and he set a team record for goals by a rookie.

In 1997–98, his brother Chris joined him on the Aeros, and Rob put up a solid 29 goals, which led the Predators to sign the 27-year-old as a free agent in May 1998. Success has followed this guy around. Valicevic was a part of two NCAA championship teams with Lake Superior State in 1992 and 1993. The New York Islanders drafted him in 1991, but he never made the team and went the college route instead.

NEW JERSEY DEVILS

Which is the only team in NHL history to start four consecutive playoff rounds on the road and win the Stanley Cup?

The New Jersey Devils. Quite a remarkable record. The year was 1995, more commonly known as the year of the lockout. A 48-game regular season began on January 20, 1995. When it was all said and done the Devils were tied for fifth in their conference, ninth overall in the league. That's the lowest any team has ever finished and still gone on to win the Cup.

New Jersey opened the playoffs in Boston, shutting them out three times en route to winning the series in five games. They opened the Eastern Conference semifinals in Pittsburgh, losing the first game but winning the next four. The first two games of the conference finals were played in Philadelphia, and the Devils won both, then lost the next two at home before wrapping up the series in six games. In the Stanley Cup finals, New Jersey opened in Detroit against the heavily favoured Red Wings but the Devils swept the series in four straight.

This edition of the New Jersey franchise can be aptly called the road warriors. In that 1995 playoff run, they broke a league mark for road wins in one playoff year with 10. Coincidentally, in the year 2000—when they won their second championship—the Devils also rang up 10 road wins, as did the L.A. Kings in 2012. The previous record was eight, held by seven teams. Colorado did it twice. The Devils also own the NHL record for the most road wins in one regular season, 28, set in 1998–99.

NEW YORK ISLANDERS

Which team holds the all-time record for most consecutive playoff series wins? Whom did the streak start against, and whom did it end against?

That would be the New York Islanders, who in a run for the ages won 19 playoff series in a row between 1980 and 1984. A bit of background will make the streak seem all the more impressive. In 1979–80, the NHL grew, adding four teams from the WHA. The playoffs were also expanded, with 16 teams qualifying instead of 12. And first-place finishers in each of the league's four divisions would no longer earn a bye into the second round. All playoff teams would be required to win four rounds to claim the Cup. Finally, the preliminary round was extended from a best-of-three to a best-of-five series.

In 1980, the Islanders opened the playoffs with a three-games-to-one victory over Los Angeles. They followed that up with wins over Boston (in five games), Buffalo (six games) and, in the finals, Philadelphia (six games). In '81 they began their defence of the Cup with a three-game sweep of Toronto, a six-game victory over Edmonton, another sweep—this time over their crosstown rivals, the New York Rangers—and a five-game win in the finals against the Minnesota North Stars. Eight rounds and counting.

The streak was endangered in the first round of the 1982 playoffs against Pittsburgh. The Isles needed a come-from-behind overtime victory in game five. John Tonelli scored the series-winning goal. Another series against the Rangers led to another win, this time in six games. Then they swept Quebec in four and Vancouver in four for their third straight Cup championship. In 1983, they beat Washington in the first round, three games to one, then the Rangers and Boston in six games each before wrapping up Cup win number four with a sweep over Edmonton.

In 1984, the Islanders once again needed overtime in the deciding game of the opening series. And for the fourth straight year, they beat the Rangers. Ken Morrow scored the winner in game five. The Islanders then beat Washington in five games and Montreal in six before finally, after four years, one month and one week, the streak ended. Their "drive for five" (Cup wins) came to a crashing halt at the hands of the Edmonton Oilers in the Stanley Cup finals. The Oilers won that series in five games.

NEW YORK RANGERS

What team has played more games on Christmas Day than any other?

Playing on Christmas Day was a long-time NHL tradition that began in 1920 and ended in 1971. A look at the six teams that played most often on December 25—along with their records—shows that, compared to their Original Six counterparts, the New York Rangers owned Christmas Day.

	GP	W	L	T
New York Rangers	38	25	11	2
Chicago Black Hawks	37	15	14	8
Boston Bruins	36	17	17	2
Toronto Maple Leafs [including the St. Pats]	32	14	14	4
Detroit Red Wings [including the Cougars and Falcons]	26	10	13	3
Montreal Canadiens	19	8	9	2

In their first 20 Christmas Day games, the Rangers recorded 17 wins. Their record is astounding when you consider that this chart encompasses an era in which the Blueshirts actually missed the playoffs five years in a row.

The first NHL game played on Christmas Day was in 1920 between the Montreal Canadiens and the Toronto St. Patricks. Toronto won the game 5–4. The first road team to win on Christmas Day was the Chicago Black Hawks, who beat the Boston Bruins, 2–1, in 1928. On the same date, the New York Americans were officially the "road" team in their 1–0 win against the Rangers. Of course, both New York teams played their home games at Madison Square Garden.

OTTAWA SENATORS

Alexei Yashin holds the Ottawa club record for the most points in one season by a rookie, with 79. He set the mark in the Senators' second season, 1993–94. Who set the record that Yashin beat?

Darren Rumble, who had 16 points as a rookie in Ottawa's first NHL season. The 63-point difference between rookie scorers is the second-biggest jump in NHL history. In 1979–80, Pierre Lacroix scored 30 points as a Quebec Nordique. The rookie defenceman had been voted Canadian Major Junior Player of the Year in 1979. He left the NHL after four seasons, and wrapped up his pro career in France in 1993. (By the way, this Pierre Lacroix isn't the former player agent who became general manager of the Colorado Avalanche.) In 1980–81, Peter Stastny accumulated 109 points in his first NHL season—79 more than Lacroix. The 24-year-old Stastny was already a five-year veteran of the Czech league, and had played for Czechoslovakia's national team at the 1976 Canada Cup and the 1980 Olympics. However, he was deemed eligible for the Calder Trophy, and he won it.

PHILADELPHIA FLYERS

In 1979–80, the Philadelphia Flyers set the record for longest undefeated streak. How many games did it run? Whose record did they break? Which team did the streak start against? Who ended it? And through it all, which was the only NHL team they did not play?

No doubt about it, this is one of my favourite topics. The Philadelphia Flyers started the 1979–80 campaign indifferently. They won the first game of the season against the New York Islanders, 5–2, but were smoked in their second game 9–2 by a very physical Atlanta Flames squad. In the third game on their schedule, the Flyers beat the Toronto Maple Leafs, 4–3. The date was

October 14, 1979. It would be 11 weeks before their next loss.

The streak lasted 35 games, during which Philadelphia racked up 25 wins and 10 ties—and, of course, no losses. The Flyers broke the previous mark of 28 games, set by the 1977–78 Montreal Canadiens. The Habs in turn had broken a record of 23 shared by two teams, the 1940–41 Boston Bruins and the 1975–76 Philadelphia Flyers. The Flyers' record-setting 29th game was a 5–2 win over Boston at the Garden on December 22, 1979. The streak finally ended on January 7, 1980, in Minnesota, where the North Stars dealt them a 7–1 pasting.

Now, considering that Philadelphia's streak lasted 35 games, and there were 21 teams in the NHL at the time, you'd think they would have played against everybody at least once. They did—except for one team, and what's really odd is that it was a team in their division: the Washington Capitals. The Flyers' next meeting with the Caps came four games after the loss to Minnesota. When they did finally meet, Philadelphia won, 7–4.

In case you were wondering if the Flyers started another streak after the collapse against Minnesota, no, they did not. They recovered to win against Winnipeg, but that was followed by a loss to Montreal. Still, the streak was phenomenal, and by season's end it had propelled the Flyers to first place overall with 116 points. They advanced to the Stanley Cup finals, where they engaged in a great series against the New York Islanders that was decided in overtime of game six on Bobby Nystrom's winning goal at 7:11.

PHOENIX COYOTES

Who was the third coach in Phoenix Coyotes history and what unique distinction does he share among the coaching fraternity?

Bobby Francis was the third man to become coach of the Coyotes since their move to Phoenix in 1996. As of the beginning of the 2011–12 season, there had been 343 coaches in the history of the NHL. What sets Francis apart is that he and his father, legendary Rangers boss Emile Francis, form one of only four father–son combinations to coach in the league. Emile Francis coached the Rangers longer than anybody else in their history, 654 games, while racking up the most wins, 342, and the best winning percentage, .602, of any Rangers coach. Nicknamed "the Cat" from his playing days as a goaltender, the elder Francis also coached the St. Louis Blues and was a general manager of those two teams, as well as the Hartford Whalers.

The Patricks are hockey's royal family. Lester Patrick and his two sons, Murray and Lynn, all coached, and Lynn's son Craig was the GM of the Penguins for nearly 17 seasons. He's also a former New York Rangers coach and general manager. His brother Glenn is a former NHL player with St. Louis, California and Cleveland, and he coached in the AHL for four seasons and in the ECHL for three. Lester's brother Frank was a coach, and another of Lester's grandsons—one of Murray's boys, Dick Patrick—is president of the Washington Capitals.

The Wilsons are the other father–son combination that coached in the NHL. Larry coached the Detroit Red Wings in 1976–77, while his son Ron recently completed his fourth tenure as a head coach, this time with the Toronto Maple Leafs. Larry's brother Johnny was also a long-time NHL coach, putting in time behind the benches of four different teams between 1969 and 1980.

The Wilson brothers are one of nine sets of brothers to have coached in the NHL. The others include Sprague and Odie Cleghorn; the aforementioned Lester and Frank Patrick; Lester's sons Murray and Lynn; Lionel and Charlie Conacher; Frank and George Boucher; Barclay and Bob Plager; Bryan and Terry Murray; and four of the six Sutter brothers: Brian, Darryl, Duane and Brent.

Every one of the above named played in the NHL except for two men: Dick Patrick and Bryan Murray. Bobby Francis played 14 games for Detroit in 1982–83.

PITTSBURGH PENGUINS

Who scored the first playoff series–winning goal in Pittsburgh history?

Michel Briere. The Penguins missed the playoffs their first two years in the NHL, 1967–68 and 1968–69, but finally made it to the post-season in 1970. They met the Oakland Seals in the quarter-finals and swept them in four games, winning the series in overtime of game four on Briere's goal.

Briere's series-winning goal was scored at 8:28 of the first overtime period on April 12, 1970. The Penguins lost the next round, against the St. Louis Blues, in six games. That series ended on April 30. Fifteen days later, Briere was critically injured in a car accident. He died from the injuries a year and a day after he scored the series-winning goal, on April 13, 1971. His number, 21, was retired by the Penguins and no player has worn it since.

Briere had been a tremendous scorer in junior hockey, racking up 159 and 161 points in his two seasons with the Shawinigan Bruins. He was the Penguins' second pick in the 1969 amateur draft—Rick Kessell was their first choice. Kessell played a total of 135 games in the NHL, 84 of them with Pittsburgh.

ST. LOUIS BLUES

What former St. Louis Blue was the first player in NHL history to record 50 or more assists in 10 straight years?

You could guess on this one until you're blue in the face and never get it. It was Foam Lake, Saskatchewan's Bernie Federko. The run started in his third NHL season, 1978–79, when Federko notched 64 helpers that year. In the nine seasons that followed, he posted totals of 56, 73, 62, 60, 66, 73, 68, 52 and 69. If he hadn't missed 14 games in the 1988–89 season he would have made it 11, as he ended up only five assists short of 50. In 1989, he was traded to Detroit, where he racked up a decent 40 assists in his only season as a Red Wing. His number, 24, was retired by St. Louis on March 16, 1991.

Federko's record-setting 50th assist of the 1987–88 season came on February 21, 1988, in a 5–4 St. Louis victory over Mario Lemieux and the Pittsburgh Penguins. Doug Gilmour scored the goal. It was a power-play marker scored at 17:14 of the second period. Mark Hunter also drew an assist on the play. By the way, Wayne Gretzky holds the record in this unofficial category, having picked up 50 or more assists in 13 straight seasons.

SAN JOSE SHARKS

What NHL team made the biggest improvement, in terms of points, from one season to the next?

The 1993–94 San Jose Sharks. They improved by a remarkable 58 points over their 1992–93 total of 24. The other compelling statistical story for the Sharks was the change in the goals-against column, from 414—the third-highest total of all time—to 265, a difference of 149. The Quebec Nordiques of 1992–93 made the second most significant jump, when they doubled their 1991–92 point total from 52 to 104. The Winnipeg Jets are third, with a 48-point jump in 1981–82. The 1967–68 Boston Bruins improved by 40 points, good for fourth. And tied for fifth are the 1986–87 Detroit Red Wings and the 1996–97 Dallas

Stars. Both of these teams increased their totals by 38 points over the year before.

TAMPA BAY LIGHTNING

The Tampa Bay Lightning has played regular-season and playoff games in five different rinks in the state of Florida since the team's inception in 1992. How many of them can you name?

In its first season, 1992–93, the Lightning played its home games at Expo Hall. Out of 40 home dates at the 10,425-seat arena, 24 were sellouts. On December 9, 1992, the Lightning played a neutral-site game at the Miami Arena, which a year later would become the Florida Panthers' first home. Tampa lost that game, 6–5, to the New York Rangers.

In 1993–94, the team began a three-year run in a building called the ThunderDome, located in nearby St. Petersburg. Originally built as an indoor baseball stadium—a purpose it now serves as the home of the Tampa Bay Rays—the ThunderDome, now called Tropicana Field, can claim to have hosted the two largest crowds ever to see NHL hockey prior to the Heritage Classics and the Winter Classic games. Tampa's first home opener in the ThunderDome—a 2–0 loss to their cross-state rivals, the Panthers, on October 9, 1993—was played before 27,227 fans, at that time the largest crowd to see a regular-season game in the NHL. The second of the team's three home playoff dates in 1996 against the Philadelphia Flyers drew 28,183, which is still a playoff record attendance. Tampa lost that game, 4–1, and the series, in six games. In 1993–94, the Lightning also played five home games at the Orlando Arena. Its record in that five-game stretch was 1–3–1.

Rink number five, the Lightning's current home, is the Ice Palace. It opened on October 20, 1996, for a 5–2 win over the Rangers, played before a crowd of 20,543. In August 2002, the naming rights of the Ice Palace were sold, and it became known as the St. Petes Times Forum. In January 2012, the name changed to the Tampa Bay Times Forum, in keeping with the name change of the newspaper that is the title sponsor.

TORONTO MAPLE LEAFS

On February 1, 1976, Darryl Sittler of the Toronto Maple Leafs scored a record 10 points in an 11–4 victory over the Boston Bruins. There are a series of questions arising from that famous night. What were Sittler's goal and assist totals? Who was the Boston goalie? Who was the backup goalie, and why didn't he play? Who scored the lone Toronto goal on which Sittler did not get a point?

Darryl Sittler had six goals and four assists in a remarkable offensive outburst. The Saturday-night game was number 13,529 in NHL history. In all those games, no one had ever had such a night, and nobody since then has been as prolific. The Boston goalie was Dave Reece. It was the 14th NHL game of his career—all of them with Boston that year—and it would be his last. After the contest, he was shipped out to the Springfield Indians of the American Hockey League. Reece's record in Boston that year was 7–5–2 with two shutouts. Borje Salming, Bobby Schmautz and Jean Ratelle recorded the next highest point totals that night with four each. Salming had two goals and two assists for the Leafs, Schmautz had one goal and three assists and Ratelle had two goals and two assists, including his 350th career marker. The time of Sittler's record-breaking point, 9:27, is part of an interesting string of coincidences with the numbers 2 and 7, 27 of course being Darryl's sweater number. The game was played between the second-place Bruins against the seventh-place Leafs. It started at 8:07 and ended at 10:27. As mentioned, Sittler's record-breaking point, his ninth, was a goal scored at 9:27 of the third period, and the six goals in total gave Sittler 27 on the season.

The backup goalie who stayed on the bench throughout the whole debacle was none other than Hall of Famer Gerry Cheevers. He had just returned to Boston from a three-and-a-half-year stint with Cleveland in the WHA and had yet to make his first start. Bruins coach Don Cherry did not want to put him in the shooting gallery, so it was up to Reece to weather the storm.

Sittler had 10 points, but the Leafs scored 11 goals, which raises the question, who scored the goal on which Sittler didn't get a point? The answer is George Ferguson, who scored at 11:40 of the second period, assisted by Inge Hammarstrom and Scott Garland. Toronto had 21 shots on goal in the second period, scoring six times. In all, the Leafs had 40 shots on goal, while Leaf goaltender Wayne Thomas faced 32.

Sittler's big night topped the NHL's previous single-game mark by two points. Rocket Richard and Bert Olmstead had each had eight-point games for the Montreal Canadiens, in 1944 and 1954 respectively.

One other player, a Bruin, achieved a milestone on Sittler's big night. Johnny Bucyk had a goal and an assist, giving him a career total of 1,283 points and moving him ahead of Detroit's Alex Delvecchio into second place on the all-time list. Only Gordie Howe had scored more career points in the NHL at that time. Thirty-six years later Bucyk, sits in a respectable 24th spot with a total of 1,369 points.

VANCOUVER CANUCKS

Only one team in the history of the NHL has scored two penalty-shot goals in the same game. What is the team, who were the players, and who was it against?

The date was February 11, 1982. In a game against the Detroit Red Wings, referee Kerry Fraser awarded two penalty shots to the Canucks, both of them in the third period. Thomas Gradin scored on the first one. Ivan Hlinka scored on the second, with 30 seconds left in the game, to tie the score at four.

The Detroit goalie was Gilles Gilbert. Gilbert might want to avoid going out on February 11. Eleven years earlier to the day, on February 11, 1971, he was the losing goalie for the Minnesota North Stars in a game against the Montreal Canadiens. The score was 6–2. Scoring a hat trick for Montreal that night was Jean Beliveau. The three goals were numbers 498, 499 and 500 in Beliveau's career.

WASHINGTON CAPITALS

The record books all contain data detailing the fastest goals by a rookie. But nobody lists the fastest point by a rookie, which in fact came three seconds quicker than the fastest goal. Who accomplished this feat?

In his first NHL game, Bobby Carpenter of the Washington Capitals assisted on a goal 12 seconds into the first period against the Buffalo Sabres. Ryan Walter scored the goal. Washington lost the game, 5–3. Carpenter and teammate Chris Valentine, a fellow rookie, went on to set the Washington rookie record for points in a season with 67.

The fastest goal by a rookie was scored by Gus Bodnar of the Toronto Maple Leafs, 15 seconds into a game against the New York Rangers on October 30, 1943. Toronto won, 5–2.

WINNIPEG JETS

After a sixteen-year absence, the Winnipeg Jets made a triumphant return to the NHL in 2011. Some of their firsts will be documented elsewhere in

the book, but their coach has some notoriety arising from his time as a player in the 1970s. Any idea what that relates to?

Claude Noel was a graduate of the Kitchener Rangers when he signed as a free agent with a minor-league hockey franchise called the Buffalo Norsemen. The Norsemen played in the North American Hockey League, which famously was the league that the movie *Slap Shot* was based on, specifically on the season during which Noel played. One incident that receives a fair amount of attention in the movie was the re-enactment of a pre-game brawl. The teams involved in real life were Noel's Buffalo Norsemen and the Johnstown Jets. Playing at that time for the Jets was current NHL coach Bruce Boudreau. Both of these current NHL coaches skated in the on-ice re-enactment of this scene, which depicted the minor-league life of many of the players at that time. Noel would play briefly in the NHL, seven games for the Washington Capitals, wearing sweater numbers 20 and 23 during the 1979–80 season.

WAYNE GRETZKY hoisted the Stanley Cup in 1984, 1985, 1987 and 1988. With 894 goals, 1963 assists, 2757 points plus another 382 playoff points, he was the greatest offensive force in sports history. If one statistic makes my case, it's this: for six straight seasons, starting in 1981-82, Gretzky finished 65 or more points ahead of the NHL's second-place scorer. Those runners-up were Mike Bossy, Peter Stastny, Paul Coffey, Jari Kurri, Mario Lemieux and Kurri again; Gretzky led them by 65, 72, 79, 73, 74 and 75 points.

Bruce Bennett Studios/ Getty Images

2

STANLEY CUP ANECDOTES

THE STANLEY CUP IS THE ultimate goal of every hockey player and every National Hockey League team. Originally purchased for the equivalent of $48.67, the Cup was first awarded in 1893 to the Montreal Amateur Athletic Association. The man who initiated this tremendous tradition, Sir Frederick Arthur Stanley—a.k.a. Lord Stanley of Preston, the 16th Earl of Derby—witnessed numerous hockey games during his stay in Ottawa as Canada's governor general. His sons had become accomplished hockey players on a team called the Rideau Rebels. Taken with their enthusiasm, Lord Stanley bought the silver mug and called it the "Dominion Hockey Challenge Cup," although it became known soon enough as the Stanley Cup. It's interesting to note that Stanley never saw a game in which teams competed for his trophy; he went home to England in the summer of 1893 and never returned to Canada.

In this chapter, you'll find some of my favourite Stanley Cup anecdotes, covering the NHL years from 1918 until 2012. I've tried to avoid duplicating material found in the NHL's *Official Guide and Record Book*, although in some cases the record or statistic has proven to be too compelling to overlook.

1918 (March 30)
Winner: Toronto Arenas
Cup-winning goal scorer: Corbett Denneny
Opponent: Vancouver Millionaires
Score of final game: 2–1. Toronto won the best-of-five series, three games to two.

The Arenas became the first NHL team to win the Stanley Cup. Their opponents, the Vancouver Millionaires, were the winners of the PCHA (Pacific Coast Hockey Association) playoffs. From 1918 until 1926, as many as three leagues in Canada competed for the Cup: the NHL, the PCHA (from 1918–1924) and the WCHL (Western Canadian Hockey League, shortened to the Western Hockey League in its final season) from 1921–1926. Winning a league championship only gave a team the right to take a step further down the Stanley Cup trail.

In 1918, Toronto beat the Montreal Canadiens in the NHL final, winning a two-game, total-goals series by an aggregate score of 10–7. Scoring his first professional goal in game one was Toronto's Jack Adams, who beat the equally legendary Montreal goaltender, Georges Vezina.

The Arenas went on to host Vancouver in the Stanley Cup final. The PCHA was still playing seven-man hockey, while the NHL had switched to the six-man game we know today. (The WCHL also played six-man hockey.) It was agreed that, whenever a PCHA team was involved, the teams would alternate between six and seven players. Toronto won games one, three and five of this series, played with "eastern" rules, while Vancouver won games two and four with the seventh man.

1919 (March 30)
Winner: None. This was the first of two times in NHL—or Stanley Cup—history that no champion was declared.
Opponents: Seattle Metropolitans and Montreal Canadiens
Score of final game: The score of the fifth and final game, played just before the series was cancelled, was 4–3 Montreal.

The teams were tied at 2–2–1 when the finals were called due to the Spanish influenza epidemic. Game four was a scoreless draw—the rule in those days was that teams played 20 minutes of sudden-death overtime, and if the game was still not decided it was declared a tie. Thus, what had started out as a best-of-five series would have to be extended. A sixth game was scheduled to be played on April 1, 1919.

With four of his nine players ill, Montreal manager George Kennedy requested to finish the series using substitute players from Victoria, but Seattle declined and the series was abandoned. "Bad" Joe Hall of the Habs died of influenza on April 5. This remains the only time events outside the league kept the Cup from being awarded.

There was some talk that Seattle might take the Cup, considering that they'd scored more goals than Montreal in the five games that had been played, but PCHA president Frank Patrick, along with Seattle vice president J.F. Douglas and director C.W. Lester, declined to accept the trophy on those terms. Another suggestion offered, this time by the NHL, was that Montreal, having beaten the defending Cup champs—the Toronto Arenas—should be awarded the Cup. However, this idea was rejected as well.

1920 (April 1)
Winner: Ottawa Senators
Cup-winning goal scorer: Jack Darragh
Opponent: Seattle Metropolitans
Score of final game: 6–1. Ottawa won the best-of-five series, three games to two.

The Metropolitans were the PCHA champs, having beaten the Vancouver Millionaires in the western playoffs. Just as the rules alternated from game to game, the location of the Stanley Cup finals rotated each year between east and west. This year it was the NHL champion's turn to play host. However, bad ice forced a move from Ottawa to Toronto's Mutual Street Arena—where artificial ice was available—for games four and five.

This was also the only year in which a Cup finalist had to change its uniforms. It was decided that Seattle's red, white and green striped jerseys resembled Ottawa's red, white and black too closely, so the Senators graciously agreed to play in white sweaters. Jack Darragh scored a hat trick in the fifth and final game.

1921 (April 4)
Winner: Ottawa Senators
Cup-winning goal scorer: Jack Darragh
Opponent: Vancouver Millionaires
Score of final game: 2–1. Ottawa won the best-of-five series, three games to two.

En route to the Cup finals, Ottawa beat the Toronto St. Patricks to move on to play against the Vancouver Millionaires. The 1921 NHL playoffs produced a number of interesting firsts. For the first time, brothers played against each other in the NHL playoffs—Ottawa's Cy Denneny faced his brother Corbett of Toronto. The first hat trick by a defenceman in NHL playoff history was recorded on March 10, 1921, when the Senators' George Boucher scored three times to pace his team to a 5–0 win in the first game of a two-game, total-goals series.

Sprague Cleghorn had played almost the whole season with Toronto, but Ottawa picked him up for the trip out west after their victory over the St. Pats. This practice, commonly known as picking up a "ringer" or replacement player, was in place until 1925. If a team lost a starter to injury, it could fill the spot with another player from its respective league. The extra player was allowed to play most times, although not always. In this case, the move gave Ottawa a defence of Cleghorn and Eddie Gerard, arguably the toughest blueline twosome in NHL history.

In Vancouver, 11,000 fans witnessed game one of the Cup finals—the largest crowd to see a hockey game in Canada to date. Fred "Cyclone" Taylor played his final playoff game in game five of the series. Jack Darragh became the first player to score back-to-back Cup winners since the formation of the NHL in 1917, a feat that would not be duplicated for 62 years. Mike Bossy of the New York Islanders—in 1982 and 1983—is the only other person to accomplish this.

1922 (March 28)
Winner: Toronto St. Patricks
Cup-winning goal scorer: Cecil "Babe" Dye
Opponent: Vancouver Millionaires
Score of final game: 5–1. Toronto won the series, three games to two.

Babe Dye's Cup-winning goal was one of four he scored in the final game. Scoring for Vancouver was Jack Adams. This was the WCHL's first season, and the Regina Capitals were the new league's champion. The Millionaires played a two-game, total-goals series against Regina to determine who would meet the St. Patricks in the finals. Vancouver defenceman Art Duncan scored a hat trick in the second game of that playoff round, helping the Millionaires to a 4–0 win in that game and a 5–2 series victory. Duncan and George Boucher were the only two defencemen to score playoff hat tricks until Bobby Orr did it in 1971.

1923 (March 31)
Winner: Ottawa Senators
Cup-winning goal scorer: Harry "Punch" Broadbent
Opponent: Edmonton Eskimos
Score of final game: 1–0. Ottawa won the best-of-three series, two games to none.

Eddie Gerard of the Senators played on his fourth Cup winner in a row. In addition to Ottawa's victories in 1920, '21 and '23, he was a replacement player for the Toronto St. Patricks' 1922 championship team. The Senators played a best-of-five series against the PCHA's Vancouver Maroons, winning three games to one, before taking on the Eskimos in a best-of-three affair. In the final game, Ottawa's King Clancy played all six positions, the only time this has ever been done—in Stanley Cup or regular-season play. Up front he filled in for

Frank Nighbor, Harry Broadbent and Cy Denneny, and he replaced Frank Boucher and Eddie Gerard on the blue line. When goalie Clint Benedict received a penalty and had to serve it himself, as all goalies did in those days, he tossed his stick to Clancy and said, "Here, kid. Take care of things until I get back." A classic quote. It was quite common in the early NHL years for players to play close to the entire game, if not all of it. A substitute or spare would see only spot duty, which makes Clancy's feat that day even more remarkable.

1924 (March 25)
Winner: Montreal Canadiens
Cup-winning goal scorer: Howie Morenz
Opponent: Calgary Tigers
Score of final game: 3–0. Montreal won the best-of-three series, two games to none.

Due to poor ice conditions, the second game of the series was transferred from Montreal's Mount Royal Arena to Ottawa, where artificial ice was now available. The four Boucher brothers were the biggest such combination in the NHL until the six Sutters came along. All four Bouchers were involved in the 1924 post-season: Bill and Bob were members of the Canadiens, and they played against George, an Ottawa Senator, in the NHL finals, before encountering Frank, who was with the Vancouver Maroons, in a Stanley Cup semifinal series.

The 1924 Cup win was Howie Morenz's first. Here are some statistics on the sizes of the players in the NHL at this time and the kind of money they could make playing on a Stanley Cup–winning team. The line of Morenz, Aurel Joliat and Billy Boucher averaged 145 pounds—Morenz, at 160, was the heaviest. Because of the large crowds—between 6,000 and 7,000—gate receipts were good and the players benefitted: each member of the victorious Canadiens took home $600, while the Vancouver players received $201 apiece. Oddly enough, the semifinals were a better draw at the box office than the finals, so there was only $183 in each Calgary Tiger's pay envelope.

1925 (March 30)
Winner: Victoria Cougars
Cup-winning goal scorer: Wilfred "Gizzy" Hart
Opponent: Montreal Canadiens
Score of final game: 6–1. Victoria won the best-of-five series, three games to one.

The Cougars were the last non-NHL team to win the Stanley Cup. Down to just two teams, the PCHA had ceased operations at the beginning of the 1924–25 season, and Vancouver and Victoria—the eventual league champs—transferred to the WCHL.

Victoria's goaltender, Harry Holmes, won his fourth Cup with his fourth different team. He was with the Cougars, the Toronto Arenas in 1918, Seattle Metropolitans in 1917 and the Toronto Blueshirts in 1914. Only one other person in Stanley Cup history has done this. Jack Marshall was his name. He played for the Winnipeg Victorias in 1901, the Montreal Amateur Athletic Association in 1902, the Montreal Wanderers in 1907 and the Toronto Blueshirts in 1914—where he was a teammate of Holmes.

1926 (April 6)
Winner: Montreal Maroons
Cup-winning goal scorer: Nels Stewart
Opponent: Victoria Cougars
Score of final game: 2–0. Montreal won the best-of-five series, three games to one.

This was the last season in which a team from outside the NHL played for the Stanley Cup. In 34 seasons of competition, stretching from 1893 until 1926, teams from 14 leagues had contested the Cup. The WCHL dropped the word "Canadian" from its name, operating as the WHL for this, its last season. Lester Patrick, the 42-year-old coach and general manager of Victoria, was pressed into emergency service in game one of his team's league semifinal series. Clint Benedict of the Montreal Maroons picked up the shutout in the Cup-clinching game. It was his fourth of the playoffs, a new Cup record. The mark has been tied by nine other goalies, but nobody has ever done better.

1927 (April 13)
Winner: Ottawa Senators
Cup-winning goal scorer: Cy Denneny
Opponent: Boston Bruins
Score of final game: 3–1. Ottawa won the best-of-three series, two games to none.

There were two ties in this series. As was the case in 1919, any game that was still tied after 20 minutes of overtime was ruled a draw. This was the Senators' fourth Cup win in eight seasons, but it would prove to be the last championship in the team's history. It would be 31 years before another team surpassed Ottawa's total of nine Cup championships: the Montreal Canadiens won their 10th in 1958.

Billy Couture of the Boston Bruins became the first player to be expelled for life from the NHL; he was turfed for attacking referee Jerry Laflamme and his assistant Billy Bell at the end of the last game of the 1927 finals. Several fights broke out at game's end, and numerous fines and suspensions were handed out by league president Frank Calder, the most serious of which was to Couture.

The New York Rangers' Lorne Chabot became the first rookie goalie in NHL history to earn a shutout in his first playoff game. The Rangers tied Boston 0–0 in game one of the semifinals. Hal Winkler was the Bruins goalie and, on November 16, 1926, he became the first goalie in NHL history to record a shutout in the first regular-season game of his career. Winkler was a Ranger at the time, and they blanked the Montreal Maroons, 1–0. The Rangers sold Winkler to Boston six weeks later to make room for Chabot.

Cy Denneny joined his brother as a Stanley Cup–winning goal scorer. They were the first of only two brother combinations to accomplish this feat. The Richards were the other—Maurice in 1956, Henri in 1966 and 1971.

1928 (April 14)
Winner: New York Rangers
Cup-winning goal scorer: Frank Boucher
Opponent: Montreal Maroons
Score of final game: 2–1. New York Rangers won the best-of-five series, three games to two.

April 7, 1928, is a legendary date in hockey history. Game two of the finals was played that night. Rangers goalie Lorne Chabot was badly cut by a Nels Stewart shot. New York had no other goalie under contract, and although Alex Connell of the Ottawa Senators and Hugh McCormick, a minor-league goalie from London, Ontario, were in attendance, the Maroons management denied them permission to play. So Lester Patrick, the Rangers' 44-year-old coach and general manager, put on the pads and finished the game in goal. Odie Cleghorn—Sprague's brother—was a former player and a current coach with the NHL's Pittsburgh Pirates, and he was allowed to help out behind the New York bench. Nels Stewart managed to put one past the "old man" and the game went into overtime tied at one. Ranger Frank Boucher scored his second goal of the game at the 7:55 mark of the first overtime period and New York got the win. It was agreed that Joe Miller, who'd played for the New York Americans during the regular season, would fill in for Chabot for the remainder of the series. This made the Rangers the first Stanley Cup–winning team to use three goalies in one playoff year.

The entire series was played at the Montreal Forum. Ice was unavailable at New York's Madison Square Garden, because the arena played host to the circus every April. The circus took precedence over everything, even the Stanley Cup finals. This scheduling conflict occurred a number of times in the Rangers' history, and in my opinion it cost them one, if not two, Stanley Cup championships.

1929 (March 29)
Winner: Boston Bruins
Cup-winning goal scorer: Bill Carson
Opponent: New York Rangers
Score of final game: 2–1. Boston won the best-of-three series, two games to none.

This was the first Stanley Cup final between two American teams. Carson's winning goal was scored with 1:58 to play and was the only goal of the two games that was not scored unassisted. Harry Oliver had the lone helper. Boston's rookie goalie, Cecil "Tiny" Thompson, was outstanding, picking up three shutouts in five games played and posting a goals-against average of 0.60. Two members of the Toronto Maple Leafs distinguished themselves by tying for the playoff scoring lead despite not playing in the Cup finals. Andy Blair and Ace Bailey each recorded three points and were tied with Butch Keeling of the Rangers.

1930 (April 3)
Winner: Montreal Canadiens
Cup-winning goal scorer: Howie Morenz
Opponent: Boston Bruins
Score of final game: 4–3. Montreal won the best-of-three series in two straight.

The Bruins' losses in the finals marked the only time during the 1929–30 season that they were handed back-to-back defeats. The Canadiens led 4–1 going into the third period of game two, only to have Boston score twice. Cooney Weiland, the league's scoring champ that year, had a goal disallowed late in the game that would have forced overtime.

1931 (April 14)
Winner: Montreal Canadiens
Cup-winning goal scorer: Johnny Gagnon
Opponent: Chicago Black Hawks
Score of final game: 2–0. Montreal won the best-of-five series, three games to two.

This was Chicago's first trip to the finals. The Hawks were coached by Dick Irvin Sr., who used four different line combinations—a common strategy today, but very unusual in those days. The previous year saw the size of the rosters expanded from 12 players to 15, and Irvin made full use of every man. Irvin's approach suggests that more players were needed to slow down the fast-skating Montreal Canadiens, who were commonly referred to as "the Flying Frenchmen." It was a great final and Chicago nearly pulled it off.

Earlier in the playoffs, Boston's Art Ross became the first coach to pull his goalie, Tiny Thompson, for an extra attacker. It happened during game two of the first round against the Canadiens. Montreal won 1–0—however, they did not score into the empty net. Despite losing in the semifinals the Bruins' Cooney Weiland, the previous season's scoring champion, led the playoffs in scoring with 9 points in the five games he played. This was only the second time a player not in the final was the post-season scoring leader, the first such occasion coming two years earlier in 1929.

1932 (April 9)
Winner: Toronto Maple Leafs
Cup-winning goal scorer: Irvine "Ace" Bailey
Opponent: New York Rangers
Score of final game: 6–4. Toronto won the best-of-five series in three straight.

This series is commonly referred to as the "tennis series," because the scores of the three Toronto victories were 6–4, 6–2, 6–4. Each of the three games took place at a different "Garden" rink. Game one took place at Madison Square Garden, but the circus again displaced the Rangers, so the second game was played at Boston Garden, a site chosen by Ranger management to serve as their "home" ice. Finally, for game three, the teams met at Maple Leaf Gardens.

In game one of the finals, Harvey "Busher" Jackson recorded a hat trick in the second period for the Leafs. He became the first player to score three goals in one period in playoff action. Toronto coach Dick Irvin, who'd been with Chicago in 1930–31, became the first man to coach two different Cup finalists in two straight seasons.

1933 (April 13)
Winner: New York Rangers
Cup-winning goal scorer: Bill Cook
Opponent: Toronto Maple Leafs
Score of final game: 1–0. New York won the best-of-five series, three games to one.

Bill Cook scored the winner in overtime while the Rangers were enjoying a two-man advantage—Bill Thoms and Alex Levinsky were in the penalty box for Toronto. The talk of the playoffs, however, was the first-round matchup between Toronto and Boston. That series lasted the full five games, with four of them going into overtime. Toronto won the fifth and deciding game, 1–0, after 104 minutes and 46 seconds of extra time. At the time, it was the longest game in history; it remains the second-longest to this day. Ken Doraty scored the winner, assisted by Andy Blair, who was the first player in NHL history to sport a mustache.

1934 (April 10)
Winner: Chicago Black Hawks
Cup-winning goal scorer: Harold "Mush" March
Opponent: Detroit Red Wings
Score of final game: 1–0. Chicago wins the best-of-five series, three games to one.

This was Chicago's first championship. For the second year in a row the Cup-clinching game went into overtime. Mush March's winning goal was scored at 10:05 of the second overtime period. This was the longest it would take to play a Cup-deciding game for 62 years. Chicago outshot Detroit 53–40. The Hawks' captain was their goalie, Charlie Gardiner. He is the only goaltender in history to captain a Cup winner. Two months later, on June 13, 1934, Gardiner passed away suddenly and tragically from a brain operation.

1935 (April 9)
Winner: Montreal Maroons
Cup-winning goal scorer: Lawrence "Baldy" Northcott
Opponent: Toronto Maple Leafs
Score of final game: 4–1. The Maroons won the series in three straight.

This was the first all-Canadian final since 1926. Leaf owner and general manager Conn Smythe made headlines after game two in Toronto when he got into a fight with a fan. This was the Maroons' second and final Cup win. Their coach and manager was Tommy Gorman, who'd also coached and managed Chicago to their 1934 championship, becoming the only NHL bench boss to win the Cup two years in a row with two different teams.

1936 (April 11)
Winner: Detroit Red Wings
Cup-winning goal scorer: Regis "Pep" Kelly
Opponent: Toronto Maple Leafs
Score of final game: 3–2. The Wings beat Toronto three games to one.

This was the first of Detroit's eleven Stanley Cup wins. They opened the playoffs against the Montreal Maroons, beating them three straight. To this day, game one of that series remains the longest game in NHL history. It lasted until the 16:30 mark of the sixth overtime period before Modere "Mud" Bruneteau scored the winner. The final score was 1–0. Hec Kilrea assisted on the goal. More information on this night can be found in Chapter 5.

1937 (April 15)
Winner: Detroit Red Wings
Cup-winning goal scorer: Marty Barry
Opponent: New York Rangers
Score of final game: 3–0. Red Wings won the best-of-five series, three games to two.

Once again the circus invaded Madison Square Garden, with the result that only one game of the finals was played on the Rangers' home ice. The other four were all held in Detroit. Marty Barry had a big night in game five, with two goals—including the Cup winner—and an assist for a total of three points.

The Wings were the second Stanley Cup–winning team in history to use three goalies in one playoff year. Starter Normie Smith was bothered by injuries and was replaced by Earl Robertson and Jimmy Franks. Robertson was the Cup-winning goalie, picking up the shutout.

In first-round action, Lionel Conacher of the Montreal Maroons took the first-ever penalty shot in the NHL playoffs. The date was March 25, 1937, and the Maroons were shut out 4–0 by the Boston Bruins. (Obviously, Conacher missed.) The shot was awarded by referee John Mitchell after Red Beattie fell on the puck near the Boston net. Tiny Thompson made the save. The first round of the playoffs was now a best-of-three series, replacing the two-game, total-goals format.

1938 (April 12)
Winner: Chicago Black Hawks
Cup-winning goal scorer: Carl Voss
Opponent: Toronto Maple Leafs
Score of final game: 4–1. Chicago won the best-of-five series, three games to one.

The Hawks used three goalies in the finals—Alfie Moore in game one, Paul Goodman in game two, and regular netminder Mike Karakas in games three and four—after a broken toe kept Karakas out of the first two games. It would be 32 years before another team, the 1970 St. Louis Blues, used three goalies in the finals.

The winning Hawks lineup featured eight Americans, six of whom were fairly prominent in terms of hockey trivia: Mike Karakas, Carl Voss, Virgil Johnson, Roger Jenkins, Elwyn "Doc" Romnes and Carl "Cully" Dahlstrom.

In 1936, Karakas was the first goalie to win the Calder Award (given to the NHL's rookie of the year). Voss was the first-ever winner of the Calder Award in 1933 with Detroit. (He's also one of only two winners to start his rookie season with one team and finish with another. He was originally a Ranger. Eddie Litzenberger, in 1955, was the other. The Montreal Canadiens sold him to Chicago in mid-season.) Later on, Voss became the NHL's referee-in-chief. Dahlstrom was the Calder Trophy winner in 1938. (The Calder Award officially became known as the Calder Trophy in 1937.) Johnson would take the third penalty shot in NHL playoff history—almost six years to the day after their Cup win, on April 13, 1944. It was against Bill Durnan of the Canadiens and he did not score. Jenkins was the first NHL player to wear number 88, in 1934–35, when he was a member of the Montreal Canadiens. Romnes won the Lady Byng Trophy in 1936, breaking a string of seven Lady Byngs in eight years by Frank Boucher of the New York Rangers.

1939 (April 16)
Winner: Boston Bruins
Cup-winning goal scorer: Roy Conacher
Opponent: Toronto Maple Leafs
Score of final game: 3–1. Boston won the best-of-seven series, four games to one.

This was the first year that the Cup finals were a best-of-seven series. Once again, the first round of the playoffs produced the most memorable hockey. Boston beat the New York Rangers in seven games. Four of the seven games went into overtime, with the Bruins winning three of them. All three game-winning goals for the Bruins were scored by Mel Hill, earning him the nickname "Sudden Death." He remains the only NHL player ever to score three overtime goals in one playoff series.

1940 (April 13)
Winner: New York Rangers
Cup-winning goal scorer: Bryan Hextall Sr.
Opponent: Toronto Maple Leafs
Score of final game: 3–2. Rangers won the best-of-seven series, four games to two.

Hextall's Cup winner was scored in overtime. He was the father of NHLers Dennis and Bryan Jr., the grandfather of Ron Hextall and the great-grandfather of Brett Hextall, Ron's son, who was drafted by the Phoenix Coyotes in 2008 and who completed his first season of pro in the AHL in 2011–12. The Hextalls recently became the latest family to have their names engraved on the Stanley Cup. With the L.A. Kings victory in 2012, Ron Hextall will see his name engraved as their assistant general manager, joining his grandfather seventy-two years later.

The Chicago Black Hawks chartered a plane to fly to Toronto for a first-round game. It was the first time an NHL team flew to a playoff game. The time saved did not help the Hawks, who were swept 2–0 in the best-of-three series.

1941 (April 12)
Winner: Boston Bruins
Cup-winning goal scorer: Bobby Bauer
Opponent: Detroit Red Wings
Score of final game: 3–1. Boston won the best-of-seven series in four straight.

This was the first four-game sweep in the Cup finals. In a first-round matchup, Nick Metz of Toronto became the first player to record three assists in one period of a playoff game. It happened in the second period of game three of the semifinals against Boston. He also scored a goal, giving him a four-point night. The final score was 7–2 for Toronto, who ultimately lost the series.

1942 (April 18)
Winner: Toronto Maple Leafs
Cup-winning goal scorer: Pete Langelle
Opponent: Detroit Red Wings
Score of final game: 3–1. Toronto won the best-of-seven series, four games to three.

This was the famous come-from-behind win for Toronto. Down three games to none in the finals, the Leafs won the next four games to take the Cup. It would be 33 years before another team duplicated that feat: the 1975 New York Islanders came back to beat Pittsburgh in the quarterfinals, and then in 2010 the Philadelphia Flyers made it three teams when they were down 3–0 to the Boston Bruins and ironically 3–0 in game seven before orchestrating their comeback to win game seven 4–3 and take the series four games to three. However, the Leafs remain the only team to perform this comeback in the finals.

During the summer of 1993 I had the privilege of meeting Carl Liscombe, who was with the Red Wings his entire career. Fifty-one years later, he was still very bitter over King Clancy's refereeing in game five of the series, won 9–3 by Toronto. He told me that Clancy, an ex-Leaf player, was as biased as any official could possibly be. Liscombe scored in that game and actually finished second in the playoff scoring race with 14 points in 13 games.

This was Toronto's eighth trip to the finals in 11 years, yet it was their first Cup win since 1932. A crowd of 16,218 fans took in game seven at Maple Leaf Gardens, at that time the largest ever to see a hockey game in Canada.

1943 (April 8)
Winner: Detroit Red Wings
Cup-winning goal scorer: Joe Carveth
Opponent: Boston Bruins
Score of final game: 2–0. Detroit won the best-of-seven series in four straight.

This was the first season in which all the playoff series were best of seven. Things would stay that way for 32 years—in 1975, the NHL introduced a best-of-three preliminary round. Harvey "Busher" Jackson, formerly of Toronto but now with Boston, became the first player to score a shorthanded goal in overtime. It happened in game three of the semifinals against Montreal—a 3–2 Bruins win that gave them the series, four games to one.

1944 (April 13)
Winner: Montreal Canadiens
Cup-winning goal scorer: Hector "Toe" Blake
Opponent: Chicago Black Hawks
Score of final game: 5–4. Montreal swept the best-of-seven series, four games to none.

The Canadiens became the first team to win eight straight games in the NHL playoffs. They lost game one of the semifinals to Toronto, won the next four, and then swept Chicago in the finals. This was Rocket Richard's first Stanley Cup win. It was also the playoff year that featured the game in which Richard was named all three stars. That happened on March 23, 1944, after Montreal beat Toronto 5–1 and the Rocket got all five goals.

1945 (April 22)
Winner: Toronto Maple Leafs
Cup-winning goal scorer: Walter "Babe" Pratt
Opponent: Detroit Red Wings
Score of final game: 2–1. Toronto won the best-of-seven series, four games to three.

Detroit almost repeated Toronto's feat of the 1942 finals. The Leafs won the first three games of the series, and then lost the next three to Detroit. However, the Leafs hung on to win game seven on home ice. Walter "Babe" Pratt became the first defenceman to score a Stanley Cup–winning goal. Of the seven games in the finals, five were shutouts. Three of the shutouts belonged to Toronto—all in a row and all recorded by Frank "Ulcers" McCool. It's still an NHL record for one playoff year shared by five other goaltenders, Clint Benedict, John Ross Roach, Brent Johnson, Patrick Lalime and Jean-Sebastien Giguere. Benedict is also known as the first goalie to ever wear a mask in the NHL, which he did in 1930 with the Montreal Maroons. Roach, as previously mentioned, was the first goalie to wear the "C" as team captain with Toronto in 1924–25. Brent Johnson is the son of former NHL goaltender Bob Johnson, making them just the fifth father–son combination to both play in the NHL as goaltenders. In another interesting twist, Brent's grandfather is former Detroit Red Wing great Sid Abel. Patrick Lalime still holds the NHL record for the longest undefeated streak to start an NHL career, 16 games, 14–0–2 with the Pittsburgh Penguins in 1996–97. And Jean-Sebastien Giguere is currently one of only five players to win the Conn Smythe Trophy as playoff MVP on a losing team, which he did with Anaheim in 2003. Four years later, he was a Cup-winning goalie with the Ducks in their five-game victory over the Ottawa Senators.

1946 (April 9)
Winner: Montreal Canadiens
Cup-winning goal scorer: Hector "Toe" Blake
Opponent: Boston Bruins
Score of final game: 6–3. Montreal won the best-of-seven series, four games to one.

One of the notable features of this series was the ongoing battle between the Reardon brothers. Boston's Terry and Montreal's Kenny never actually dropped the gloves, but they hit each other, ran each other and generally whacked each other for the entire series. The Winnipeg natives were teammates in Montreal during the 1941–42 season. Blake's Cup-winning goal was his second in three years.

1947 (April 19)
Winner: Toronto Maple Leafs
Cup-winning goal scorer: Ted "Teeder" Kennedy
Opponent: Montreal Canadiens
Score of final game: 2–1. Toronto won the best-of-seven series, four games to two.

Ted Kennedy became the youngest player to score a Stanley Cup–winning goal with his tally in game six. He was 21 years, four months and seven days old. Kennedy also assisted on the other goal in the 2–1 Toronto victory. This was the first Cup final series between the Leafs and the Canadiens. Rocket Richard was suspended for game three after slashing shut the eye of Vic Lynn and cutting open Bill Ezinicki's skull. There were six rookies on this edition of the Leaf squad. At the other end of the spectrum, the 1967 Leafs won the Cup with seven players who were 36 or older.

1948 (April 14)
Winner: Toronto Maple Leafs
Cup-winning goal scorer: Harry Watson
Opponent: Detroit Red Wings
Score of final game: 7–2. Toronto won the best-of-seven series in four straight.

Game two of the finals featured a brawl that saw both goalies, Turk Broda of Toronto and Harry Lumley of Detroit, mixing it up. But it was a minor flare-up compared to game three of Toronto's semifinal series against Boston. Several fights during that match precipitated a wild ending that saw Bruins fans involved not only with the Leafs but with their own players. Boston's Pete Babando was tagged with a $100 fine for assaulting a fan. There were no other injuries or suspensions. Toronto won the series, four games to one.

Gordie Howe scored his first playoff goal on April 4 in game six of the Red Wings' semifinal win over the Rangers. The goalie was Charlie Rayner.

1949 (April 16)
Winner: Toronto Maple Leafs
Cup-winning goal scorer: Cal Gardner
Opponent: Detroit Red Wings
Score of final game: 3–1. Toronto swept the best-of-seven final.

Toronto became the first NHL team to win the Cup three straight times. Fleming MacKell, a 19-year-old Leaf rookie, got his name on the Cup for the first of two times. He became the first Cup-winning player whose father had also played on a championship team. Jack MacKell won two Cups with the Ottawa Senators, in 1920 and 1921.

1950 (April 23)
Winner: Detroit Red Wings
Cup-winning goal scorer: Pete Babando
Opponent: New York Rangers
Score of final game: 4–3. Detroit won the best-of-seven series, four games to three.

This was the first final to go into overtime in game seven. Detroit also won its semifinal series against Toronto in overtime of game seven. Two of the Rangers' "home" games were played at Maple Leaf Gardens in Toronto, as Madison Square Garden hosted the circus. It was the first time since 1920 that Toronto had hosted a Cup final game without a local team playing.

Gordie Howe was injured in the first game of the semifinals against Toronto. He suffered a skull fracture in a collision with Ted Kennedy. He did not return for the rest of the playoffs.

The playoff scoring leader was Pentti Lund of the Rangers. The Finn became the second European-born player to lead the playoffs in scoring. Johnny Gottselig, of the 1938 Chicago Black Hawks, was the first. He was born in Russia.

1951 (April 21)
Winner: Toronto Maple Leafs
Cup-winning goal scorer: Bill Barilko
Opponent: Montreal Canadiens

Score of final game: 3–2. Toronto won the best-of-seven series, four games to one.

The 1951 finals are the only series in NHL playoff history in which every game went into overtime. For the record, the game-winning goal scorers were Sid Smith, Ted Kennedy, Harry Watson and Bill Barilko for Toronto. Rocket Richard scored the winner for Montreal in game two. It was Richard's third overtime goal of the playoffs, tying a record first set by Mel "Sudden Death" Hill in 1939. All of Hill's goals had come in the same series, the semifinals against the Rangers.

Barilko's Cup-winning goal has been immortalized by the rock group the Tragically Hip in their song "Fifty Mission Cap." Barilko died later that summer on a fishing trip. His remains were not found until June 7, 1962. In an eerie coincidence, the Leafs did not win another championship until 1962.

Game two of the semifinal between Toronto and Boston was declared void with the score tied at one. The province of Ontario had a Sunday curfew law and no sporting event could be played past midnight. So at 11:45 p.m. on Saturday night, after one period of overtime had been played, the game was called. Barilko had scored for Toronto, Johnny Peirson for Boston. It would be 37 years before another playoff game went unfinished: the fourth game of 1988 finals between the Bruins and Edmonton Oilers. A blown electrical transformer left the Boston Garden in darkness. In both instances, league officials ordered that the suspended games be replayed in their entirety. Toronto won its 1951 rematch.

A lot is made about roughness and dirty play in today's NHL, but it's amazing what you'll find if you research the game's history. The suspended game between Toronto and Boston featured 22 penalties. The following Bruins were injured: Johnny Peirson suffered a fractured cheekbone; Dunc Fisher required 12 stitches to close a gash on his head; Pete Horeck, 10 stitches over one eye; and Murray Henderson, three stitches over an eye. Ted Kennedy of Toronto needed numerous facial and scalp stitches. Play was halted to give rink attendants time to scrape the blood off the ice. During one fight along the boards, Boston coach Frank Patrick took a swing at one of the Leaf players. The Leafs' chairman of the board, W.H. MacBrien, raced out of his seat—where he had been sitting with Canada's governor general—to berate referee Red Storey. A classic contest, to say the least.

1952 (April 15)
Winner: Detroit Red Wings
Cup-winning goal scorer: Metro Prystai
Opponent: Montreal Canadiens
Score of final game: 3–0. Detroit swept the best-of-seven series.

In terms of trivia, the most memorable feature of the 1952 finals would be the malfunctioning clock in game one. With Detroit leading 2–1, Habs coach Dick Irvin pulled goalie Gerry McNeil. Detroit's Ted Lindsay scored into the empty net and the time was announced as 19:44. The siren to end the game did not sound until a full minute after the time had ticked off the score clock—it was later determined that there was indeed another minute left to play after Lindsay's goal. Coach Irvin was naturally incensed. He was adamant that he would not have pulled McNeil had he known there was so much time left in the game.

Pete and Jerry Cusimano were responsible for starting a Red Wing tradition. Their father owned a fish and poultry shop, so they brought an octopus to the game with them. The creature's eight legs represented the eight playoff victories needed to win the Cup. The brothers threw it onto the ice, hoping it would bring the team good luck in their eighth playoff game. Detroit won, and a superstition was born.

Detroit swept both its playoff rounds, becoming the second team to win eight consecutive playoff games. However, they were the first to do so without a loss. (The '46 Canadiens had lost the first game of the semifinals before winning eight in a row.)

This was Detroit goalie Terry Sawchuk's finest moment. The ace netminder shut out the Habs in games three and four, allowing a total of two goals in the four games. His four shutouts in the post-season tied an NHL record, and his goals-against average in the eight wins was 0.62.

Toronto's Walter "Turk" Broda became the first goalie to play in 100 playoff games when he faced the Red Wings in a 1–0 loss in game two of the semifinals in Detroit. The other semifinal series produced one of the most dramatic goals ever scored in hockey. And by who else: Maurice "the Rocket" Richard.

Richard's Canadiens were in a battle with Boston that would last the full seven games. In the second period of game seven, Richard was hit by Bruins defenceman Leo Labine and was knocked unconscious, either by Labine's knee, the ice, or a combination of the two. He needed six stitches. Late in the third period, with the score tied at one, coach Dick Irvin looked down the bench and saw Richard in place. Richard, bandaged and bloody, took the ice for his shift. He picked up a pass from Emile "Butch" Bouchard and started up the ice. He wove through four Bruins, then fought off Bill Quackenbush before beating "Sugar" Jim Henry for the tie-breaking goal with four minutes to play. After the game, Bruins coach Lynn Patrick was quoted as saying, "A truck couldn't have stopped Richard on that play." Montreal won the game, 3–1, and the series, 4–3.

1953 (April 16)
Winner: Montreal Canadiens
Cup-winning goal scorer: Elmer Lach
Opponent: Boston Bruins
Score of final game: 1–0. Montreal won the best-of-seven series, four games to one.

If the 1953 playoffs were famous for anything, it was the stunning defeat of Detroit at the hands of the Bruins. Terry Sawchuk recorded his third straight playoff shutout in game one of the semis against Boston, won 7–0 by Detroit. (Sawchuk had shut out Montreal in games three and four of the 1952 finals.) But legendary left winger Woody Dumart, in his second-last NHL season, shut down scoring sensation Gordie Howe and the Bruins won the semifinal in six games.

Jacques Plante made his playoff debut for Montreal in the semifinals against Chicago and played games one and two of the finals before giving way to Gerry McNeil, who appeared in the last three games. One fact that strikes me about the Cup-winning goal: in the celebration that followed the goal, Rocket Richard broke teammate Elmer Lach's nose. You always had to watch out for the Rocket, even when the game was over.

1954 (April 16)
Winner: Detroit Red Wings
Cup-winning goal scorer: Tony Leswick
Opponent: Montreal Canadiens
Score of final game: 2–1. Detroit won the best-of-seven series, four games to three.

For the second time in NHL history, the finals went to overtime of the seventh game. The series ended when Tony Leswick scored the flukiest Cup-winning goal of all time. He picked up a cross-ice pass from Glen Skov and lobbed the puck into the air so he could get to the bench for a line change. Perennial all-star defenceman Doug Harvey reached up to grab the puck and it tipped off the fingers of his glove and rolled over the shoulder of goalie Gerry McNeil into the net. Game over, Cup won.

The goal, scored at 4:29 of overtime, sparked a wild celebration on the ice of the Detroit Olympia. The Canadiens left the ice without shaking hands. Former Red Wing and then-Hab Gaye Stewart said that the players wanted to come back out and congratulate the Wings, but management forbade it. Dick Irvin, the coach of the Canadiens, was quoted as saying, "If I had shaken hands, I wouldn't have meant it, and I refuse to be hypocritical." Such was life in the NHL in the raucous '50s.

1955 (April 14)
Winner: Detroit Red Wings
Cup-winning goal scorer: Gordie Howe
Opponent: Montreal Canadiens
Score of final game: 3–1. Detroit won the best-of-seven series, four games to three.

Despite the absence of Rocket Richard, the Canadiens made it to the finals and took Detroit to seven games. Richard had been suspended for the last three games of the regular season and all of the playoffs after striking Boston's Hal Laycoe repeatedly with several sticks and punching linesman Cliff Thompson in a game on March 13, 1955. It was the second-harshest sentence in NHL history for an on-ice incident, next to Billy Couture's lifetime ban in 1927. The suspension sparked the most infamous incident in hockey history on St. Patrick's Day, March 17—an event now known as the "Richard Riot."

On the statistical front, Gordie Howe set a new playoff point-scoring mark with 20. The previous mark of 18 was held by Toe Blake in 1944 and Newsy Lalonde in 1919, both with Montreal. Red Kelly of the Wings picked up the first misconduct of his career. He took exception to a hard slash from Montreal's Butch Bouchard, ended up fighting him, and they both had misconducts tacked onto their fighting penalties. Dick Irvin recorded his 100th playoff victory as a coach when the Habs won game six of the finals, 6–3. He was the first coach to reach that plateau. Unlike the year before, the teams did shake hands at the conclusion of game seven.

1956 (April 10)
Winner: Montreal Canadiens
Cup-winning goal scorer: Maurice Richard
Opponent: Detroit Red Wings
Score of final game: 3–1. Montreal won the Cup in five games.

Montreal and Detroit met in the finals for the third time in a row. Game five was the last of Montreal captain Butch Bouchard's career. He accepted the Stanley Cup and skated around the rink, pursued by one of the Cup guardians, who slipped on the ice as he tried to grab Bouchard. Of course, all of this totally delighted the crowd. It may have been the first time that a player actually skated around the rink with the Cup, although some sources credit Ted Lindsay with doing this after a previous Cup win by Detroit. Jean Beliveau's 12 playoff goals tied the record set by Rocket Richard in 1944.

1957 (April 16)
Winner: Montreal Canadiens
Cup-winning goal scorer: Dickie Moore
Opponent: Boston Bruins
Score of final game: 5–1. Montreal won the best-of-seven series in five games.

The stage seemed to be set for another Detroit–Montreal final, but the Bruins upset the first-place Detroit club in the semifinals. The Bruins had won seven and tied three of their 14 regular-season games against Montreal, but their good fortune was not to carry over to the playoffs. Rocket Richard scored four goals in game one and the Habs never looked back. All three playoff series featured brawls. The worst was in game two of the semifinals between Detroit and Boston: there were six fights, 22 penalties, and a lengthy delay while Wings goalie Glenn Hall had 18 stitches put into a cut on his chin. Of course, he returned to action.

1958 (April 20)
Winner: Montreal Canadiens
Cup-winning goal scorer: Bernie Geoffrion
Opponent: Boston Bruins
Score of final game: 5–3. Montreal won the series in six games.

For the second year in a row it was a Montreal–Boston final. With the series tied at two wins each, the Canadiens won game five in overtime. Rocket Richard scored the winner. It was the last overtime goal of his career—and his sixth, which stood as a record for 48 years until surpassed by Joe Sakic. It also was his 18th game-winning goal in the playoffs, a mark that has been surpassed by only four men: Wayne Gretzky and Brett Hull each with 24, and Claude Lemieux and Joe Sakic, who each had 19 game winners. The Rocket also scored seven goals in a four-game sweep of the Red Wings in the semifinals. He was 36 years old.

1959 (April 18)
Winner: Montreal Canadiens
Cup-winning goal scorer: Marcel Bonin
Opponent: Toronto Maple Leafs
Score of final game: 5–3. Montreal won the series, four games to one.

And then along came the Leafs. With a brash, tough-talking coach in Punch Imlach, Toronto finally halted a skid that had seen the team miss the playoffs two years in a row and made the finals for the first time in eight seasons.

The best series of the playoffs was the semifinal round between Toronto and Boston. It went seven games, with the Leafs winning on a goal by Gerry Ehman with 2:33 left to play.

The Cup win by the Habs was their fourth in a row, something no other NHL team had ever done. The Cup-winning goal scorer, Marcel Bonin, turned to an interesting pastime in the off-season to make a few bucks and stay in shape: he wrestled bears in the circus. Bonin had a phenomenal playoff that year with 10 goals in 11 games and a total of 15 points. He was second to teammate Dickie Moore in post-season scoring by two points. There were no playoff hat tricks this year, something that would not happen again until 2001, 42 years later.

1960 (April 14)
Winner: Montreal Canadiens
Cup-winning goal scorer: Jean Beliveau
Opponent: Toronto Maple Leafs
Score of final game: 4–0. Montreal swept the finals.

This was the second and last time that a team won eight straight games to win the Cup. Many people still consider this edition of the Habs to be the greatest team of all time. They won their fifth straight Cup and their twelfth overall. Game four of the finals was the last NHL game that Maurice Richard ever played, and he picked up his final playoff point, the 126th of his career. It was an assist on the third goal in a 4–0 Montreal win. His brother, Henri, scored the goal; Dickie Moore drew the other assist; the time was 16:40 of the second period. In game three, he'd scored his last goal, against Johnny Bower. The same linemates figured in the scoring: Henri and Dickie Moore assisted.

1961 (April 16)
Winner: Chicago Black Hawks
Cup-winning goal scorer: Ab McDonald
Opponent: Detroit Red Wings
Score of final game: 5–1. Chicago won the series, four games to two.

This was Chicago's third Cup win. The Black Hawks ended Montreal's bid for a sixth straight championship with a very emotional win in the semifinals. Although the series went six games, the turning point came in game three, which went to a third overtime period before Murray Balfour scored on the power play. Dickie Moore was in the box for Montreal. The Habs had two goals called back, and coach Toe Blake was incensed. He confronted referee Dalton MacArthur on the ice after the game and threw a punch at him. That action cost him $2,000—which, up until then, was the largest fine in hockey history.

This would be the only Stanley Cup victory in the careers of Bobby Hull and Stan Mikita. For the record, Gordie Howe outpointed Bobby Hull and Stan Mikita, 8–7, in the finals. Howe also set a career mark for playoff assists in game two of the finals, a 3–1 Red Wings win over Chicago. His two helpers in that game gave him a total of 61, passing Doug Harvey's mark of 59.

1962 (April 22)
Winner: Toronto Maple Leafs
Cup-winning goal scorer: Dick Duff
Opponent: Chicago Black Hawks
Score of final game: 2–1. Toronto won the series, four games to two.

Stan Mikita set a new playoff record for points with 21—6 goals and 15 assists. Don Simmons was the winning goalie for Toronto in games five and six, substituting for an injured Johnny Bower. This was an era that still saw the superstars of the game involved in the rough stuff as much as the lesser lights. Stan Mikita and Frank Mahovlich were kicked out of game four after a brawl deteriorated into a stick-swinging duel. The home team won games one through five. Toronto broke that string in the sixth game, played in Chicago. The game was scoreless until 8:56 of the third, when Bobby Hull excited the crowd with a goal. It took 10 minutes to clear the ice of debris. Moments later, Bob Nevin tied it for Toronto. The winner was scored by Dick Duff after Tim Horton took the puck from end to end and passed to him.

1963 (April 18)
Winner: Toronto Maple Leafs
Cup-winning goal scorer: Eddie Shack
Opponent: Detroit Red Wings
Score of final game: 3–1. Toronto won the series in five games.

Eddie Shack probably never scored an easier goal than the one that became the Cup winner. Kent Douglas fired a shot that hit a Red Wing player and caromed off Shack's stick into the net behind Detroit goaltender Terry Sawchuk. Bob Pulford of the Leafs took a penalty late in the game and the Wings removed Sawchuk for an extra attacker, but Dave Keon cemented the win with an empty-net goal. Dick Duff, who scored the Cup-winning goal the year before, set an NHL record in game one of the finals that still stands: he scored two goals in 1:08 at the start of the game. It remains the fastest two goals to start a game in NHL playoff history. Nineteen sixty-three is also notable for being the only year in which not one overtime game was played in the playoffs.

1964 (April 25)
Winner: Toronto Maple Leafs
Cup-winning goal scorer: Andy Bathgate
Opponent: Detroit Red Wings
Score of final game: 4–0. Toronto won the series in seven games.

This was the series in which Bobby Baun scored his famous overtime goal in game six—a goal that many people have incorrectly identified as the Cup winner. For the record, Baun's ankle was cracked by a Gordie Howe shot late in the game. He had the doctors freeze it, and 3:07 into overtime, he took a shot that hit Bill Gadsby's stick and went over Terry Sawchuk's right shoulder. That tied the series at three wins apiece.

Game two of the series had also been decided in overtime—Larry Jeffrey scored the winner for Detroit. Two of the other games were decided by such late goals that they may as well have been in overtime. Bob Pulford scored a shorthanded goal with two seconds left in game one for a 3–2 Toronto win. Alex Delvecchio scored with 17 seconds to play in game three for a 4–3 Detroit win.

Gordie Howe became the career playoff point leader when he scored a goal against Chicago in game five of the semifinals. The point was number 127 of his playoff career, eclipsing Rocket Richard's 126.

1965 (May 1)
Winner: Montreal Canadiens
Cup-winning goal scorer: Jean Beliveau
Opponent: Chicago Black Hawks
Score of final game: 4–0. Montreal won the series in seven games.

In first-round action, Gordie Howe of Detroit surpassed another of Rocket Richard's records in game three against Chicago. His career playoff penalty total now stood at 194 minutes, passing the Rocket's 188. Detroit's Norm Ullman also got into the record book in game five of the same series, when he scored two goals in five seconds during a 4–2 Detroit win. They were—and still are—the fastest two goals in Stanley Cup playoff history. Unfortunately for these record setters, their luck ran out and they lost a hard-fought seven-game series to the Hawks.

Game seven of the finals saw Montreal's Jean Beliveau add his name to the record book a few more times. Beliveau scored the fastest Cup-winning goal in NHL history. The time was 14 seconds. Beliveau was the inaugural winner of the new Conn Smythe Trophy as most valuable player in the playoffs. The Cup-winning goal he scored was his second, tying him with Jack Darragh, Howie Morenz and Toe Blake for most career Cup-winning goals.

For the first time, a playoff series was played in the month of May. Unlike in later years, when expansion led to an increased regular-season schedule and more playoff rounds, this was strictly a result of the regular season beginning later. In the span of five years, between 1959 and 1964, the starting date moved from October 5 to October 12, as training camps grew longer and teams played more exhibition games. The move was also considered to be better for the fans. In addition, none of the playoff rounds was completed in fewer than six games. So, instead of the playoffs ending in the last week of April, they would now begin stretching into May.

1966 (May 5)
Winner: Montreal Canadiens
Cup-winning goal scorer: Henri Richard
Opponent: Detroit Red Wings
Score of final game: 3–2. Montreal won the best-of-seven series in six games.

Game two of the Detroit–Chicago semifinal made history: it was the first nationally televised game in the United States. The date was April 10 and the hometown Hawks were pounded 7–0 by the Wings.

The Cup-winning goal was a controversial one. Henri Richard was upended by the Wings' Gary Bergman. Sliding along the ice, both players crashed into Detroit goalie Roger Crozier—not, however, before the puck slid off Richard's elbow and into the net. Gary Bergman told me in a conversation in 1993 that, before he or Red Wings coach Sid Abel could complain, referee Frank Udvari was leaving the ice. I guess a video goal judge would have been handy at that time. Montreal coach Toe Blake played a role as well, ordering his players to jump onto the ice as soon as the goal light came on, leaving as little room as possible for discussion. They say that history repeats itself, and this story is eerily similar to the ending of the 1999 finals.

Richard's goal meant that, for only the second time, a set of brothers was on record as scoring Cup-winning goals. Rocket Richard had popped the winner for Montreal in 1956. The Denneny brothers—Corb in 1918 with the Toronto Arenas and Cy with the 1927 Ottawa Senators—make up the other set.

Roger Crozier was the second winner of the Conn Smythe Trophy—becoming the first goalie, and the first member of the losing team, to win the award.

1967 (May 2)
Winner: Toronto Maple Leafs
Cup-winning goal scorer: Jim Pappin
Opponent: Montreal Canadiens
Score of final game: 3–1. Toronto won the series in six games.

This was the last Stanley Cup final series played in the Original Six era—the NHL expanded to 12 teams for the 1967–68 season—and to date it is the last Stanley Cup championship won by the Toronto Maple Leafs. Game three in Toronto featured an amazing goaltending duel between Montreal's Rogie Vachon and Toronto's Johnny Bower. By the time the Leafs' Bob Pulford scored the winner at 8:26 of the second overtime period, Toronto had outshot Montreal 62–54. The Leafs won the game 3–2.

The final face-off of game six was won by a Toronto defenceman. Staying true to his game plan, Leaf coach Punch Imlach had veteran blueliner Allan Stanley take the draw against the indomitable Jean Beliveau. Stanley tied up Beliveau's stick while Red Kelly raced in and threw the puck to Pulford, who passed it to captain George Armstrong. Armstrong put it into the empty net—Hab goalie Gump Worsley had been pulled for an extra attacker. Game and series over. Seven of the Leafs—Bower, Terry Sawchuk, Marcel Pronovost, Tim Horton, Stanley, Red Kelly and Armstrong—were 36 years old or older. Dave Keon was the Conn Smythe Trophy winner.

1968 (May 11)
Winner: Montreal Canadiens
Cup-winning goal scorer: J.C. Tremblay
Opponent: St. Louis Blues
Score of final game: 3–2. Montreal beat St. Louis in four straight games.

As a result of civil unrest in the wake of the assassination of Rev. Martin Luther King Jr., three NHL playoff games were postponed.

All four games in the Stanley Cup finals were decided by one goal, two of them in overtime. The Blues, with six former Habs on their roster, were being called Montreal West in some circles.

Montreal coach Toe Blake retired after this Cup win, the Canadiens' 15th, citing the pressure as being too much for him. He had been coach for 13 seasons, winning the Cup eight times. He had also played for the Canadiens for 13 years, and it took Montreal 13 games to win this last Cup for him.

In the quarterfinals, Wayne Connelly of Minnesota scored the first penalty-shot goal in playoff history, against the Los Angeles Kings and their legendary goaltender, Terry Sawchuk. (Connelly had been the West Division's top goal scorer, with 35.) The date was April 9, 1968, and the final score was 7–5 Minnesota. The Stars won the series but lost in the semis to St. Louis in seven games. Leading the way for the Stars was Bill Goldsworthy with 15 points in the fourteen playoff games he played. He led the playoffs in points despite not making the Cup final, first time that had happened since 1931.

St. Louis goalie Glenn Hall won the Conn Smythe Trophy. For the second time in four years, the Smythe went to a member of the losing team.

1969 (May 4)
Winner: Montreal Canadiens
Cup-winning goal scorer: John Ferguson
Opponent: St. Louis Blues
Score of final game: 2–1. Montreal swept the best-of-seven series.

Several records were set in the early rounds of these playoffs. Boston and Toronto engaged in on-ice warfare in their quarterfinal series. In game one—a 10–0 Boston shellacking—the Leafs' Forbes Kennedy set new marks for the most penalties in one period (six) and one game (eight), and most penalty minutes in one period and one game (34 and 38 respectively). Of the four marks, the only one he still holds is the one for most penalties in a game, and he now shares it with Kim Clackson of the Pittsburgh Penguins, who equalled it in 1980.

Boston set a record that still stands in game one, scoring six power-play goals. Meanwhile, Bruins centre Phil Esposito tied the record for 10 points in one series originally set by Dickie Moore. It has long since been shattered and is now held by another Bruin: Rick Middleton, who in 1983 picked up 19 points in a seven-game quarterfinal series against Buffalo.

The Bruins won game two, 7–0. Games three and four in Toronto were closer, but the series was still over in four straight.

Jean Beliveau scored the only overtime goal of his career in game six of the semifinals against Boston. It was the series-clinching goal, scored against Gerry Cheevers on April 24 at 11:28 of the second overtime. It was after midnight (Eastern time) when this game ended, and I remember it very well because it was the first game I ever watched from start to finish. I was a very lucky nine-year-old who had pleaded with his father and mother to stay up well past his bedtime. They consented, seeing as it was an important playoff game. The next day, I fell asleep in Mrs. McKaskill's fourth-grade class, and when she woke me I jumped up and yelled, "He scores!"

1970 (May 10)
Winner: Boston Bruins
Cup-winning goal scorer: Bobby Orr
Opponent: St. Louis Blues
Score of final game: 4–3. Boston won the best-of-seven series in four straight.

For the first—and so far, only—time in NHL history, there were no Canadian teams in the playoffs. Neither Montreal nor Toronto qualified.

As in the previous two seasons, most hockey fans felt that the East Division semifinal between Boston and Chicago was the real Cup final series. The winner of that series was expected to roll over the West's representative. Phil Esposito shattered the one-season playoff point record, picking up 13 goals and 14 assists for 27 points in 14 games. The record had previously been held by Stan Mikita, with 21 in 1962.

Bobby Orr set a new standard for defencemen with 20 points—four more than Toronto's Tim Horton in 1962. And his nine goals were four more than Earl Seibert had for Chicago in 1938.

The Pittsburgh Penguins became the first team in NHL history to win their first four playoff games. The Penguins swept Oakland thanks to an overtime goal by Michel Briere in game four.

Of course, this was the season of The Goal. On Mother's Day—May 10, 1970—Bobby Orr scored what has been voted the greatest goal in NHL history. It was scored in overtime, and Orr had no sooner scored than he went flying through the air after being tripped by Noel Picard. More on the goal—and its incredible connection with the number four—can be found in Chapter 7.

1971 (May 18)
Winner: Montreal Canadiens
Cup-winning goal scorer: Henri Richard
Opponent: Chicago Black Hawks
Score of final game: 3–2. Montreal won the best-of-seven series, four games to three.

The main event of note in this playoff year was the Montreal Canadiens' quarterfinal upset of the Boston Bruins in seven games, courtesy of the astounding goaltending of Ken Dryden. (The Bruins had set 37 team and individual scoring records during the 1970–71 season.) Dryden, who had played in only six regular season games, would take part in all 20 of Montreal's playoff games and win the Conn Smythe Trophy.

Bobby Orr became the first defenceman to record a hat trick in a playoff game since Art Duncan in 1922. It happened in the fourth game against Montreal, a 5–2 Boston win.

On April 22, 1971, the Minnesota North Stars beat Montreal in game two of their semifinal matchup, becoming the first expansion club to win a playoff game against an Original Six team. Montreal would go on to win the series in six games.

In the finals, Montreal won game seven at Chicago Stadium—the first time since 1945 that a visiting team had won a seventh game in the Cup finals. The Habs' Frank Mahovlich tied Phil Esposito's year-old record for points in one playoff season, with 27.

1972 (May 11)
Winner: Boston Bruins
Cup-winning goal scorer: Bobby Orr
Opponent: New York Rangers
Score of final game: 3–0. Boston won the series in six games.

The Bruins won their fifth championship—and their second in three years. Orr scored his second Cup-winning goal, becoming only the second non–Montreal Canadien (Ottawa's Jack Darragh was the other) to notch two Cup winners. Orr also became the first player to win the Conn Smythe Trophy twice. His goal in Boston's 5–2 loss to New York in game three of the finals was the 17th playoff marker of his career—propelling him past Red Kelly on the all-time list among defencemen.

It was the Rangers' first appearance in the finals since 1950. In fact, their first-round win over Montreal marked the first time they had won a playoff series since the 1950 semifinals. In between, they missed the post-season 12 times. The Rangers' coach in 1972 was Emile Francis, who had been the Blueshirts' backup goalie to Charlie Rayner in 1950.

1973 (May 10)
Winner: Montreal Canadiens
Cup-winning goal scorer: Yvan Cournoyer
Opponent: Chicago Black Hawks
Score of final game: 6–4. Montreal won the series in six games.

Montreal and Chicago met in the finals for the fifth time since 1931. The Canadiens had won on all four previous occasions, and they soon made it five in a row. Yvan Cournoyer was the offensive story with 15 goals and 10 assists. He won the Conn Smythe Trophy. Henri Richard got his name on the Cup for the 11th time as a player, breaking the record held by his long-time teammate Jean Beliveau. In game three of the finals, Richard also set a new mark for career playoff games with 165, passing Red Kelly.

1974 (May 19)
Winner: Philadelphia Flyers
Cup-winning goal scorer: Rick MacLeish
Opponent: Boston Bruins
Score of final game: 1–0. Philadelphia won the series in six games.

After seven NHL seasons, a team from the 1967 expansion had won the Stanley Cup. Not one member of the Flyers had played on a Cup winner before. Game five of the finals featured an NHL record 43 penalties. There were six separate fights. Boston won the game 5–1. The Bruins had not been shut out all season before they lost the final game, 1–0.

The final minutes of the Cup-deciding game proved extremely dramatic. With 2:22 to go in the third period and the Flyers nursing a 1–0 lead, referee Art Skov called Bobby Orr for holding after he'd made a terrific effort to get back and knock Bobby Clarke off the puck on a breakaway. The call was a weak one at best and came only minutes after Johnny Bucyk had been whistled off for interference on Rick MacLeish—who had taken a dive. (I often wonder if referees look back at tape from the '70s and feel a twinge of guilt about how easily they were fooled by the diving.)

Flyer coach Fred Shero further developed his enigmatic reputation. The former minor-league player and part-time NHLer had become a studious coach, particularly in terms of preparation and execution of a game plan. He used an array of motivational tools, including messages posted in and around the dressing room. Two of the more famous that season were, "Get to the puck by the shortest route and arrive there in ill humour," and this gem, prior to game six in Philadelphia: "Win today and we walk together forever."

The Bruins would have a new coach for the start of the 1974–75 season. His name: Donald Stewart Cherry.

1975 (May 27)
Winner: Philadelphia Flyers
Cup-winning goal scorer: Bob Kelly
Opponent: Buffalo Sabres
Score of final game: 2–0. Flyers won the series in six games.

Thanks to the expansion of the playoffs from eight teams to 12 and the addition of a best-of-three preliminary round, the playoffs ran later than ever this year.

In the second game of a first-round tilt between the New York Rangers and Islanders, another record for penalties was set. Fifty penalties were called in the Rangers' 8–3 win, which tied the series at a game apiece. In the third game, on the strength of J.P. Parise's overtime goal, the Isles advanced and began a remarkable series of comebacks. In the quarterfinals against the Penguins, they became only the second team in NHL history to win a best-of-seven series after falling behind three games to none. In the semifinals against Philadelphia, they nearly duplicated the feat, dropping the first three games, then winning games four, five and six, before losing the seventh.

Parise's overtime winner in that third game against the Rangers came 11 seconds into the extra period, making it the fastest in NHL history. The old mark of 19 seconds had been set in 1969 by Ted Irvine of the Los Angeles Kings.

Dave Schultz of the Flyers brawled his way to a new record for career playoff penalty minutes. He ended the post-season with a career total of 273, bettering John Ferguson's mark of 260.

The third game of the 1975 finals went down in hockey history as the "fog game." The temperature hit 87 degrees Fahrenheit and a dense mist rose off the ice inside Buffalo's Memorial Auditorium. The officials were forced to stop play no fewer than 12 times and ask the players to skate laps of the rink to dissipate the fog. After skating through a full three periods and almost all of an overtime session, Buffalo's Rene Robert scored the winner on a sharp-angled shot that Flyer goalie Bernie Parent said he never saw because of the fog. Parent played well enough overall to win the Conn Smythe Trophy for the second year in a row, becoming the first player to do so.

1976 (May 16)
Winner: Montreal Canadiens
Cup-winning goal scorer: Guy Lafleur
Opponent: Philadelphia Flyers
Score of final game: 5–3. Montreal won the series in four straight.

This year, two players tied a record first set in 1919 by Newsy Lalonde and matched by Rocket Richard in 1944: Toronto's Darryl Sittler and Philadelphia's Reggie Leach each scored five goals in a game. Sittler's five goals came in game six of the Leafs' quarterfinal matchup against the Flyers. The Leafs won that game, 8–5, but lost the series.

Leach fired home his five in the fifth game of the semifinals against the Bruins. The final score was 6–3 and the win eliminated Boston from the playoffs. Leach went on to score 19 playoff goals. There have been previous publications stating that Newsy Lalonde was a 19-goal scorer in the 1919 playoffs but a review of the game sheets now has him at 17 in the ten games the Montreal Canadiens played that playoff year. So Leach's 19 goals is the record which was subsequently tied by Jari Kurri in 1985. Leach also became the third person to win the Conn Smythe Trophy while playing on a losing team.

The finals produced a real quirk given the Broad Street Bullies were involved: there was only one fighting major in the four game series, Andre Dupont versus Mario Tremblay. An odd statistic given the Flyers willingness to drop the gloves was a key to their success in the previous two seasons. Some people point to the emergence of Larry Robinson on defence for Montreal as a key element in terms of a deterrent.

1977 (May 14)
Winner: Montreal Canadiens
Cup-winning goal scorer: Jacques Lemaire
Opponent: Boston Bruins
Score of final game: 2–1. Montreal won the series in four straight.

This tremendous year for Montreal included a regular-season record of 60–8–12. The Habs scored 387 goals while allowing only 171. Although Detroit would surpass Montreal's standard of 60 wins—with 62 in 1995–96—the Canadiens' point total of 132 has stood the test of time, up to and including the 2011–12 season.

Don Kozak of the Los Angeles Kings scored six seconds into game four of the quarterfinals against the Boston Bruins. Gordie Howe of Detroit and Chicago's Ken Wharram shared the previous mark for fastest goal off the start of a game—nine seconds. The Kings won the game, 7–4, but lost the series, four games to two. Montreal's Bob Gainey got in on the act in Montreal's semifinal matchup against the New York Islanders. In the sixth game of the series, he opened the scoring seven seconds into the first period. The final score was 2–1 and the Habs won the series, four games to two.

Clark Gillies of the Islanders scored game-winning goals in four straight games: in game two of the preliminary round against Chicago, and the first three games of New York's quarter-final series against Buffalo. (Billy MacMillan scored the winner in game four as the Isles swept the Sabres.) It's a unique distinction, and one that's rarely mentioned.

Guy Lafleur won the Conn Smythe Trophy.

1978 (May 25)
Winner: Montreal Canadiens
Cup-winning goal scorer: Mario Tremblay
Opponent: Boston Bruins
Score of final game: 4–1. Montreal won the series in six games.

The year 1978 is one that rekindles many memories for Toronto Maple Leaf fans. It had been 11 years since their last Cup victory, and the city was buzzing after a thrilling overtime victory over the New York Islanders in game seven of the quarter-finals. Lanny McDonald scored the big goal. The euphoria was short-lived when the Montreal Canadiens swept Toronto in four games in the semifinals.

The Habs and Bruins had a tremendous rivalry in the late 1970s, one that would culminate a year later in a phenomenal seven-game semifinal series. The most-talked-about moment in the '78 playoffs happened in game four of the finals between Montreal and Boston. In this tilt, an infamous fight between Stan Jonathan and Pierre Bouchard took place at 6:28 of the first period. Jonathan broke Bouchard's nose in a bloodbath that saw linesman John D'Amico hit as well. John Wensink and Gilles Lupien also fought and were given majors and gross misconducts. These were the first fights of the series. Four more followed in game five. Larry Robinson was the Conn Smythe Trophy winner.

1979 (May 21)
Winner: Montreal Canadiens
Cup-winning goal scorer: Jacques Lemaire
Opponent: New York Rangers
Score of final game: 4–1. Montreal won the series in five games.

For the second time in their history, the Canadiens won the Cup four years in a row. They lost the first game on home ice and were down 2–0 in game two before rallying and winning that game—and the next three. Ken Dryden became the first goalie to record an assist in the finals. He picked up the helper on the last goal of game three, a 4–1 Montreal win. Jacques Lemaire scored the goal, while Steve Shutt picked up the other assist.

The talk of the playoffs was the semifinal series between Montreal and Boston, decided in overtime of game seven on Yvon Lambert's goal at the 9:33 mark. It was May 10, the anniversary of Bobby Orr's Cup-winning goal in 1970. The final score was 5–4 for Montreal, and it was, in my opinion, the greatest hockey game Guy Lafleur ever played. He had three points in the third period, including the tying goal scored on a power play with 1:14 on the clock. The Habs had the man advantage because Boston had been called for too many men on the ice at 17:26. It was an infamous moment in Bruins history. Jean Ratelle noticed that there were six Bruin skaters on the ice, and he climbed back over the boards before the referee could catch the error. But an overanxious Stan Jonathan raced into the play and checked Mark Napier, and this time the ref made the call. Peter McNab served the bench minor for the Bruins, which was handed out a minute and 25 seconds after Boston had taken a 4–3 lead on a goal by Rick Middleton.

Bob Gainey won the Conn Smythe Trophy, and Jacques Lemaire joined the elite circle of two-time Cup-winning goal scorers.

1980 (May 24)
Winner: New York Islanders
Cup-winning goal scorer: Bobby Nystrom
Opponent: Philadelphia Flyers
Score of final game: 5–4. The Islanders won the series in six games.

This was the first of four straight Cup wins for the Islanders. The Cup-winning goal was scored in overtime, and it's very easy to remember the time: 7:11, just like the popular convenience store chain. John Tonelli and Lorne Henning assisted on Nystrom's marker. The Islanders began their quest for the Cup with a first-round win over the Los Angeles Kings. This would be the first of 19 consecutive playoff series victories for the Islanders, an NHL record that, quite likely, will never be matched.

In the first round, a 52-year-old grandfather by the name of Gordie Howe played his final game in the NHL. The date was April 11, 1980—30 years to the day after Howe suffered a skull fracture that many observers thought would end his career. Howe picked up a goal and an assist in the three-game series against Montreal. The goal, his last ever in the NHL, was the 869th of his career (including playoffs). He scored it against Denis Herron in game two of the series on April 9. It was the last Hartford goal in an 8–4 loss and it was assisted by his son, Mark.

In game two of the finals, an 8–3 Flyers win played on May 15, 1980, Paul Holmgren of the Flyers became the first American-born player to record a hat trick in playoff action.

Bryan Trottier won the Conn Smythe Trophy and set a new playoff record for points with 29, eclipsing the previous mark of 27 set by Phil Esposito in 1970 and tied by Frank Mahovlich in 1971.

1981 (May 21)
Winner: New York Islanders
Cup-winning goal scorer: Wayne Merrick
Opponent: Minnesota North Stars
Score of final game: 5–1. The Islanders won the series in five games.

The Islanders became only the third American team to win back-to-back Stanley Cups. The Philadelphia Flyers (in 1974 and '75) and Detroit Red Wings (on two occasions, in 1936 and '37, and again in 1954 and '55) are the others. John Tonelli assisted on the Cup-winning goal for the second year in a row.

In the quarterfinals, Anders Hedberg of the New York Rangers scored only the second penalty-shot goal in playoff history, against Mike Liut of St. Louis in a 6–4 New York victory. The Rangers won that series, but the Islanders swept them four straight in the semifinals.

Robert "Butch" Goring of the Islanders won the Conn Smythe Trophy. In game three of the finals, he became the first player in NHL history to score a playoff hat trick for two different teams. He had previously scored three goals for the Los Angeles Kings in a 1977 game against Atlanta and goalie Phil Myre.

Mike Bossy's 35 points broke teammate Bryan Trottier's year-old record for most points in one playoff year.

1982 (May 16)
Winner: New York Islanders
Cup-winning goal scorer: Mike Bossy
Opponent: Vancouver Canucks
Score of final game: 3–1. The Isles won the series in four straight.

Bryan Trottier led the playoffs in scoring with 29 points as the Islanders won their third straight Cup championship. Although the series was a sweep, Vancouver was very much a factor in the first two games: game one went into overtime, while the second game was also close at 6–4. Game one turned on a poor clearing attempt by veteran defenceman Harold Snepsts in the dying seconds of the extra period. Mike Bossy pounced on the puck and scored the second overtime goal of his career with two seconds left on the clock.

In first-round action, Mikko Leinonen of the New York Rangers set a playoff record with six assists, helping New York beat Philadelphia 7–3 in game two. This broke the previous record of five, held by six players—including Wayne Gretzky in 1981.

One of the biggest upsets in playoff history took place in the first-round series between Edmonton and Los Angeles. The Oilers had finished 48 points ahead of the Kings in the regular season. In a wild best-of-five series game one was a 10–8 win for L.A., as the teams combined to set a playoff record for most total goals in one game that still stands. Edmonton won game two and took a 5–0 lead in game three. Then the Kings staged the biggest comeback in playoff history, emerging with a 6–5 win. Daryl Evans scored the winner. Edmonton tied the series at two, but Los Angeles did the unthinkable again, winning the fifth and final game in Edmonton, 7–4. Bernie Nicholls scored the series-winning goal. The Kings lost the next round to Vancouver, four games to one.

Mike Bossy won the Conn Smythe Trophy.

1983 (May 17)
Winner: New York Islanders
Cup-winning goal scorer: Mike Bossy
Opponent: Edmonton Oilers
Score of final game: 4–2. Islanders swept the series.

Mike Bossy became the second player to score back-to-back Cup-winning goals. (Ottawa's Jack Darragh was the first, in 1920 and '21.)

Wayne Gretzky became the second player in NHL history to rack up two four-goal games in one playoff year. The first came in the first round, against the Winnipeg Jets. The goalie was Brian Hayward. The second was in the quarterfinals against the Calgary Flames and goalie Reggie Lemelin. Newsy Lalonde of Montreal was the only other player to accomplish this feat. In 1919, he had a five-goal game against Ottawa and goalie Clint Benedict, and a four-goal game against Seattle and goalie Harry "Happy" Holmes. Gretzky set a new playoff mark for points in one playoff year with 38, despite being kept goalless in the finals. This was due in no small part to Billy Smith, who blanked the Oilers 2–0 in game one and held them to six goals in the series. He ran his career playoff record to 73–24 and was the obvious choice for the Conn Smythe Trophy.

1984 (May 19)
Winner: Edmonton Oilers
Cup-winning goal scorer: Ken Linseman
Opponent: New York Islanders
Score of final game: 5–2. The Oilers won the series in five games.

The Montreal Canadiens were the story of the playoffs for a couple of very different reasons. First of all, there was rookie goalie Steve Penney's attempt to emulate Ken Dryden. Penney had played four regular-season games, compared with Dryden's six in 1971. Both men led their teams to first-round upsets of the Boston Bruins. Penney and the Habs went on to enjoy a six-game victory over Quebec, then won the first two games of their conference final series with the Islanders before the bubble burst and the Isles won the next four games and the series.

The other reason that the Canadiens were the topic of conversation was the final game of their series with Quebec. It was played on Good Friday and the Habs won the game 5–3, but not before fans witnessed an NHL rarity, back-to-back bench-clearing altercations. During a full-scale brawl at the conclusion of the second period, Quebec's Louis Sleigher sucker-punched Montreal's Jean Hamel. There was a 40-minute delay while the penalties were sorted out. Twelve players were kicked out of the game, but they were not informed of the fact, so they all returned to the ice to start the third period. Before the officials could even think of starting the period, Montreal's Mark Hunter immediately set out to get Sleigher—and at one point was on top of his brother Dale, although they did not throw any punches. Surprisingly, this game did not set any playoff penalty records.

The Oilers won their first Stanley Cup at the same time as they ended New York's "drive for five." It was a passing of the torch between dynasties. Mark Messier was the Conn Smythe Trophy winner. The 23-year-old finished third in playoff scoring and was a driving force in the Oilers' first Cup win.

1985 (May 30)

Winner: Edmonton Oilers
Cup-winning goal scorer: Paul Coffey
Opponent: Philadelphia Flyers
Score of final game: 8–3. The Oilers won the series in five games.

The Winnipeg Jets won their first-ever playoff series, beating the Calgary Flames three games to one in the first round. The Oilers, en route to their second Cup championship, swept the Jets in their division final series. In game four of that series, Wayne Gretzky tied his own playoff record of seven points in one game. He won the Conn Smythe Trophy. Edmonton's Cup win was somewhat anticlimactic due to a rash of injuries suffered by the Flyers. Jari Kurri tied Reggie Leach's record of most goals in one playoff year with 19.

Brad Park of the Detroit Red Wings appeared in his 17th straight playoffs—a record at that time.

The Islanders became the first team in NHL history to overcome a 2–0 deficit in a best-of-five series. They beat the Washington Capitals 2–1 in game five. Their luck ran out in the second round against the Flyers, where they were beaten in five games.

Philadelphia's Tim Kerr set two scoring marks in the first round against the Rangers. He scored four goals in one period—three of them on the power play. The four goals in one period is a mark he shares with Mario Lemieux, the power play goal record Kerr still holds by himself to this day.

The best story from this playoff year came in the first round between Montreal and Boston. The year before, Canadiens rookie Steve Rooney had planned a wedding, never thinking he'd be with Montreal—let alone in the midst of a great playoff series—in the spring of '85. He was simply a promising American-born rookie who was graduating from Providence College. The wedding date now conflicted with game three of the series against Boston. Rooney got married before the game and immediately after the service was whisked to Boston Garden, complete with police escort. In that game, he scored his first career playoff goal, helping Montreal win the game 4–2. The Habs won the series in five games before losing to archrival Quebec in the next round.

1986 (May 24)

Winner: Montreal Canadiens
Cup-winning goal scorer: Bobby Smith
Opponent: Calgary Flames
Score of final game: 4–3. Montreal won the Cup in five games.

This was Montreal's 23rd Stanley Cup win—its first in seven years. The Habs had not gone more than seven years without a championship since 1944. Montreal won the Cup with 10 rookies, a record. They were Claude Lemieux, Brian Skrudland, Stephane Richer, Kjell Dahlin, Steve Rooney—who was still considered a rookie after playing only three regular-season games the previous season—David Maley, Mike Lalor, Randy Bucyk, John Kordic and Patrick Roy. In game two of the finals, Skrudland scored the fastest overtime goal in NHL playoff history at the nine-second mark. Twenty-year-old Patrick Roy won the Conn Smythe Trophy, becoming the youngest recipient in history. The series between Montreal and Calgary was the first all-Canadian final since 1967.

Winnipeg set an unusual record in its first-round loss to Calgary. The Jets used four goalies—Brian Hayward, Daniel Berthiaume, Dan Bouchard and Marc Behrend—the most any team has ever employed in one playoff series. Calgary went on to beat Edmonton in the Smythe Division final in seven games. This was the series in which Edmonton defenceman Steve Smith banked the puck into the Oilers net off his own goalie, Grant Fuhr. He was attempting to pass the puck to his defence partner Don Jackson, but misplayed the angle badly. There were still 15 minutes to play, but the Flames hung on for what can only be described as a huge upset, winning 3–2. Calgary's Perry Berezan was credited with the goal. One other statistical note; for the first time since 1968, the playoff scoring leader came from a team that did not make the finals. Bernie Federko and Doug Gilmour each recorded 21 points for the St. Louis Blues during their nineteen game run through the semifinals.

1987 (May 31)
Winner: Edmonton Oilers
Cup-winning goal scorer: Jari Kurri
Opponent: Philadelphia Flyers
Score of final game: 3–1. The Oilers won the Cup in seven games.

This year's finals were the first in 16 years to go the distance. Still, they were overshadowed by the drama of an earlier game seven, in the Patrick Division semifinals between the New York Islanders and Washington Capitals. (For the first time, the first-round series were best-of-seven instead of best-of-five.) The deciding game of that series was the fifth-longest NHL game at that time and it still sits in the number ten spot for the longest OT games as of 2012. Pat LaFontaine scored the series winner at 8:47 of the fourth overtime period. The game ended at 1:55 a.m. The goalies who played all 128 minutes-plus were Kelly Hrudey for the Islanders and Bob Mason for the Capitals. In the next round, the Isles encountered yet another seven-game series, although this time they were defeated by the Philadelphia Flyers.

In the Wales Conference finals against Montreal, it was just like old times for the Flyers. Prior to game six, the teams staged a 10-minute brawl. It started when Philadelphia's Eddie Hospodar jumped Montreal's Claude Lemieux, who'd been following a pre-game ritual of shooting the puck into the opposition net. Flyers backup goalie Chico Resch was also involved at the outset and soon both teams were on the ice and going at it. Fines totalling $24,500 were handed out in the wake of the skirmish, and Hospodar was suspended for the remainder of the playoffs.

Flyer goalie Ron Hextall became the seventh goalie, and third rookie, to win the Conn Smythe Trophy. He also was the fourth player from a losing team to cop the award.

1988 (May 26)
Winner: Edmonton Oilers
Cup-winning goal scorer: Wayne Gretzky
Opponent: Boston Bruins
Score of final game: 6–3. The Oilers swept the series.

This championship is significant because it was Wayne Gretzky's last. He would be traded to Los Angeles on August 9 as part of a blockbuster deal that involved multiple players, draft choices and millions of dollars.

For the first time since 1927, a game in the Stanley Cup finals was suspended. It was also the first playoff game to be suspended since 1951. (Details on these two previous occurrences can be found in their respective years.) The reason? Simply, the power went out at Boston Garden and they couldn't get it switched back on. It happened in game four, at 16:37 of the second period. Craig Simpson had just scored for Edmonton, tying the game at three, when the lights flickered and went out. Emergency lighting was available to help the spectators leave the building, but there was no light for the players on the ice—or more importantly, for the television cameras. The game was replayed in Edmonton, and the Oilers won—making them the only NHL team in history to sweep a Cup final in five games.

Although the game was ruled null and void, the points accumulated by the players counted towards their personal stats. Among the statistical leaders in the playoffs was the ever-present Number 99. Gretzky picked up 31 assists to break his own record, and he became only the third player to win the Conn Smythe Trophy twice. (Bobby Orr in 1970 and '72 and Bernie Parent in 1974 and '75 were the others.)

Elsewhere in this post-season, which from a trivia standpoint could only be described as extraordinary, replacement officials were needed for game four of the Wales Conference finals. The series pitted the New Jersey Devils, making their first playoff appearance, against the Boston Bruins, who had beaten the Montreal Canadiens in the playoffs for the first time since 1943—a span of 45 years and 19 series. New Jersey coach Jim Schoenfeld took exception to the officiating of referee Don Koharski in game three, and he confronted the ref as he left the ice at the end of the game. They bumped and Koharski fell. Schoenfeld screamed that unforgettable phrase, recorded by the TV cameras: "Have another doughnut, you fat pig!" The NHL immediately suspended Schoenfeld, but he obtained a court order and was behind the bench for game four. Referee Dave Newell and linesmen Ray Scapinello and Gord Broseker refused to work the game. Replacement officials Vin Godleski, Paul McInnis and Jim Sullivan were recruited. The Devils won the game 3–1 but lost the series in seven games.

In their first-round win over the Islanders, New Jersey became the first team to allow a shorthanded goal in overtime since 1943. It was scored by New York's Brent Sutter in game four, and it tied the series. But New Jersey prevailed in six.

Patrik Sundstrom, also of the Devils, set a new playoff mark in the third game of round two against the Washington Capitals. He picked up three goals and five assists in a 10–4 win. So noteworthy and newsworthy items were associated with all three rounds in which the Devils played. Even the way they qualified for the playoffs was dramatic: in their last game of the season, they beat Chicago on a John MacLean overtime goal to squeak in ahead of the Rangers and Pittsburgh.

1989 (May 25)
Winner: Calgary Flames
Cup-winning goal scorer: Doug Gilmour
Opponent: Montreal Canadiens
Score of final game: 4–2. The Flames won the Cup in six games.

Calgary got a chance to avenge its loss to Montreal in 1986 and the Flames made good. This was to date their only Cup win. They went to the finals in 2004 and those three series are their only playoff series victories since 1989. The Flames won the Cup at the Montreal Forum, and for years it has been erroneously reported that this was the first Cup win by a visiting team on Forum ice. True, but only as far as the Canadiens are concerned. However, the New York Rangers won the Cup at the Forum in 1928, against the Montreal Maroons. Another misconception surrounds the Cup-winning goal. Many people think Lanny McDonald scored it, and he did score in the game, but it was Gilmour who recorded the third Flames goal, the Cup winner.

In game five of the Patrick Division final, Mario Lemieux tied Patrik Sundstrom's record from the season before with an eight-point game against Philadelphia. The Penguins won the game 10–7 but lost the series in seven games.

Flyers netminder Ron Hextall duplicated a feat he had accomplished during the regular season in 1987–88. He shot the puck the length of the ice in game five of Philadelphia's first-round matchup against Washington and became the first goalie in NHL history to score a goal in the playoffs. Philadelphia won the game, 8–5, and the series in six games. Hextall's goal was scored short-handed—Jeff Chychrun was the Flyer in the penalty box. Hextall made news a little later in the playoffs as well. At the conclusion of game six of the conference finals against Montreal, he raced out of his crease to attack Montreal's Chris Chelios. There was 1:37 to play and Montreal had the game and the series in hand. Hextall felt he had to make amends for a hit Chelios had put on Brian Propp in game one of the series. He drew a match penalty for the attack and was suspended for 12 games at the start of the next season.

Calgary's Al MacInnis won the Conn Smythe Trophy and became the fourth defenceman in history to lead the playoffs in scoring (Pierre Pilote, Bobby Orr and Larry Robinson were the others).

1990 (May 24)
Winner: Edmonton Oilers
Cup-winning goal scorer: Craig Simpson
Opponent: Boston Bruins
Score of final game: 4–1. The Oilers won the Cup in five games.

The Oilers won their fifth Cup title in seven years, making them the closest thing to a dynasty as you're likely to get. Winning without Wayne Gretzky made the accomplishment even more special. The Oilers finished fifth overall—a far cry from their glory years—but they rode the hot goaltending of Bill Ranford to their second final-round matchup against Boston in three years. Game one produced the most compelling story of the playoff. As it dragged on—and on—the thinking was that it would have significant implications for the rest of the series, and it did. The Oilers' Petr Klima finally ended it at 15:13 of the third overtime. It became—and remains to date—the longest game played in the Stanley Cup finals, beating by 83 seconds the mark set in 1931 between Chicago and the Montreal Canadiens. The Hawks' Cy Wentworth scored the deciding goal in that game, but the Habs prevailed in the series.

There were four penalty shots called throughout the 1990 playoffs. In game two of the finals, Klima, who had ended the game-one marathon, was awarded one of them, against Reggie Lemelin. He missed. In the conference finals, Washington's Kelly Miller missed against the Bruins' other goalie, Andy Moog. Randy Wood of the Islanders was denied by Mike Richter of the Rangers in the first round. Calgary's Al MacInnis was the only one to succeed. He popped one against Kelly Hrudey of Los Angeles in the first round.

Edmonton's Mark Messier broke a Wayne Gretzky record—actually, one that they shared:

most career shorthanded goals in the playoffs. The former teammates were tied with 10 until game one of the Smythe Division semifinals. The Oilers lost the game, 7–5, despite Messier's record-breaking goal, but they did win the series. Messier retired with a total of 14 shorthanded goals in the playoffs, that still is an NHL record. Bill Ranford, who strung together a shutout streak of 154 minutes and 24 seconds, won the Conn Smythe Trophy.

1991 (May 25)
Winner: Pittsburgh Penguins
Cup-winning goal scorer: Ulf Samuelsson
Opponent: Minnesota North Stars
Score of final game: 8–0. The Penguins won the Cup in six games.

This was the first trip to the finals for the Penguins. It also marked the first time since 1934 that neither team had previously won a Stanley Cup. (In 1934, it was Chicago against Detroit.) The Penguins lost the first game of every series they played. But they rebounded to beat New Jersey in seven, Washington in five, Boston in six (after losing the first two games), and finally Minnesota. Their 8–0 victory in the deciding game was the largest margin of victory ever in a Cup-clinching game. Mario Lemieux missed most of the season due to injury but he was firing on all cylinders in the post-season. His 44 points gave him the Conn Smythe Trophy and still represents the second-highest total of all time behind Gretzky's 47 in the 1985 playoffs.

Speaking of Gretzky, he passed his former teammate and linemate, Jari Kurri, for the most career goals in the playoffs. Kurri had returned to Finland in 1991 and left the NHL with 92 playoff markers. Gretzky scored number 93 in game four of the Smythe Division semifinals against Vancouver. The Kings won the game 6–1 and took the series in six games. One other statistical note in this post-season, not one series ended in a four-game sweep. It would be 11 years before that happened again.

1992 (June 1)
Winner: Pittsburgh Penguins
Cup-winning goal scorer: Ron Francis
Opponent: Chicago Blackhawks
Score of final game: 6–5. The Penguins swept the series.

The 1992 playoffs started later than ever before, thanks to the first work stoppage in NHL history. The issues that prompted a walkout by the NHL Players' Association were settled after 10 days and all series began play on April 18. As a result of the delay, NHL hockey was played in the month of June for the first time.

Six of the eight first-round matchups went the full seven games; in three of them, the winning team overcame a 3–1 deficit. Pittsburgh came back to beat Washington, Vancouver did the same against Winnipeg, and Detroit came back against Minnesota.

Game six of the Red Wings–North Stars series had historic overtones as video replay was used for the first time to review a goal. The decision would have a bearing on the outcome of the game and, ultimately, the series. Neither team scored in regulation time—the first time this had happened in 13 years. Eighteen minutes into overtime, Sergei Fedorov roofed a quick shot that appeared to go into the net, yet it bounced out so quickly that play continued. At the next stoppage in play, league official Wally Harris reviewed the play and concluded that the puck had indeed entered the net. A goal was awarded to Fedorov, and a seventh game would be played. Detroit won that game, and the series.

In game three of the Penguins–Capitals tilt on April 23, 1992, Pittsburgh coach Scotty Bowman became the all-time leader in playoff wins when he led the Pens to a 6–4 victory. Bowman passed Al Arbour, who had 114 victories—all with the New York Islanders. Bowman's league total now sits at 223 wins, the most all-time.

Boston swept Montreal for the first time in 64 years. Meanwhile, Chicago was on a roll. The Hawks established an NHL record with 11 straight post-season wins as they marched into the Cup finals against the Penguins. Their hot play continued early in game one against Pittsburgh, as the Hawks built up a 3–0 lead, but the Pens came back to win 5–4 and ended up defeating Chicago in four straight. Oddly enough, the Penguins had been on a seven-game winning streak prior to the finals, so the sweep gave them 11 in a row, tying the mark set by the Blackhawks just a few days earlier. Mario Lemieux became only the second player to win the Conn Smythe Trophy in consecutive years. (Flyer goalie Bernie Parent, in 1974 and '75, was the other.)

1993 (June 9)
Winner: Montreal Canadiens
Cup-winning goal scorer: Kirk Muller
Opponent: Los Angeles Kings
Score of final game: 4–1. The Canadiens won the Cup in five games.

The Montreal Canadiens won their 24th Stanley Cup title, beating Wayne Gretzky and the Kings. It was L.A.'s first trip to the finals. The Kings rode the hot hand of a rejuvenated Wayne Gretzky, who led all scorers with 15 goals and 25 assists for 40 points. He would have been a surefire Conn Smythe Trophy winner had a certain Mr. Patrick Roy not gotten in the way—literally and figuratively.

The Kings beat Toronto in a hotly contested semifinal series. In games six and seven, Gretzky's greatness shone through. With his team trailing three games to two, the Great One scored his fourth career overtime goal, sealing a 5–4 win. Then, in the seventh game, he recorded his ninth career playoff hat trick as L.A. won again by a 5–4 count. A pair of non-calls added a bit of controversy to the series. In game six, the Leafs' Doug Gilmour was not penalized for a head butt on L.A. defenceman Marty McSorley. In the same match, Gretzky went unpunished for a high stick on Gilmour that drew blood—he should at least have been assessed a minor penalty, if not a double minor or ejection from the game. It's no surprise that Leaf fans are quick to remember the high stick, but for some reason they forget about the head butt. Bottom line: the better team won the series.

The Maple Leafs set a record for the most games played in one playoff year by a team that did not make the finals: 21. All three rounds in which they participated went the distance.

The finals, which marked the 100th anniversary of the Stanley Cup, featured the greatest team of all time against arguably the greatest player of all time. En route, Montreal shattered the record for consecutive overtime wins. The Habs ended up with 10 straight wins in OT, meaning that Patrick Roy had played 96:38 of consecutive shutout hockey when one goal meant losing the game. A remarkable record. The previous record had been held by the 1980 New York Islanders, with six. The Habs' seventh win came in game three of the Wales Conference finals against the Islanders. The final score was 2–1, Guy Carbonneau was the goal scorer, and the time of the goal was 12:34 of the first overtime period. Twenty-eight overtime games were played in 1993—outstripping the previous high of 16, set in 1991—and Montreal took part in 11 of them.

A couple of notes from the finals. The Kings won game one, 4–1, and was in control of the second game, leading 2–1 late when Marty McSorley was penalized for using an illegal stick with too much of a curve. With the man advantage, Habs coach Jacques Demers pulled Patrick Roy for an additional attacker and Eric Desjardins scored on the power play, forcing overtime. Fifty-one seconds into the extra frame, Desjardins scored again to win the game, tie the series and become the first defenceman in NHL history to record a hat trick in the finals. Montreal did not lose another game, winning two more in extra time. John LeClair became the 13th player to score winning goals in back-to-back overtime games. Patrick Roy won the Conn Smythe Trophy, his second.

1994 (June 14)
Winner: New York Rangers
Cup-winning goal scorer: Mark Messier
Opponent: Vancouver Canucks
Score of final game: 3–2. The Rangers won the Stanley Cup in seven games.

Vancouver returned to the finals after 12 years, New York after 15. And what a series it was. It was, in my opinion, the most competitive, most exciting Stanley Cup final since 1971. Along the way their captain and leader, Mark Messier, elevated his already-legendary status when he guaranteed a win over New Jersey in game six of their seven-game semifinal on May 25, 1994.

You have to wonder what possesses an athlete to say such a thing; even more mysterious are the gifts they must possess that allow them to deliver the goods. The Rangers won game six, 4–2, led by Messier's hat trick. Truly amazing. Game seven was no less dramatic. It took a goal by Stephane Matteau at 4:24 of the second overtime period to cement the win and put the Rangers in the finals.

Upsets had been a regular occurrence in the NHL playoffs for years and 1994 was no exception. The San Jose Sharks beat the Detroit Red Wings in the first round thanks to a late goal in game seven by Jamie Baker. They very nearly pulled off another miracle against Toronto in the second round, taking a 3–2 lead in games, only to watch the Leafs rally and win games six and seven. Toronto would lose to Vancouver in five games in the conference finals. Brian Leetch of New York won the Conn Smythe Trophy, becoming the first non-Canadian to win the award.

1995 (June 24)
Winner: New Jersey Devils
Cup-winning goal scorer: Neal Broten
Opponent: Detroit Red Wings
Score of final game: 5–2. The Devils won the Cup in four games.

The New Jersey Devils became the sixth expansion franchise since 1967 to win the Stanley Cup. The Philadelphia Flyers, New York Islanders, Edmonton Oilers, Calgary Flames and Pittsburgh Penguins were the others. The Devils started life as the Kansas City Scouts in 1974, then became the Colorado Rockies before finally settling in New Jersey in 1982.

The 1994–95 season has become known as the year of the lockout. A labour dispute between the NHL owners and the players association was finally resolved more than three months after the season was scheduled to begin. Play finally started on January 20, 1995. Each team played a 48-game schedule—the shortest regular season since 1941–42.

Paul Coffey became the highest-scoring defenceman in NHL playoff history on May 27, 1995. His goal and assist in Detroit's 6–2 win over San Jose gave him 166 career points, two more than Denis Potvin. Coffey retains the title, with 196 points. As of 2012, Nick Lidstrom now sits in second spot with 183 points, Ray Bourque is third with 180. The win enabled Detroit to sweep the Sharks and advance to the semifinals.

June 24 was the date of the Devils' victory over Detroit in game four of the finals. It was the latest the Cup winner had ever been decided. Had the series gone the full seven games it was scheduled to end on July 1. Claude Lemieux of the Devils won the Conn Smythe Trophy with 13 goals in 20 playoff games.

1996 (June 10)
Winner: Colorado Avalanche
Cup-winning goal scorer: Uwe Krupp
Opponent: Florida Panthers
Score of final game: 1–0. The Avs won the Cup in four straight.

This was the second sweep in a row in the finals. A record seven playoff games went into two or more overtime periods, breaking the previous mark of six. The record-breaking seventh game turned out to be the final game of the playoffs, in which Colorado beat Florida 1–0 in a great goaltending duel between Patrick Roy and John Vanbiesbrouck.

Uwe Krupp's Cup-winning goal, scored on a shot from the point, came at 4:31 of the third overtime period, ending what was at the time the longest Cup-deciding game in history. Earlier in the series, Colorado's Joe Sakic set a record for game-winning goals in one playoff year, since broken by Brad Richards—more on that note in the 2004 section. His 18th and final goal of the playoffs, scored in game three, was his sixth game-winner. Sakic would also win the Conn Smythe Trophy.

The Tampa Bay loss to Philadelphia gained them credibility but it would still be eight years until they really made some playoff noise. They also set a unique mark in that their first two playoff victories came in overtime. After losing game one against Philadelphia, the Lightning won games two and three in sudden death. Brian Bellows and Alex Selivanov were the goal scorers. The Lightning remain the only team to accomplish this feat.

1997 (June 7)
Winner: Detroit Red Wings
Cup-winning goal scorer: Darren McCarty
Opponent: Philadelphia Flyers
Score of final game: 2–1. The Wings won the Stanley Cup in four games.

For the third year in a row, the finals produced a sweep. Detroit won its eighth Cup and first in 42 years.

Patrick Roy broke another record with his 89th career playoff win—a 7–0 shutout of Chicago in game five of the Western Conference quarterfinals. The previous mark had been held by Billy Smith of the New York Islanders.

There was NHL playoff action in the city of Ottawa for the first time in 67 years. Back in 1930, the Senators had lost to the New York Rangers in a two-game, total-goals series. The modern-day version of the Sens lost a scintillating seven-game series to the Buffalo Sabres. In game seven, Derek Plante scored at 5:24 of overtime on a shot that goalie Ron Tugnutt got a piece of but could not hold on to.

Goaltender Mike Vernon of Detroit won the Conn Smythe Trophy in the closest vote ever. He edged out his teammate, Steve Yzerman. Nothing, of course, could have prepared the hockey world—and specifically the Red Wings—for the tragedy that would take place six days after the final game. A limousine carrying several team players and personnel went off the road and struck a tree. Defenceman Vladimir Konstantinov suffered a serious head injury that ended his career; Slava Fetisov had chest lacerations and a bruised lung; and team masseur Sergei Mnatsakanov sustained severe head injuries. Nobody was killed, but it was a terrible tragedy that shook the Red Wings.

1998 (June 16)
Winner: Detroit Red Wings
Cup-winning goal scorer: Martin Lapointe
Opponent: Washington Capitals
Score of final game: 4–1. The Wings win the Stanley Cup in four games.

Detroit became the first repeat Cup winner since the 1992 Pittsburgh Penguins. For coach Scotty Bowman, this was Cup win number eight, tying him with his mentor, Toe Blake. Bowman was also the bench boss for that Penguin victory in 1992.

For the fourth year in a row, the finals were wrapped up in four games. The turning point of the series came in game two. Detroit overcame a two-goal deficit in the third period and went on to win the game, 5–4. It was the first comeback of this nature in 42 years. (Game one of the 1956 finals between Montreal and Detroit was the last time a team erased a two-goal third-period deficit and went on to win.)

Upsets ruled the Eastern Conference playoffs, as Ottawa prevailed over New Jersey, Montreal over Pittsburgh, and to a lesser extent, Buffalo over Philadelphia, the previous year's runner-up. The greatest repercussions were felt in New Jersey, where head coach Jacques Lemaire resigned after the loss. Ottawa lost the next round to Washington. The Capitals went all the way to the finals despite owning one of the two worst playoff records ever on home ice. Their six losses tied the mark for home futility with the 1987 Philadelphia Flyers—who also made the finals that year. Steve Yzerman, the heart and soul of the Red Wings, won the Conn Smythe Trophy.

1999 (June 19)
Winner: Dallas Stars
Cup-winning goal scorer: Brett Hull
Opponent: Buffalo Sabres
Score of final game: 2–1. The Stars won the Stanley Cup in six games.

Finishing first overall has become the kiss of death for many NHL teams that have gone on to crash and burn at some point in the playoffs. When the Dallas Stars won the Cup in 1999, it was only the seventh time since 1980 that a regular-season champion was able to claim the playoff title, too.

Most of what would happen in these playoffs was overshadowed by the retirement of Wayne Gretzky. The rumours became truth on April 16, 1999, when Gretzky made the announcement, and the Ranger played his final game two days later, against Pittsburgh at Madison Square Garden.

Colorado equalled a dubious record, racking up six losses on home ice—matching Washington's mark of the year before, which also belonged to the '87 Flyers. Unlike those teams, however, the Avalanche did not make the finals.

The Stars and the St. Louis Blues played four overtime games in a six-game second-round series, ultimately won by Dallas. Each team won twice in overtime. The Stars' Joe Nieuwendyk equalled Joe Sakic's record of six game-winners in one playoff year. Last, but certainly not least, in these playoffs, Brett Hull's Stanley Cup–winning goal was scored at 14:51 of the third overtime period, ending the longest Cup-deciding game to date. It was 10 minutes and 20 seconds longer than game four of the 1996 finals. The marathon fell 22 seconds shy of being the longest game ever played in the Stanley Cup finals, a mark still held by the first game of the 1990 series between Boston and Edmonton. It did, however, secure the number two spot in that category.

I mentioned that Gretzky's retirement overshadowed nearly everything that happened in the playoffs. Unfortunately, it could not eclipse the fallout surrounding Hull's Cup winner. Hull was clearly in the crease when he beat Buffalo's Dominik Hasek. A review of the videotape should have overturned the goal and play should have resumed. But with members of the media scampering onto the ice among the players, and the fans going wild, an immediate decision was made to try and sweep the controversy under the rug.

The league's director of officials, Bryan Lewis, reasoned that Hull had preceded the puck into the crease and therefore was "allowed" to be in the crease when the puck came to him. The argument was weak at best, but it was all the NHL had and they stuck with it. The situation did finally prompt the league to change the rule back to something more closely resembling a common-sense, "no-harm, no-foul" approach to in-the-crease infractions and goal nullifications. Joe Nieuwendyk won the Conn Smythe Trophy.

2000 (June 10)
Winner: New Jersey Devils
Cup-winning goal scorer: Jason Arnott
Opponent: Dallas Stars
Score of final game: 2–1. The Devils won the Cup in six games.

For the second year in a row the Cup was won on an overtime goal. Jason Arnott atoned for an earlier penalty and converted a Patrick Elias pass to net the winner. Along the way, the Devils overcame a three-games-to-one deficit in the Eastern Conference finals against the Philadelphia Flyers.

The Flyers were the talk of the post-season for a number of reasons, including their surprising decision to let Eric Lindros play in games six and seven against New Jersey. But there was also their upset win over Buffalo in the first round, followed by a tough series against Pittsburgh. Down two games to none, Philadelphia won game three in overtime. Andy Delmore's game-winning goal completed a hat trick, making him the 12th defenceman to record a hat trick in the post-season. For the record, the others are Art Duncan, George Boucher, Bobby Orr, Dick Redmond, Denis Potvin, Doug Halward, Paul Reinhart, Al Iafrate, Gary Suter, Brian Leetch and Eric Desjardins.

Nothing could prepare the teams and the fans for the fourth game, which ended at 2:37 a.m. (Eastern time). I watched every second of it. The time of Keith Primeau's winning goal was 12:01 of the fifth overtime period. Only two games in NHL history were longer, both of them played more than 75 years earlier. (For reference, I describe them in the sections on 1933 and 1936.) Philadelphia's Brian Boucher and the Penguins' Ron Tugnutt were the goalies. Flyers defencemen Dan McGillis played 61:05 of action in the marathon event. His defence partner Luke Richardson was nine seconds short of the full sixty, officially clocking in at 59:51. It was one of the most incredible hockey games I've ever seen. And it ended on a beauty of a goal. Primeau raced—if I can use that term—down the right side and turned on a dime, going inside on Darius Kasparaitis. He then fired a bullet to the top corner that Tugnutt had no chance of stopping. It was a legit goal, no fluke. Philadelphia won the next two games and went on to face New Jersey but blew a tire after four games of that series.

Coach Larry Robinson of the Devils became the 14th person in NHL history to win the Stanley Cup as both a player and a head coach. The others are Jacques Lemaire, Terry Crisp, Al Arbour, Tom Johnson, Toe Blake, Joe Primeau, Hap Day, Jack Adams, Cooney Weiland, Frank Boucher, Lester Patrick, Cy Denneny and Eddie Gerard. Honourable mention goes to Art Ross, who coached Boston to their Cup win in 1939 and was a Cup winner as a player prior to the formation of the NHL. Scott Stevens of New Jersey won the Conn Smythe Trophy.

2001 (June 9)
Winner: Colorado Avalanche
Cup-winning goal scorer: Alex Tanguay
Opponent: New Jersey Devils
Score of final game: 3–1. Colorado won the Stanley Cup in seven games.

The year of Bourque. In what would be his final season in the NHL, 22 years after his career began, Raymond Bourque finally got to carry the Stanley Cup. The move to hand the Cup to a veteran player has become as much a part of the winner's tradition as the team photo and the parade around the ice. Colorado Captain Joe Sakic received the Cup from Commissioner Gary Bettman, and upon hoisting it high for his second time after a previous Cup win in 1996, he turned it over to Bourque. It was a classic Stanley Cup moment and made for a great image as we all witnessed the sheer elation exuded by Ray Bourque in his second season in Colorado after 20 years in Boston.

In a statistical highlight from those playoffs, Alex Mogilny tied an NHL record with four points in one period of playoff hockey for the New Jersey Devils. His offensive outburst came in game two of the Devils' second-round victory over the Toronto Maple Leafs when he picked up one goal and three assists to stake the Devils to a 4–1 lead. The Leafs tied the game in the third; however, their run fell short, and the Devils would win the game in overtime on a Randy McKay goal and take the series in seven games. Mogilny had the biggest multi-point game, but nobody registered a hat trick during the 2001 playoffs. This was the first time that had happened since 1959. Dominik Hasek of the Buffalo Sabres set a record on May 2 when he faced his fourth career playoff penalty shot, stopping Martin Straka in a game won 5–2 by the Sabres. The previous mark of three shots faced was held by John Vanbiesbrouck.

The upset of the playoffs was a six-game defeat of the Detroit Red Wings courtesy of the L.A. Kings. The seventh-seed Kings lost the first two games but roared back to win four straight, including a mini-miracle on Manchester moment in game four where they were down 3–0 with six minutes to play, tied the game and won it in overtime. (More on the Miracle on Manchester can be found in the 1982 subsection.) L.A. would lose the next round in seven games to the eventual Cup champions. Patrick Roy won his third Conn Smythe Trophy, a record that stands to this day.

2002 (June 13)
Winner: Detroit Red Wings
Cup-winning goal scorer: Brendan Shanahan
Opponent: Carolina Hurricanes
Score of final game: 3–1. Detroit won the Stanley Cup in five games.

Carolina made their first appearance in the Cup finals, but it was Detroit that got back to their winning ways with Cup number three on Steve Yzerman's watch and number nine for head coach Scotty Bowman, who broke former head coach Toe Blake's record with that victory, and number ten for the Red Wing franchise since their first Cup in 1936. Statistical notes this playoff year included the following: For the first time since they joined the NHL in 1979 and 1980, respectively, both Edmonton and Calgary missed the playoffs. There were no series sweeps for the first time since 1991, but it was the year of the playoff shutout with 25 accumulated by all teams, an NHL record.

Leading the way for goaltenders were Ottawa's Patrick Lalime and St. Louis's Brent Johnson, who in almost synchronized fashion were engineering shutouts in unison. Both men recorded shutouts on April 20, Ottawa over the Flyers 3–0, St. Louis over Chicago 2–0. Johnson made it two in a row with a 4–0 win for his Blues over the Hawks on April 21. Lalime matched that the next night, April 22, with another 3–0 win over the Flyers. Johnson notched his third in a row, tying the NHL record, on April 23, this time producing a 1–0 score over Chicago. Not to be outdone, Lalime backstopped Ottawa to yet a 3–0 win over the Flyers yet again, on April 24. In fact, the Flyers scored only two goals in the five games played, setting an NHL record for the fewest number of goals by one team in a five-game series. Lalime and Johnson tied an NHL record originally set by Clint Benedict of the 1926 Montreal Maroons and subsequently tied by John Ross Roach of the 1929 New York Rangers and Frank McCool of the 1945 Toronto Maple Leafs.

The fortunes of the finals changed on one game, as they so often do. In this case, with the series knotted at 1–1, Detroit won game three in triple overtime on a goal scored by Igor Larionov at 14:47 of the third extra frame. Carolina's overtime victory was their seventh in the 2002 playoffs. The Larionov OT goal gave him the distinction of being the oldest player, at 42 years and 172 days, to score a goal in the Stanley Cup finals. The Wings went on to win the next two games and the Cup. Chris Chelios won his second Stanley Cup, his first coming 17 seasons earlier with Montreal. That, too, is a record for time elapsed between Cup wins by a player. Peter Forsberg led the playoffs in scoring despite not playing in the finals. He recorded 27 points in Colorado's 20-game playoff run. He previously led playoff scorers in 1999 with 24 points in 19 Avalanche games, again a year in which his Colorado Avalanche did not make the finals. Nicklas Lidstrom became the first European to win the Conn Smythe Trophy.

2003 (June 9)
Winner: New Jersey Devils
Cup-winning goal scorer: Mike Rupp
Opponent: Mighty Ducks of Anaheim
Score of final game: 3–0. New Jersey won the Stanley Cup in seven games.

This was the third Cup victory for general manager Lou Lamoriello. His Devils had won in 1995, 2000 and now 2003, each time with a different head coach. Pat Burns was the winning bench boss of this series, and in light of his passing from a valiant fight with cancer almost seven and a half years later, it's a victory savoured by many in his memory.

The early story of the playoffs were the Minnesota Wild, who erased not one but two 3–1 deficits on their way to the Western Conference final. Those victories came against Colorado and Vancouver, but then they ran into a stone wall, a.k.a. Jean-Sebastien Giguere of the Ducks. Giguere, who would go on to win the Conn Smythe Trophy, albeit in a losing cause, tied the NHL record for consecutive shutouts in the first three games of the conference final, winning 1–0, 2–0 and 4–0 before giving up his first goal of the series 4:37 into game four to Minnesota's Andrew Brunette. It was the only goal Minnesota would score in the series, as Giguere stopped 122 of 123 shots faced for an incredible .992 save percentage.

Brunette made history in the first round of the playoffs while helping the Wild to a stunning victory over the Colorado Avalanche. Brunette's goal 3:25 into the first overtime period of game seven was the series winner and also was the last goal ever allowed by Patrick Roy. Brunette's name can be found elsewhere in this book, as he scored the first goal ever in Nashville Predator history. And he once had a 62-goal season as a junior in Owen Sound. Brunette suited up for the Chicago Blackhawks in 2011–12.

Anaheim was the OT darling in the 2003 post-season, winning seven times to tie the mark set the year earlier by Carolina, though still three back of the record held by the 1993 Montreal Canadiens. Included in Anaheim's run was a five-overtime marathon in game one of their second round, against the Dallas Stars, that ended 48 seconds into the eighth period on a goal by Petr Sykora. This game still ranks as the fourth longest in NHL history. Unbelievably, game two also went to OT but ended only 1:44 in on a goal by Mike Leclerc of the Mighty Ducks. Unfortunately, when it came time for their appearance in the finals, they, like every other team, couldn't figure out a way to beat New Jersey at home. Playing 13 games on home ice, the Devils were victorious in 12 of those games, and that's the most home victories in one playoff year of any team in NHL Stanley Cup history.

Coincidentally, the Devils set the NHL record for the most road losses this same season with seven, but they got it done on home ice when it mattered most, thanks in large part to the play of Martin Brodeur, who set the NHL record for the most shutouts in one playoff year with seven in the Devils' 24 games.

2004 (June 7)
Winner: Tampa Bay Lightning
Cup-winning goal scorer: Ruslan Fedotenko
Opponent: Calgary Flames
Score of final game: 2–1. Tampa Bay wins their first ever Stanley Cup in seven games.

A number of unusual events dotted this playoff year by the time it concluded in early June. Martin Gelinas became known as Captain Clutch for the Calgary Flames. He recorded the series-winning goal in three successive matchups as Calgary beat Vancouver, Detroit and San Jose before losing a thrilling Cup final in seven to Tampa Bay. There was controversy in game six of the Cup final in Calgary related to a Gelinas no-goal in the third period that could have counted as the Cup winner. There is no doubt in my mind that puck was across the line and past Tampa goalie Nikolai Khabibulin. Instead, former Flames prospect Martin St. Louis scored in overtime, and Tampa went on to win the Cup in game seven, 2–1.

Of equal interest from a historical point of view was the fact that John Grahame, the backup goalie to Khabibulin, joined his mother as the only mother–son pair to have both their names on the Cup, one as a player, and Charlotte Grahame as the director of hockey administration for the Colorado Avalanche in 2001.

The Flames, who were the first Canadian team in the final in ten years, played a total of 26 playoff contests, tying the record set by the Philadelphia Flyers in 1987.

Brad Richards set the NHL record for the most game winners in one playoff year with seven en route to winning the Conn Smythe Trophy as playoff MVP.

2006 (June 19)
Winner: Carolina Hurricanes
Cup-winning goal scorer: Frantisek Kaberle
Opponent: Edmonton Oilers
Score of final game: 3–1. Carolina Hurricanes win their first-ever Stanley Cup in seven games.

There were a number of firsts and oddities about this playoff year, not the least of which was that it presented the first Stanley Cup since 2004, as a result of the lockout in 2004–05. On the ice, the Western Conference made history in the first round when all four series were won by the lower-seeded teams (conversely, all four series in the Eastern Conference were won by the higher-seeded teams). The eighth- and lowest-seeded Edmonton Oilers proceeded to win the Western Conference and reach the finals. This was the first time that happened after the playoffs went to their current format in 1994.

This series also marked the Oilers' first trip to the Cup final since 1990, when the franchise won their fifth Stanley Cup. Meanwhile, the Hurricanes advanced to the Cup final for the first time since 2002, when they lost in five games to the favoured Detroit Red Wings.

The curiosities continue to add up. Never before had two former World Hockey Association teams played against each other for the Stanley Cup since the surviving WHA teams joined the NHL in 1979. Carolina was originally the Hartford Whalers, who in the WHA had been known as the New England Whalers. The Winnipeg Jets/Phoenix Coyotes team is the only former WHA club to never have played in a final. In 1995, the Quebec Nordiques franchise moved to Colorado, and of course they have two Cups to their credit.

The Carolina–Edmonton final was also only the second final contested by two teams that had both missed the playoffs the previous season (setting aside the 2005 Stanley Cup playoffs, which never happened). The other such final was played by Pittsburgh and Minnesota in 1991. Even more interestingly, it also proved to be the first final contested by teams that would both go on to miss the following years' playoffs. Prior to this final, only one team, the Chicago Blackhawks, had ever missed the playoffs one year, then played in the Stanley Cup Final (win or lose) the following season, and then missed the playoffs again the season after that. That would be the 1937–38 and 1938–39 editions of the Chicago Black Hawks.

The turning point of the playoffs was the decision by Carolina head coach Peter Laviolette to replace Martin Gerber with a 22-year-old rookie named Cam Ward in game two of their first-round series against the Montreal Canadiens. Despite blowing a lead in that game and eventually losing, Ward and the Hurricanes righted the ship and rolled through the playoffs en route to the Cup. Even more impressive was the fact that Cam Ward captured the Conn Smythe Trophy after not even being in the Hurricanes' playoff plans when the post-season started.

In game one of the finals, Carolina matched the biggest comeback in Cup final history, overcoming a three-goal deficit to win 5–4. In the second period, Edmonton defenceman Chris Pronger scored the first penalty-shot goal in Stanley Cup Finals history after Carolina defenceman Niclas Wallin illegally covered the puck inside his own goalie's crease. Late in the final period, Oilers goalie Dwayne Roloson suffered a series-ending knee injury in a collision and was replaced with Ty Conklin. With 32 seconds to go in regulation, Conklin misplayed the puck, and it deflected off Jason Smith's stick to the front of the empty net, allowing Rod Brind'Amour to score the winning goal.

With Roloson's injury, Jussi Markkanen started in net for the Oilers in the second game. Although Markkanen had played 37 games in the regular season—sharing the net with Roloson, Conklin and Mike Morrison — he had not played in the entire post-season; he also had not played in a game since March 1, 2006. The Hurricanes shut out the Oilers, 5–0, with five different Carolina players scoring goals. It was the first time that a team had used three goaltenders in a Cup final since May 1970, when the St. Louis Blues employed Jacques Plante, Glenn Hall and Ernie Wakely on their way to being swept by the Boston Bruins.

2007 (June 7)
Winner: Anaheim Ducks
Cup-winning goal scorer: Travis Moen
Opponent: Ottawa Senators
Score of final game: 6–2. Anaheim Ducks win their first-ever Stanley Cup in five games.

For the third straight season, a Canadian team was in the Cup finals, and for a third straight season they would lose. The Anaheim Ducks had shed the word "Mighty" from their official name, changed logos and changed sweaters to reflect the fact that the Disney Corporation no longer owned the team. They were still the Ducks, but not your older brother's Ducks from four years earlier. This team was tough, hungry, well coached, had great goaltending and was ready to play.

This was the only year the Atlanta Thrashers made the playoffs during their 12 years in the NHL. Ironically the last NHL playoff hockey in Atlanta was played by the Flames prior to their move to Calgary in 1980. That year they lost a best-of-five to the New York Rangers three games to one, with the final game being played on April 12. Twenty-seven years later to the day, the Thrashers played game one of their first-round series against the same franchise, the Rangers. The Flames' last playoff goal was scored by Guy Chouinard from the province of Quebec. The Thrashers' first playoff goal, on April 12, 2007, was scored by Eric Belanger, another player from Quebec. The Thrashers also lost in four games to the Rangers, although in their case it was a sweep in a best-of-seven.

Calgary backup goalie Jamie McLennan set a dubious NHL record in their first round matchup against the Detroit Red Wings: the least amount of time played before being ejected and subsequently suspended. He was put in to relieve Mikka Kiprusoff late in game five in Detroit, and 18 seconds into play he was ejected for slashing Johan Franzen in the midsection with his stick. He would be suspended for five games. In that same contest, won 5–1 by Detroit, the Red Wings' Daniel Cleary converted the first-ever penalty-shot goal scored by a Red Wing in Detroit. The Wings won the series but lost in the conference final to the surging Ducks. Also of statistical note, Dallas goalie Marty Turco joined the growing list of goalies with three shutouts in one playoff series, although he posted his trifecta in a seven-game loss to the Vancouver Canucks.

Included in this incredible series was the sixth-longest game to date in playoff history, game one, won 5–4 by Vancouver's Henrik Sedin with 1:54 to play in the fourth overtime period.

The Ottawa Senators were making their tenth straight appearance in the post-season and trying to shed the demons of previous failures. They did so thanks to a tremendous offence led by captain Daniel Alfredsson, Jason Spezza and Dany Heatley. Included in their three series wins was a five-game defeat of the Pittsburgh Penguins, who featured Sidney Crosby in his playoff debut. It went well statistically for Crosby with five points, including three goals, in the five-game loss, but we'd see a little more out of him and his teammates in the next two seasons. The Senators were in a good position in the finals, having won game three to close the deficit to 2–1, but things unravelled at the conclusion of the second period of game four with the game tied at two. Captain Daniel Alfredsson in a fit of anger shot the puck at Anaheim captain Scott Niedermayer. The Ducks kept their composure in the third period, rode a game-winning goal by Dustin Penner back home to Anaheim and sealed the deal with a 6–2 win. Niedermayer would win the Conn Smythe Trophy.

2008 (June 4)
Winner: Detroit Red Wings
Cup-winning goal scorer: Henrik Zetterberg
Opponent: Pittsburgh Penguins
Score of the final game: 3–2. The Detroit Red Wings won the Stanley Cup in six games.

With their fourth Cup victory in 12 years, the Detroit Red Wings cemented their hold on what fans and pundits now refer to as a modern-day dynasty. In game one of the Western Conference quarterfinals against the Minnesota Wild, Chris Chelios of the Detroit Red Wings appeared in his 248th career playoff game, passing Patrick Roy for most career playoff games of all time. Another Red Wing, Johan Franzen, tore it up in the Wings' four game sweep over their arch-rival, the Colorado Avalanche. Franzen broke a Wings record held by Gordie Howe since 1949, when Howe had scored eight goals in a series; Franzen had nine in the four-game sweep. Franzen also notched two hat tricks, becoming the first player to do so in a series since Jari Kurri in 1985, who had a four-goal game and two other hat tricks in a six-game series win for the Oilers against Chicago.

In game two of the Western Conference semi-finals in San Jose, Dallas Stars centre Brad Richards, a previous Conn Smythe Trophy winner, tied the NHL record for most points in one period of a playoff game when he recorded one goal and three assists in the third period. Game six of their series also entered the record books, and still stands, as the eighth-longest game in the history of the NHL, lasting 129:03. Stars captain Brenden Morrow ended the game at 9:03 of the fourth overtime, tapping in a power-play goal. Goalies Marty Turco and Evgeni Nabokov set team records for saves in a game with 61 and 53 respectively. The final score was 2–1 and the date was May 4, eight years to the day after the third-longest playoff game in NHL history, a five-extra-period marathon between the Flyers and the Penguins. Another NHL record set this playoff year was for penalty shots. Six were called, the most ever in a single playoff season, with only one resulting in a goal. Mike Richards of the Philadelphia Flyers got his shot past Cristobal Huet of the Washington Capitals.

Sidney Crosby and Henrik Zetterberg tied for the playoff point lead, each recording 27 points.

Zetterberg's strong play throughout the playoffs was rewarded with him winning the Conn Smythe Trophy. Nicklas Lidstrom became the first team captain born and trained in Europe to lead a Stanley Cup champion. There were three previous Cup-winning captains born in Europe: Dunc Munroe, born in Scotland, with the Montreal Maroons in 1926; Charlie Gardiner, who was also born in Scotland and is the only goalie to captain a Cup winner, with Chicago in 1934; and Johnny Gottselig, also with the Hawks, in 1938, who was born in Russia. All three were raised in Canada but born overseas. Along with Derian Hatcher, the American-born and -raised captain of the Dallas Stars who hoisted the trophy in 1999, these players represent all of the non-Canadian-born Cup-winning captains. There was one additional name, prior to the formation of the NHL, in 1915. The Vancouver Millionaires won the Stanley Cup, and although he was injured in the final series, their captain was Si Griffis from Kansas City, Missouri.

2009 (June 12)
Winner: Pittsburgh Penguins
Cup-winning goal scored by: Maxime Talbot
Opponent: Detroit Red Wings
Score of the final game: 2–1. The Pittsburgh Penguins won their third Stanley Cup in seven games over Detroit.

There was some resemblance between this Cup victory by the Pittsburgh Penguins and the championship by the Montreal Canadiens in 1971. The Penguins became the first team to win a seven-game Cup final after losing the first two on the road since the Habs did it in '71, and Max Talbot became the first player to score two goals, including the Cup winner, on the road in game seven, since Henri Richard of that Montreal team in their game-seven victory in Chicago.

As much as the talk at the conclusion of the playoffs was the surprise victory by the Penguins in Detroit in game seven, the single game that still had fans talking happened on May 4, game two of the second-round matchup between the Penguins and the Washington Capitals. The new faces of the NHL were front and centre as Sidney Crosby and Alex Ovechkin each recorded hat tricks in a 4–3 Washington win. It was a classic tit-for-tat contest, with Ovechkin getting the last shot, his third goal, the game winner, during the third period. He also finished the game with 12 shots on goal, Crosby with five. It was a phenomenal game, and the series was eventually won by the Penguins, thanks in part to some pretty weak goaltending by the Caps Semyon Varlamov, who was pulled 2:13 into the second period of the final game with the Caps down 4–0. Game, series over.

As much as the 2009 Cup win was the anointment of Sidney Crosby, the youngest captain of a Cup-winning team in NHL history, it was his teammate Evgeni Malkin who rode the consistent hand of 36 points in the Penguins 24 games to notch both the playoff scoring title and the Conn Smythe Trophy. He was the first Russian-born player to win the award. After back-to-back trips to the finals by both these teams, there was nothing to suggest that fans were not in for more of the same over the next season or two. It would turn out to be anything but the case.

2010 (June 9)
Winner: Chicago Blackhawks
Cup-winning goal scored by: Patrick Kane
Opponent: Philadelphia Flyers
Score of the final game: 4–3. Chicago won the Stanley Cup in six games.

There were several very compelling storylines from the 2010 playoffs, not the least of course was Chicago winning their first Stanley Cup since 1961. Patrick Kane's Cup-winning goal will go down as one of the more surreal, given that for a span of two or three seconds it appeared as if he was the only player and perhaps the only person in the entire rink who knew that the puck had slid under Philadelphia goaltender Michael Leighton and into the back of the net.

Chicago's Cup win set an unusual record. For the first time since the inception of the trophy in 1893, there had been seven different winners in seven consecutive seasons: Chicago, 2010; Pittsburgh, 2009; Detroit, 2008; Anaheim, 2007; Carolina, 2006; Tampa Bay, 2004; New Jersey, 2003. As we all know, this trend has continued to 2012, but the new record started with Chicago's win. There were two previous runs of six straight years with six different winners running back-to-back stretches, from 1925–30 and 1931–36.

Back to 2010. Along with the Hawks' incredible run, fans witnessed great play by their opponent in the finals, the Philadelphia Flyers, and an amazing run by the Montreal Canadiens courtesy of goalie Jaroslav Halak. In the Flyers' case, they became only the third team to come back from a 3–0 series deficit, which they did against the Boston Bruins in the second round. To put that accomplishment in perspective, they were down 3–0 in games, they had a one-goal lead late in game four when the Bruins' Mark Recchi scored his second of the game with only 32 seconds left to force overtime. How demoralizing must that have been? Yet Simon Gagne scored in the extra frame, and the Flyers began the road back. As most of you are aware, they managed to knot the series at three, only to roll into game seven and absolutely collapse in the first period when the Bruins roared out to a 3–0 lead only 14 minutes into the first frame. The Flyers' comeback began with a James van Riemsdyk goal and ended with yet another marker by Simon Gagne, which ended up as the series winner. I find it interesting to look back historically at the two previous 3–0 comebacks and cite the key goals in the fourth game that started the road back. In the case of the 1942 Leafs, a hat trick by Don Metz in game four sparked the Toronto comeback in the finals against Detroit. For the New York Islanders in 1975, it was two goals 40 seconds apart by Clark Gillies and J.P. Parise that cemented the win in game four and led the Islanders to their improbable comeback against the Pittsburgh Penguins.

The Montreal Canadiens contributed their own part to the improbable run of the 2010 playoffs. They became the first number-eight seed to knock off a number-one after being down three games to one. Jaroslav Halak gave one of the more stunning performances in NHL playoff history, enabling Montreal to shock Alex Ovechkin and the Washington Capitals. For an encore performance they knocked off Sidney Crosby and the Pittsburgh Penguins, again in seven games, thereby becoming the first Eastern Conference eighth seed to play in the conference final since the current format was introduced (Edmonton went to the Western Conference final in 2006 after finishing the regular season in eighth place). Montreal's luck ran out in that semifinal against the Flyers, with the key game being game four, played on a Saturday afternoon in Montreal. The Habs registered one shot on goal in the second period, and frankly the statisticians were being kind. I was at the game and it was a shoot-in from centre ice that happened to find its way to the net. Montreal had nothing left in the tank and lost game five 3–0 and the series in five games.

Jonathan Toews, the Blackhawks captain, was the Conn Smythe Trophy winner in 2010. But another Chicago forward made the most intriguing entry into the record books, as the culmination of the 2010 playoffs ended a three-year run the likes of which had never been seen in NHL history and only once previously in Stanley Cup history. Marian Hossa finally won his Cup in his third straight try in the finals with three different teams. He lost with Pittsburgh in 2008, flew that coop to Detroit, who, as defending champions, then lost to the Penguins in 2009. With the Hawks, Hossa got his win and a nice contract. As of this writing the hockey world will wait to see if he's fully recovered after being on the receiving end of a brutal cheap shot by Raffi Torres of the Phoenix Coyotes during the 2012 playoffs, leading to Torres's 25-game suspension.

The only other player I could find who played in three straight Cup finals with three different teams was Tommy Smith in 1911, 1912 and 1913. He was with Galt when they lost to the Ottawa Senators in 1911. He left Galt to play for Moncton, who lost the 1912 Cup to Quebec, and in an eerily similar move to Marian Hossa's, albeit 98 years earlier, he then left Moncton to play for the defending Cup champs and got his Cup win (his second, in fact) when Quebec defended their title in 1913. He had previously been with Ottawa when they won two Cup challenges in 1906 against a team from Queen's University and one from a small town south of Ottawa called Smiths Falls. Tommy Smith was inducted into the Hockey Hall of Fame in 1973.

2011 (June 15)
Winner: Boston Bruins
Cup-winning goal scored by: Patrice Bergeron
Opponent: Vancouver Canucks
Score of the final game: 4–0. Boston won the Stanley Cup in seven games.

The trend of new teams winning the Stanley Cup continued in 2011. After the devastation of a blown 3–0 series lead and a 3–0 lead in game seven to the eventual Cup finalists in 2010, the Boston Bruins simply were not going to be denied. This season, the Bruins became the kings of the seven-game series, winning three of them, a first since the NHL's best-of-seven format began in 1939. The Bruins' victory also meant a couple of other things historically: another non-Canadian captain, Zdeno Chara, hoisted the Cup, and Mark Recchi joined a very elite group of players who had won three cups with three different teams. The overall record for multiple championships on different teams is four by two players. Jack Marshall played on championship teams with the 1901 Winnipeg Victorias, 1902 and 1903 Montreal AAA, 1907 and 1910 Montreal Wanderers, and 1914 Toronto Blueshirts.

On that 1914 Toronto team was a goaltender named Harry Holmes. Although some sources cite Holmes's next victory with another team from Toronto, the Arenas in 1918 as a continuation of the franchise from 1914, I do not believe that to be the case. It's my conclusion that with those two wins and his subsequent victories with Seattle in 1917 and Victoria in 1925 he joins Marshall as a four-time winner with four different teams. The others with three and three include Frank Foyston, Jack Walker, Mike Keane, Joe Nieuwendyk, Claude Lemieux, Al Arbour, Gord Pettinger and Larry Hillman.

Recchi also broke the record set previously by Igor Larionov as the oldest player to score a goal in the Stanley Cup finals. He was 43 years and 126 days old.

The year 2011 was the first time that all three California teams—Los Angeles, San Jose and Anaheim—made the playoffs. The first round almost produced the incredible again as the

Chicago Blackhawks lost the first three games to the Vancouver Canucks before winning the next three, only to lose game seven in overtime. It was the third year in a row that these two teams had met in the post-season. The Blackhawks had won the previous two series in six games and of course were defending Cup champs. An astute play by Vancouver's Alex Burrows led to the series-winning goal at 5:22 of overtime. He intercepted an errant pass by Chris Campoli and fired a quick, hard shot that seemed to surprise Chicago goalie Corey Crawford. It was Burrows's second goal of the game.

In the second round, the Bruins and the Flyers met in a rematch of their incredible series from the season before. Not this time, Philly. The Bruins absolutely demolished the Flyers in four games straight, outscoring them 20–7 in the process. Never have the Flyers' goaltending woes been more apparent. In 11 games played, they pulled their starting goalie six times, they used three goaltenders in total and the seemingly endless rotation of Philly starters continued for a team who remain still Cupless since the Broad Street Bully heydays when they won in front of scintillating goaltending by future Hall of Famer Bernie Parent.

If there's one thing apparent about today's NHL, it's that no lead is safe, not only in a game but in a series. Case in point: the 2011 playoffs saw two more comebacks from 3–0 series deficits; and yes, the teams who gave up those leads did hang on to win, but it made for some extremely compelling hockey. Detroit did the same as Chicago had done against Vancouver, in this case losing their first three games to San Jose, then winning the next three. The Sharks, however, held on to win game seven, 3–2.

The final followed a similar path to 1971's, in which Montreal and Chicago were in a homer series until game seven, when the Habs prevailed on the road and won the Cup. Similarly, Boston lost the first two in Vancouver, held serve, so to speak, and the series continued that way until game seven, when Boston enjoyed a fairly pedestrian win, 4–0. Tim Thomas became the third American-born player to win the Conn Smythe trophy, and the Bruins had their first Cup since the halcyon days of Bobby Orr and Phil Esposito.

2012 (June 11)
Winner: Los Angeles Kings
Cup-winning goal scored by: Jeff Carter
Opponent: New Jersey Devils
Score of the final game: 6–1. Los Angeles won their first Stanley Cup in six games.

In 1967, the Kings were one of the six expansion teams to join the NHL in what's known as the "modern expansion." The earliest expansion in the NHL actually occurred in 1924, when the Boston Bruins and the Montreal Maroons joined the league. There were several other expansion teams after that, but 1967 represented the largest growth ever in league history, and the Kings were one of those six entries. After 45 years, the many players in their history should all have shared a little in the phenomenal playoff run by the long-awaited championship edition of the franchise.

The Boston Bruins and Vancouver Canucks, the Stanley Cup finalists from 2011, were eliminated in the first round, ensuring a new champion in 2012 for the record-setting ninth straight year. In the East, three of the four opening-round series went to seven games, and two of those went to overtime to decide the series. Philadelphia and Pittsburgh set new playoff scoring records in their series, while Washington totalled only a single goal more than Boston in their entire series. In the West, none of the first-round winners had ever won a Stanley Cup, and the Phoenix Coyotes won their first playoff series since moving to Phoenix from Winnipeg. All western series were decided in six games or fewer, and five of the six games in the Chicago–Phoenix series went to overtime. However, what the playoffs will be remembered for will be two things: the win by the Kings, of course, but the incredible violence as evidenced by an NHL record 12 suspensions, multiple-line brawls and myriad cheap shots that kept the league disciplinary committee hopping. In an ironic twist, there was no further discipline announced for New Jersey Devils forward Steve Bernier, who received a five-minute major and a game misconduct for a hit behind the net on L.A.'s Rob Scuderi. The Kings blew the game open with three power-play goals, and for all intents and purposes, after Bernier's penalty the final was over.

En route to their victory, the Kings became the league's ultimate road warriors, winning ten straight on the road. This set the new single-season mark, and they also extended the overall total to 12, including their last road game in the 2011 playoffs. Dustin Brown became the second American NHL captain to hoist the Stanley Cup, joining Derian Hatcher with the Dallas Stars in 1999. Kings goalie Jonathan Quick was absolutely brilliant in this playoff run, with a spectacular 1.11 GAA in the finals, which cemented his winning the Conn Smythe Trophy.

Hy Peskin/Sports Illustrated/Getty Images

MAURICE "ROCKET" RICHARD celebrates a goal against the Toronto Maple Leafs in November 1954. He remains the NHL's greatest goal scorer from the blue line to the goal line; no player was as single-minded about putting the puck in the net. His 544 regular season goals pale next to more recent totals, but his playoff goal records were surpassed only decades later, when the post-season lasted for twice as many games. Congratulating Richard is Bernard "Boom Boom" Geoffrion. Four months later, with Richard suspended, Geoffrion surpassed his linemate for the scoring lead in what was the Rocket's last real chance to win a scoring title.

3

BEST OF THE BEST

OVER THE COURSE OF MY career studying hockey statistics and trivia, I have compiled a list of 12 players who, in my opinion, were the most dominant during their respective eras. Eleven of these men are retired, Sidney Crosby represents the current group of superstars. The list begins with the first NHL season—1917–18—and continues in chronological order. These 12 men still rank as my "best of the best," and in the following questions and answers I have included a brief synopsis of their careers and the reasons why they rank so highly.

But there are other players who played alongside these superstars, men who were thought by some to have played in the shadows and who merit special attention. So, after each superstar I have listed one of these "shadow" players and included a special trivia question and answer that shows in detail how they rivalled the stars for talent, heart and performance.

1917–1925

JOE MALONE

Joe Malone's name appears at the top of the list of the year-by-year scoring leaders. The Quebec City native, born February 28, 1890, had an incredible touch around the net. In 126 NHL games, he scored 143 goals. His totals are even more impressive when you factor in his pre-NHL numbers: 338 goals in 271 games. Four times he was a league scoring leader—twice in the National Hockey Association (NHA) and twice in the NHL. Malone played on three Stanley Cup–winning teams: the Quebec Bulldogs in 1912 and '13 and the Montreal Canadiens in 1924. Always a clean, sportsmanlike player, he stood out in an era that was characterized by rough play. He didn't possess any particular skill that made him better than the rest; he just had the ability to appear out of nowhere at the right time and score, a talent that earned him the nickname "Phantom."

It is a measure of his leadership and his stature on the Quebec team that Malone was captain for seven years. To this day he still holds the NHL record for most goals in one game: seven, scored on January 31, 1920, in a 10–6 victory over the Toronto St. Pats. Malone was regarded the NHL's first superstar and he was the first player to be in the top ten scorers with three different teams: the Quebec Bulldogs, Montreal Canadiens and

Hamilton Tigers. Malone was inducted into the Hall of Fame in 1950.

Joe Malone is one of how many players to lead the NHL in scoring while on a last-place team?

Three. The others were Dave "Sweeney" Schriner of the New York Americans in 1937 and Max Bentley of Chicago in 1947. Schriner edged out Syl Apps Sr. of Toronto by one point, 46–45, while Bentley nosed out Rocket Richard by the same slim margin, 72–71.

Malone was a Montreal Canadien in the NHL's first season, 1917–18, and he set a standard of 44 goals which would stand for 27 years. Real stat buffs will notice that, although the standings show the Habs playing a 22-game schedule, Malone took part in only 20. The Westmount Arena, home of Montreal's other NHL team, the Wanderers, burned down in January 1918, four games into the NHL season. The Wanderers folded after the fire. Any further scheduled games were cancelled, which meant Malone was two games shy of a full season.

In 1919–20, Malone returned to his original team, the Quebec Bulldogs. The Bulldogs had been a charter member of the NHL in 1917. According to some sources they were organized as the Quebec Athletics, but they are most commonly referred to as the Bulldogs. They did not have sufficient operating capital to play in that first year of the NHL, nor for season number two. They finally became solvent in 1919, and their original players, who had been scattered around the NHL by way of a special waiver draft, were reclaimed. Joe Malone was one of those players.

The Bulldogs finished last in a four-team league with a record-low 8 points in a 24-game schedule. Malone scored 39 goals and added 10 assists for 49 points, good for a three-point lead over Newsy Lalonde of the Montreal Canadiens.

1917–1927
CYRIL "CY" DENNENY

Cy Denneny was as dominant a player as Joe Malone during the early years of the NHL. Both players, along with the likes of Edouard "Newsy" Lalonde and Fred "Cyclone" Taylor, were prominent in pro hockey prior to the NHL's formation.

Born in Farran's Point, Ontario, on December 23, 1897, Denneny's career began in 1914–15 with the Toronto Shamrocks of the NHA. The following season he and his brother Corbett signed with the Toronto Shamrocks. Centred by Gordon "Duke" Keats, they made for a very potent scoring line—tops in the NHA, for that matter. However, the team finished last and it wasn't until the first NHL season in 1917–18 that Cy showed what was in store for his career. By now he was in Ottawa; the Senators had spent $750 and traded Sammy Hebert to Toronto to acquire the left winger. Although Denneny was a scoring champ only once, he finished second five times. A third-place finish and two fourths rounded out his showings in the NHL's top ten.

Denneny was a typical player of the day, small in stature but well built. By all accounts he could take care of himself, and he regularly looked after his linemates as well. There are a number of oddities regarding his career. He is on record as being the scoring champion with the fewest number of assists: two. His 22 goals and 2 assists in the 1923–24 season enabled him to finish one point ahead of George Boucher of the Montreal Canadiens.

He set the NHL record for the longest consecutive goal-scoring streak, 12 games, in 1917–18, only to watch his teammate Harry "Punch" Broadbent beat it by scoring in 16 straight games in 1922. On March 7, 1921, Denneny had a six-goal game against the Hamilton Tigers and goalie Howard Lockhart. It was only 40 days after his brother Corbett, still playing for Toronto, scored six in a game against the same Hamilton team and goalie. They remain the only brother combination to each score five goals or more in an NHL game.

Denneny scored the Stanley Cup–winning goal for the Ottawa Senators the last time they won it, in 1927 against the Boston Bruins. That was his fourth championship with Ottawa and he added a fifth title as a member of those same Bruins in 1929, his last season of pro hockey.

He retired as the NHL's career scoring leader with 331 points. He was the first player in league history to record 200, and then 300, career points, and his final total of 246 goals was also tops in the NHL at the time. Cy Denneny was elected to the Hall of Fame in 1959, a very deserving inductee and without question a superstar of his day.

Who was the first brother combination to have both their names engraved on the Stanley Cup after the formation of the NHL in 1917?

The Dennenys, Cy and Corb. Corb was a two-time winner with the Toronto Arenas and the Toronto St. Pats. Cy won four Cups with the Ottawa Senators and then a final one with the Boston Bruins in 1929. The Dennenys were also part of the highest-scoring brother combination in the early days of the NHL, Cy and his brother Corbett combined for 349 goals and 475 points.

1923–1933
HOWIE MORENZ

Unlike anyone before him, Morenz cut a swath through the NHL. With blazing speed as his forte, he was acknowledged by everybody as the single most important presence in the game from the mid-1920s until the mid '30s. Born June 21, 1902, in Mitchell, Ontario, Morenz was lightning fast on his skates, earning him the moniker "the Mitchell Meteor." Later, while playing for the Stratford Midgets in the Ontario Hockey Association (OHA), the nickname became "the Stratford Streak."

An American promoter named Tex Rickard was first turned on to hockey after watching Morenz play with the Montreal Canadiens against the New York Americans. Shortly after that, Rickard obtained his own franchise, the second one in the city of New York, and called it the Rangers. Morenz was a two-time scoring champion, in 1928 and 1931, and on three occasions he won the Hart Trophy as the league's most valuable player: 1928, '31 and '32, all with Montreal.

After falling out of favour with Habs management, Morenz was traded to Chicago in 1934, and then to the Rangers in 1936. At the start of the 1936–37 season, he was back with the Habs, and playing with his old teammates rejuvenated him. But on January 28, 1937, he suffered a badly broken leg. Instead of recuperating, he experienced what was reported as a nervous breakdown and subsequent heart trouble. Morenz died unexpectedly on March 8, 1937, shocking the hockey world. His funeral was held at the Montreal Forum on March 11. The second benefit game, featuring all-stars, was held in his honour on November 7, 1937, also at the Forum. Morenz was inducted into the Hockey Hall of Fame in 1945.

What are Howie Morenz's connections to March 11?

The one date that will forever connect Morenz and the Forum is March 11. As mentioned, his funeral was held in the Forum on March 11, 1937. I find it a remarkable coincidence that 59 years later to the day, on a Monday night, the Canadiens played their last game in the Forum, one of the most historic buildings in sports, and Canadian, history. Montreal beat the Dallas Stars, 4–1, on

March 11, 1996. There's also a March 11 connection between Morenz and the popular Hall of Fame winger Bernard "Boom Boom" Geoffrion, who had married Howie's daughter. It was decided that during the 2005–06 season Geoffrion's sweater would be retired. The date picked was March 11, 2006. Regrettably, as it approached Geoffrion's health worsened, and on that very day he passed away in Atlanta. His family decided to make the trek to Montreal that same day, the 11th, for the celebration of their patriarch's life and sweater-retirement ceremony in the part of the Forum building that now memorializes its time as a sports arena. In one of the most moving of events, Morenz's sweater, number seven, was lowered from the rafters and then raised together with that of his son-in-law and a legendary player in his own right, Bernie Geoffrion, number five. Both sweaters were then lifted to the rafters, 67 years to the day after Morenz's funeral. Incredible.

1925–1937
NELSON "NELS" STEWART

Born in Montreal on December 29, 1902, Stewart was nicknamed "Old Poison" because of his habit of spitting chewing tobacco into the eyes of opposing goaltenders. He literally burst onto the NHL scene in 1925 as a 22-year-old centre with the Montreal Maroons.

By the end of his first NHL season, Stewart had made a name for himself. He was the league's scoring leader with 34 goals and 8 assists. He won the Hart Trophy and was second in the league in penalty minutes with 119—one penalty short of the total amassed by Bert Corbeau of the Toronto St. Pats and 14 minutes shy of his league leading 133 in 1927. Stewart also helped the Maroons win the Stanley Cup—in only their second season—by scoring a playoff-high six goals in eight games, including both goals in the Cup-clinching game, a 2–0 Maroons victory over the Victoria Cougars.

Over the next 12 seasons, Stewart finished in the top ten in scoring a total of nine times. With the Maroons he centred one of the roughest lines in hockey history. The combination of Stewart, Reginald "Hooley" Smith and Albert "Babe" Siebert were known as the "S" Line.

Although only Smith hung on with the Maroons until their second and final Cup win in 1935, the "S" Line would enjoy great success with Stewart leading the way. He won the Hart Trophy for the second time in 1930, and he helped the Maroons to the finals in 1928. In that series, he became part of hockey history by scoring on the Rangers' Lester Patrick in the legendary game of April 7, 1928, game in which the 44-year-old New York coach played goal in relief of injured starter Lorne Chabot. Stewart retired at the conclusion of the 1939–40 season as a New York American. He had also been with the Bruins for three-plus seasons, and although he was never on another Cup winner, he did manage to tie Larry Aurie for the league lead in goals with 23 in 1937.

Stewart was a big man for his day, standing six foot one and weighing nearly 200 pounds. Clearly he was no shrinking violet on the ice. He was involved in two of the more spectacular fights of the thirties. In 1932, while still a Montreal Maroon, he was in a war with Alex Levinsky of Toronto, and in January 1935, now a Bruin, he was suspended for his part in a brawl against his old team, the Maroons, even though he was by all accounts on the losing end of a scrap with Lionel Conacher. In the history of the NHL, only two men have led the league in scoring and led the league in penalty minutes—one was Ted Lindsay. The other was "Old Poison," Nels Stewart.

A solid contributor to NHL lore in the late '20s and early '30s, Stewart was elected to the Hall of Fame in 1962.

Who was the second player in NHL history, after Joe Malone, to be in the top ten in scoring with three different teams?

Nels Stewart accomplished this rare feat in 1938 when he tied for 10th with Neil Colville of the New York Rangers. Stewart was playing with the New York Americans at that time. Although he'd also finished the 1936–37 season in the top ten as a member of the Americans, some of his points had been picked up while with Boston. Prior to that, Stewart had cracked the top ten with the Montreal Maroons and the aforementioned Bruins. By the way, Joe Malone made the top ten in scoring with the Montreal Canadiens, Quebec Bulldogs and Hamilton Tigers.

1928–1940
EDDIE SHORE

Eddie Shore was a legend in western Canada before he played his first game in the NHL. The man who became known as "the Edmonton Express" was born in Fort Qu'Appelle, Saskatchewan, on November 25, 1902, but grew up in Cupar, another small town in Saskatchewan. He earned his nickname as a member of the Edmonton Eskimos in the Western Hockey League. Shore set precedents for toughness and tolerance of pain that were unheard of.

After gaining the confidence of Bruins general manager Art Ross during his first NHL training camp in 1926, Shore set out to make sure everyone in the league remembered his name. Ross and Shore concocted some of the first public-relations moves in hockey history. Through the pre-game warm-ups, and right up until the start of each game, Ross would delay Shore's arrival on the ice. Fans would be unsure of his playing status until he would suddenly arrive: with the band playing "Hail to the Chief," Shore would emerge wearing a matador's cloak, followed by a valet who would remove the cloak and allow Shore to play. Needless to say, this ploy would drive fans into hysterics.

In a 14-year NHL career, Shore was a four-time winner of the Hart Trophy, in 1933, '35, '36 and '38. Had there been a Norris Trophy back then, he probably would have won it many times. He has to go down in hockey history as one of the top three or four defencemen in hockey history. He helped the Bruins to their first two Stanley Cup wins in 1929 and 1939 and he was inducted into the Hockey Hall of Fame in 1945.

Who holds the NHL record for the most fights in one game?

Eddie Shore. In his era, there was no "three fights and you're out" rule, and Shore set a bloody benchmark during an era marked by rugged, turbulent play. On November 23, 1929, two days before his 27th birthday, Shore made hockey history with five separate fights in one game. The defending Cup champs were undefeated three games into the season when they travelled to Montreal to play the Maroons, the 1926 Cup winners and a team that sported a very strong and tough lineup. "Mayhem on ice" was the way one headline described the game that ended in a 4–3 Boston win. In those days, there were two referees, not one ref and two linesmen. George Malinson and Leo Heffernan had the misfortune of being assigned to this match. In the third period, they actually had to call a halt to the game to have some of the blood scraped off the ice.

Shore's first fight was with one of the famous Boucher brothers, George. George "Buck" Boucher was the biggest and the toughest of the four Boucher brothers—as his 802 career penalty minutes attest. After Boucher, Shore got into it with Dave Trottier, collapsing one of Trottier's lungs and forcing a trip to the hospital. At this point, Shore became a marked man. Long-time sparring partner Hooley Smith decided he wanted in on the action, so he and Shore hooked up. It became apparent to fans that the Maroons were operating with a different mandate: to drive Shore from the game. Fight number four took place with Mervyn "Red" Dutton (a future president of the NHL), the previous season's penalty champ and about equal in size to Shore.

But the best was left for last. There has never been a left winger in hockey history who could rival Albert "Babe" Siebert. He could hit, shoot, skate, score—and he could fight. It's not that hard for any of today's tough guys to rack up 1,000 penalty minutes over a 14-year career, but Siebert played in an era of 44- and 48-game schedules. Siebert had been knocked down behind the net and was in the process of getting up when Shore clocked him. Infuriated, Siebert got up and ran at Shore with his stick up. Sticks, gloves and then the two players were dropped in short order. It was at this point that play was halted while the blood that had accumulated on the ice was cleaned up.

The ambulances were busy that night. In all, Shore, Siebert and Trottier were admitted to hospital. Shore's chart read as follows: broken nose, four teeth lost, two black eyes, gashed cheekbone, cuts over both eyes, and a mild concussion. But before he was helped from the ice after the last bout with Siebert, Shore contributed offensively with two assists, staking his Bruins to a 4–3 lead, one they would hang on to. Not only did the evening of November 23, 1929, result in one for the record books for Edward William Shore, but it goes down as one of the most brutally violent nights in NHL history.

As is the case with all good stories, the myth gets embellished as time passes. The story is told that Shore returned to play the next game, which coincidentally was against the Maroons, three nights later at Boston Garden. Such was not the case. Shore missed that game and didn't return until a week later in Pittsburgh. For the record, the rematch was tame—only 12 minor penalties were called in a 6–1 Montreal win that ended Boston's undefeated streak. However, Bruins president Charles Adams caused a furor among those at the league office when he presented Shore with a $500 cheque prior to the team's next home game, against the Montreal Canadiens. He was quoted as saying that the money represented $100 for each facial scar that Shore received at the hands of the Maroons. Can you imagine that happening today?

1939–1944
"BOSTON" BILL COWLEY

Bill Cowley filled the buffer period between the Eddie Shore and Rocket Richard eras in the NHL—that is, roughly the time between the late '30s, when Shore's dominance was on the wane, and the 1943–44 season, when Richard really kicked into gear. Cowley was one of the league's most consistent performers during the interval. In my opinion, Bill Cowley centred the most underrated line in the history of the NHL: Cowley, "Sudden Death" Mel Hill and Roy Conacher. Many who saw him play call him the greatest passer the game has ever known.

Born in Bristol, Quebec, on June 12, 1912, Cowley began his NHL career with the St. Louis Eagles during their only year in the NHL, 1934–35. Before the next season began, the members of the Eagles were dispersed in a special waiver draft. With their first pick in the draft—the sixth overall—the Bruins claimed Cowley for the price of $2,250. He played in Boston for the next 12 seasons, and from 1937 until 1945 he was among the top ten scorers in every year but one. In 1941, Cowley was the NHL scoring champ with 62 points in 46 games played, a whopping 18 points ahead of his nearest competitor. Or, more accurately, competitors: there was a five-way tie for second place between Bryan Hextall Sr. and Lynn Patrick of the Rangers, Gord Drillon and Syl Apps of Toronto and Syd Howe of Detroit. The 18-point margin smashed the previous record set in 1928 by Howie Morenz, who outpaced his teammate and linemate Aurel Joliat by 12 points.

Many hockey fans know the name Mel "Sudden Death" Hill. He scored three overtime goals in the first round of the 1939 playoffs as Boston beat the Rangers in seven games. Bill Cowley assisted on all three of those goals and led the playoffs in scoring with 14 points, helping Boston to its second Stanley Cup championship.

The following year saw the emergence of the Kraut Line, featuring the great Milt Schmidt, Bobby Bauer and Woody Dumart. Lost in the shadows was the trio of Cowley, Hill and Roy Conacher. Many experts of the day, including Detroit's GM Jack Adams, said that Cowley was one of the greatest stickhandlers of all time and, had he played with Dumart and Bauer, his numbers would have been even more impressive.

Cowley was the recipient of the Hart Trophy on two occasions: 1941 and 1943. However, it was in 1943–44 that he really produced in spectacular fashion, accumulating 71 points in just 36 games. His average of 1.97 points per game stood as the highest points-per-game average for 37 years until a lad named Wayne Gretzky came along. In 1980–81, the Great One scored 164 points in 80 games for an average of 2.05. Gretzky later increased that standard to 2.77 in 1983–84 which is still the NHL record.

"Boston" Bill Cowley retired in 1947 as the NHL's career leader in assists and points. He'd outstripped Frank Boucher in the assist category and overtaken his old St. Louis Eagle teammate Syd Howe as the all-time points king. Both of Cowley's marks were eventually eclipsed by the Canadiens' Elmer Lach. Cowley was elected to the Hall of Fame in 1968.

What was Bill Cowley's contribution in the first Stanley Cup final to be played in a best-of-seven format?

The year was 1939 and Boston defeated the Toronto Maple Leafs four games to one. Bill Cowley and linemate Roy Conacher tied for the scoring lead with seven points in the five games; however, Cowley was the overall leader that playoff year with 14. In game five, won 3–1 by Boston on April 16, 1939, Conacher scored the Cup-winning goal at 17:34 of the second period, assisted by Cowley and Eddie Shore.

1944–1957
MAURICE "THE ROCKET" RICHARD

Born August 4, 1921, in Montreal, Quebec, Richard was the catalyst for the birth of a Montreal style of hockey that continued for 40-plus years: "firewagon" hockey. Richard and the Habs employed a fast-paced system that was likened to a firewagon racing to a burning building.

Richard's passion for sports was fuelled during his early days at home in Bordeaux, a suburb north of Montreal. Excelling in baseball and hockey, he even entered a Golden Gloves boxing tournament and did quite well. Opponents on the ice would find out about this particular talent for years to come.

After several setbacks due to injury, Richard exploded on the NHL scene in 1943–44, scoring 32 goals in the regular season and helping the

Habs win the Cup with another 12 goals in nine playoff games. It was Montreal's first Cup win in 13 years, dating back to the glory days of Howie Morenz. Put on a line with Hector "Toe" Blake and Elmer Lach, Richard and his mates became known as the Punch Line, and two years later they led the Canadiens to another Stanley Cup.

Richard was a goalie's nightmare. Long-time Toronto netminder Johnny Bower told me in an interview once that the happiest day of his life was when the Rocket retired in 1960. Richard became the first man to score 50 goals in a season, in 1945; the first to score 500 in a career, in 1957; and he captained the Canadiens to the last four of their five straight Cup wins in the late 1950s. He won the Hart Trophy in 1947, was a 14-time member of the All-Star team—selected to the First Team eight times—and he still sits in second place for career overtime goals in the playoffs with six, behind only Joe Sakic's mark of eight.

Richard never led the league in points, but he did take the goal-scoring crown on five occasions. In his honour, the league commissioned the Maurice Richard Trophy for leading the league in goals, which was awarded for the first time in 1999. The first winner was Teemu Selanne of Anaheim, with 47 goals.

Aside from the goal-scoring exploits and his team's winning ways, Richard had a desire to play and win, coupled with a temper best characterized as volatile. During an altercation with Hal Laycoe of the Bruins on March 13, 1955, Richard hit linesman Cliff Thompson and was subsequently suspended for the remainder of the season and the entire playoffs. There were three games left in the regular season. The Canadiens' next home game was against Detroit on March 17, 1955. That date will forever be infamous for the "Richard Riot." Montreal fans were so incensed by the judgment handed down by league president Clarence Campbell that they rioted, causing $500,000 in damages citywide. Richard later appeared on radio and television in an attempt to calm the waters.

Maurice Richard was inducted into the Hockey Hall of Fame in 1961, becoming only the second player for whom the Hall's waiting period was waived. (Dit Clapper was the first.) The Rocket is still regarded by many as the purest goal scorer, and the most dominant player from the blue line to the net, that the game has ever known. Richard died on May 27, 2000, and his body lay in state in the Molson Centre for an entire day. Over 115,000 people filed past his casket in a display of affection and respect. He was given a full state funeral on May 31.

Who holds the rather unusual NHL record of being awarded a penalty shot just 12 seconds after a game had begun?

Rocket Richard. It's not a stat you would find in any record book, but the Rocket does have the distinction of being the player who took the earliest penalty shot ever in a game. Twelve seconds into Montreal's match against Chicago on New Year's Day 1952, Chicago's Jimmy Peters, himself a former Canadien, hauled down Bert Olmstead, who was in all alone. In those days, any player who was on the ice when the infraction occurred could take the shot. Richard was on the ice, so there was no doubt he would get the call. This was the third and final penalty shot of the Rocket's career. He was stopped on his first attempt on March 17, 1945—10 years to the day before the Richard Riot—by Chicago goalie Doug Stevenson. He scored on January 19, 1950, against Turk Broda of the Toronto Maple Leafs.

If you're really observant you'll notice that Richard's first penalty shot was awarded the day before he became the first man to score 50 goals.

That was on March 18, against Boston. Imagine: the Rocket could have scored the historic marker on a penalty shot on home ice. Only one player ever recorded a 50th goal on a penalty shot: Mario Lemieux, in 1997 against goalie John Vanbiesbrouck. It would be the last regular-season goal of Lemieux's career (prior to his comeback in 2000–01). Only one player scored his final NHL goal on a penalty shot: King Clancy of the Leafs, in 1936, against Mike Karakas of the Chicago Black Hawks.

But I digress! Back to the Rocket.

Richard scored on the 1952 penalty shot and Montreal went on to win the game 3–0. So, besides being the quickest penalty-shot goal in NHL history, it is also the quickest game-winning goal in Montreal Canadiens history. It's only five seconds slower than the NHL record in that category: Charlie Conacher of Toronto scored a goal seven seconds into a game on February 6, 1932, a 6–0 Leaf victory over Boston.

1947–1960
"TERRIBLE" TED LINDSAY

As the league evolved in the late 1940s and early '50s there was a slew of players who would rate as excellent candidates to be the "shadow," if you will, to the indomitable Maurice Richard. Max Bentley of Chicago, Toronto and the Rangers, Montreal's Elmer Lach and Ted Kennedy of Toronto are only a few. The man I've chosen was, without a doubt, Richard's main adversary in those days.

Lindsay was born in Renfrew, Ontario, on July 29, 1925. His dad, Bert Lindsay, was a goalie for eight pro seasons in the NHA, PCHA and the NHL—where he spent a season with the Toronto Arenas in 1918–19.

Ted played most of his 17 years with the Detroit Red Wings, with the exception of the period from 1957 until 1960 when he was in hockey's purgatory: Chicago. Lindsay will always be known as the left winger on one of the top lines in NHL history—the Production Line, which featured Gordie Howe on right wing and Sid Abel at centre. In 1950, this was the third line in NHL history to finish one-two-three in scoring. The first two were Boston's Kraut Line, in 1940, and the Punch Line of Montreal, in 1945.

Lindsay was the NHL's scoring leader in 1949–50 with 78 points in 69 games played. His 141 penalty minutes were third in the league behind Bill Ezinicki of Toronto and Gus Kyle of the Rangers, but they represented the highest total by any scoring leader in NHL history, breaking the mark of 119 set by Nels Stewart in 1925–26. (Lindsay's mark would be eclipsed by Jean Beliveau, with 143 in 1956. In 1964, Stan Mikita broke that record with 146, then outdid himself the following year with 154. That total remains the all-time high for a scoring leader.) Ted Lindsay captained Detroit for four seasons, 1952–1956. During that time the Red Wings finished first three times, played in three finals and won two Cups. Lindsay had 221 points and 467 PIMs.

On January 25, 1951, Lindsay and Ezinicki staged the brawl of the year at the Detroit Olympia. Ezinicki lost a tooth and got two black eyes, a broken nose and 19 stitches. Lindsay needed five stitches and his knuckles were badly cut and swollen. Both players were fined $300 and suspended for three games.

A nine-time all-star—including eight appearances on the First Team—Lindsay proved over his career that he could score as well as play it tough. His one Art Ross Trophy is backed up by seven other top ten finishes in scoring, including three times in the runner-up spot.

Lindsay's battles off the ice to form the first players' union have been well documented and were the subject of a movie and a book, both called *Net Worth*. His efforts were "rewarded" with a trade to Chicago on July 23, 1957, less than a week before his 32nd birthday. He and goalie Glenn Hall were sent to the Black Hawks in exchange for Hank Bassen, Johnny Wilson, Forbes Kennedy and Bill Preston.

After three years in Chicago, the fiery left winger hung up the blades. Four years later he took one final kick at the can, coming out of retirement to play for the Wings in 1964–65. When he retired for good after that season, his 379 career goals were tops among left wingers, and he was the all-time leader with 1,808 penalty minutes. Lindsay was a four-time Cup winner with the Red Wings and was one of the game's fiercest competitors. He was elected into the Hall of Fame the year after he retired in 1966, becoming the third player for whom the Hall waived its waiting period.

Who are the only three players to lead the NHL in goals one season and penalty minutes in another?
Ted Lindsay, Nels Stewart and Rocket Richard. Nels Stewart was the first, leading the league in goals in 1925–26 and in penalty minutes the following year. Rocket Richard led the league in goals on five occasions and in penalty minutes in '52–53. Lindsay was the goal-scoring leader in 1947–48 with the Red Wings and the penalty leader in '58–59 with Chicago. At the time, Lindsay's 184 minutes in 1959 were the second-highest total ever recorded. Only Lou Fontinato of the Rangers, with 202 minutes in 1955–56, had been more belligerent. Lindsay wore number 15 during his one-season comeback with Detroit in 1964–65; his old number, 7, had been taken by Norm Ullman.

1950–1968
GORDIE HOWE
Born March 31, 1928, in Floral, Saskatchewan, Gordie Howe defied all probability by playing in hockey's major leagues for 32 years. The fourth of nine children, Howe quit school early to work in construction. At the age of 15, he took an overnight train to Winnipeg, where he attended his first training camp, that of the New York Rangers. The well-known story describes Howe becoming homesick and returning to Saskatchewan. The next year, however, he attended Detroit's training camp in Windsor, Ontario, where he was offered his first contract by the Wings' general manager/coach, Jack Adams. It would be another two years before Howe suited up for the parent club, by which time he was a strapping, slope-shouldered, six-footer weighing 205 pounds.

It wasn't until his fifth year in the league that Howe had more points than penalty minutes in a season. The change may have been prompted by a conversation with Adams, who said, "Gordie, we know you can fight, but can you play the game?" Play he did: he led the NHL in scoring in each of the next four years—1950–51 through 1953–54—then added two more titles in 1957 and 1963. He was in the top ten in NHL scoring in 21 straight years. In 1952–53, he set a record for points, with 95, that stood for six years. Howe got his name on the Stanley Cup four times, but an injury en route to his first Cup win in 1950 nearly killed him. His skull was fractured badly after a collision with the boards—and Ted Kennedy of Toronto—and he missed the rest of that year's playoff action. Fortunately, it would turn out that very little could stop the man known as "Mr. Hockey."

Howe played out his first NHL career in Detroit retiring in 1971, only to come back two years later and play with two of his sons, Mark and Marty, for the Houston Aeros of the World

Hockey Association. Would the 45-year-old embarrass himself and the game of hockey? Not likely. Twice in six WHA seasons he topped the 100-point mark; on another occasion he had 99. Howe retired after one more year in the NHL with the Hartford Whalers in 1979–80. He played in all 80 games, scored 15 goals, turned 52 years of age and became a grandfather.

Arguably the greatest ambassador in the history of the game, Howe's ability to play at such a high level for three decades is a feat that will never be duplicated. Howe was inducted into the Hockey Hall of Fame in 1972.

Besides Ray Bourque, what other NHL player once had 19 shots on goal in a regular-season NHL game?

Gordon Howe of the Detroit Red Wings. Again, this is not a statistic that you will find in the NHL's *Official Guide and Record Book*, for the very understandable reason that statistics in a number of categories were incomplete for many years—in fact, right up until the modern expansion of 1967.

On the night of January 27, 1955, the Detroit Red Wings and New York Rangers skated to a 3–3 tie. The fact that Howe was held scoreless and pointless was in those days significant enough; however, his total of 19 shots against goalie Gump Worsley takes on greater significance when you consider the final total that night: Detroit 31, New York 18. That's right: Howe had more shots than the entire Ranger team. The Blueshirts tied the game on a goal by Gordie's brother, Vic Howe, at 11:57 of the third period. It was Vic's second career goal, and was assisted by Pete Conacher and Ron Murphy. Vic would only score three goals in his NHL career. It's interesting that one of them came on a night when his much more famous brother recorded the greatest offensive output of his lifetime, yet did not appear in the scoring summary.

1955–1971
JEAN "LE GROS BILL" BELIVEAU

This natural scoring sensation was born August 31, 1931, in Trois-Rivieres, Quebec. One would think that his fate would be to play for the Habs, but in the early 1950s that appeared to be anything but a lock. The scoring star of the Quebec Aces of the Quebec Senior Hockey League felt no pressure to make the jump to the NHL and the Montreal Canadiens for a very simple reason: he could earn more money and enjoy a better quality of life in the minor pro league known as the QSHL.

Beliveau first wore the Canadiens' red, white and blue on December 16, 1950, when both he and Bernie Geoffrion were called up from the ranks of the Quebec Junior Hockey League—Beliveau from the Quebec Citadelle, Geoffrion from the Laval Nationale. Beliveau and Geoffrion played in a game against the Rangers and it ended 1–1. A little more than a month later they were both called up again. The date was January 27, 1951, and Montreal beat Chicago 4–2—both juniors scored.

Montreal was able to get Geoffrion under contract fairly easily. However, when he graduated from the Citadelle, Beliveau opted instead to remain in Quebec, where he was treated like a superstar—and paid like one. Occasionally, as he had done as a junior, he would test the NHL waters with Montreal, who owned his big-league rights. In fact, the Habs also owned the QSHL. It was one of two leagues that they purchased outright to protect a single player. The other was the Eastern Ontario Junior Hockey League, which they bought in the late 1950s to protect their claim on Bobby Rousseau.

Beliveau's next appearance as a Hab was on December 18, 1952, and it left no doubt that he was ready for NHL prime time. He scored a hat trick against the Rangers in a 6–2 win, had numerous scoring chances in a 6–3 loss to Boston and then added two more goals in a rematch with the Bruins the next night as Montreal won 4–3. Hab fans languished for several years knowing full well that this giant of a man could be a key ingredient to reclaiming the Cup, which they had not won since 1946. Montreal did win the Cup in the spring of 1953 without Jean Beliveau, but management had made up its mind that signing the reluctant star was priority number one.

In the fall of 1953, Beliveau became a full-time member of the Montreal. Frank Selke Sr., general manager of the Canadiens, discovered the trick to getting the big man on board. As he so eloquently put it, "I just opened the vault and said, 'Jean, help yourself.'" Beliveau hit his stride in his second NHL season, when he finished third in scoring behind two teammates, Bernie Geoffrion and Rocket Richard, and made his first trip to the finals, where Montreal lost the Cup in seven games to Detroit. The next 16 years would see the tall Number 4 win an Art Ross Trophy in 1956, two Hart Trophies—in 1956 and 1964—and the inaugural Conn Smythe Trophy in 1965. Six times he was a First-Team All-Star, and four times he made the Second Team. He became the fourth player to record 500 career goals and only the second to score 1,000 career points. Beliveau also captained the Canadiens for 10 seasons and he played on a total of 10 Stanley Cup–winning teams. In those 10 victories, Beliveau played 108 games and accumulated 129 points.

Beliveau's final season, 1970–71, best exemplified his career. At the age of 39, he led his team in scoring, finishing in a tie for ninth in the league. For the 17th time, he entered the playoffs—although, unlike so many times before, the Canadiens were huge underdogs going into the quarterfinals against the powerful Boston Bruins. Down 1–0 in games and trailing 5–2 at the end of two periods of game two in Boston, Beliveau ignited a comeback with two quick goals as the Habs went on to win the game 7–5 and the series four games to three.

After a hard-fought series against Minnesota that went six games, the Habs won the Cup—their 17th championship, Beliveau's 10th and last—with another nail-biter of a series against Chicago. The series went to seven games, and the Canadiens won the final game 3–2. "Le Gros Bill" played in all 20 playoff games and accumulated 22 points—including 16 assists, which at that time was a playoff record. And he was nearly 40.

To this day, Jean Beliveau is revered in a similar vein as Gordie Howe. They are two of the greatest ambassadors the game of hockey has ever seen. Beliveau possessed dignity both on and off the ice, and his quiet charisma instilled in his teammates a certain kind of pride and a feeling that wearing the red, white and blue was an honour, one that should be repaid with a Cup win. Beliveau was elected to the Hall of Fame in 1972. His number, 4, was retired by Montreal to honour both him and Aurel Joliat.

Who sits in second spot behind Bill Mosienko for the fastest three goals by one player in an NHL regular-season game?

Jean Beliveau. Bill Mosienko's famous hat trick was scored in 21 seconds on March 23, 1952. It's one of the greatest feats of all time. Somewhat forgotten is Beliveau's threesome, scored in 44 seconds on November 5, 1955, in a 4–2 Montreal win over Boston. In fact, Beliveau scored all four Habs goals in that game.

Beliveau's three goals—at 0:42, 1:08 and 1:26 of the second period—were all scored over the course of the same Montreal power play, during which they held a two-man advantage. Prior to 1957, a player served out the entire penalty, regardless of how many goals were scored. The Bruins goalie was Terry Sawchuk, who had been acquired from Detroit in the off-season.

There's one other statistical note about Beliveau that I love. The night of Beliveau's first hat trick in NHL history, December 18, 1952, he was wearing number 12, not 4. He did not take number 4 on a full-time basis until his first full season in 1953–54.

1960–1972
BOBBY HULL

Robert Marvin Hull was born on January 3, 1939, in Pointe Anne, Ontario. The man they called "the Golden Jet" burst onto the NHL scene during the 1957–58 season. If you look closely at the TV footage of Rocket Richard's 500th career goal on October 19, 1957, you'll notice a young man wearing number 16 skating off the ice to the Chicago bench as the Rocket is being congratulated. It was Hull's fifth NHL game. Who could have known that the 18-year-old would be the man to break the Rocket's record of 50 goals in one season and who would also surpass his career mark of 544 regular-season goals?

Hull combined tremendous speed with raw power and strength. After a stellar junior career in St. Catharines, he was expected to pay immediate dividends in Chicago, and he did. In 1958, he finished second to Toronto's Frank Mahovlich for the Calder Trophy. In his third season, at the age of 21, he won his first scoring championship. The following year, 1961, he won his one and only Stanley Cup championship and, the year after that, he had his first 50-goal season. With the curved "banana" blade now at his disposal, he possessed a shot that not only travelled about 100 miles an hour but also tended to move unpredictably, making it a goaltender's nightmare. During the 1965–66 season, Hull became the first player to score 50 goals more than once and then, on March 12, he scored his 51st goal, breaking the Richard record that had stood for 21 years.

Hull's scoring prowess and his powerful slapshot are legendary, but the true measure of his significance in the hockey world is best demonstrated by the instant credibility he gave the fledgling World Hockey Association in 1972. Winnipeg was so enamoured with him that they took their name, the Jets, from his nickname, the Golden Jet. He was greeted as a national hero and he repaid the team and the fans by taking the Jets right to the top of their division. In 411 WHA games, Hull scored 303 goals. Although the NHL looked down upon the upstart organization, a number of prominent players got their pro hockey start there, most notably Wayne Gretzky and Mark Messier.

History regards Hull as the greatest left winger of all time—and as far as goal scoring is concerned that would be correct. But I maintain that Albert "Babe" Siebert brought a more complete package of skills to the Montreal Maroons in the late 1920s and early '30s. Hull was a three-time Art Ross Trophy winner in 1960, '62 and '66, and he won the Hart Trophy winner in 1965 and '66. Bobby and his son Brett are the only father–son combination each to win the Hart Trophy. Bobby was inducted into the Hockey Hall of Fame in 1983.

What player drew an assist on Bobby Hull's historic 51st goal during the 1965–66 season, even though he was actually on the bench when the goal was scored?

Lou Angotti. The goal came 10 days after Hull recorded number 50 against Detroit goalie Hank Bassen. (Twenty-four years later, Hank's son Bob and Bobby's son Brett would be teammates on St. Louis.) After that game, Hull and the Hawks were shut out in three straight games as the whole team tried to get the puck to Bobby at every opportunity. Finally, Hull told the boys to concentrate on playing hockey and the goal would come on its own. Sure enough, in the very next game, on March 12 against the Rangers, he scored the historic goal at 5:34 of the third period. It was a typical Hull play: Bill Hay passed the puck to Lou Angotti, who was heading off on a line change, but not before he passed the puck to Hull. Hull carried the play up ice and, with Angotti on the bench, he fired a bullet past Cesare Maniago from just over the blue line. The goal prompted a seven-minute standing ovation from the crowd of 16,666.

Hull would finish the season with a total of 54 goals. He later broke his own mark with 58 in 1968–69. That mark was in turn overtaken by Phil Esposito's 76-goal outburst in 1970–71, which was eclipsed in 1981–82 by Wayne Gretzky's 92-goal performance.

1960–1970
STAN MIKITA

For starters, Stan Mikita is not his real name. He was born Stanislav Gvoth on May 20, 1940, in Sokolce, Czechoslovakia. At the age of eight, he was sent on his way to St. Catharines, Ontario, for what he thought would be a short visit with his Uncle Joe and Aunt Anna Mikita, who had immigrated to Canada years earlier. Little did he know it was a trip that would change his life. The political climate in Czechoslovakia was uncertain, and it had been arranged that little Stanislav, now known as Stan, would begin a new life in southern Ontario.

It wasn't long before the youngster who had travelled so far took up his new country's favourite pastime, hockey. By the age of 16, he'd joined the local junior team, the St. Catharines Teepees. As was the case with Jean Beliveau, Mikita's NHL debut came during a call-up. It was November 1958, and within 24 hours of getting the call, Mikita was facing off against the big Number 4 from Montreal, Jean Beliveau. That first taste of NHL action lasted three games, and although Mikita didn't score he did pick up an assist on a goal by Ted Lindsay. But he would soon be no stranger to NHL scoresheets.

Mikita racked up 541 regular-season goals, but I doubt if there is a player anywhere who could claim that his first big-league goal was more of a fluke. It was October 7, 1959, and the Black Hawks were hosting the New York Rangers at Chicago Stadium. Mikita was on a line with Bobby Hull and Eric Nesterenko. The rebound of a Hull shot hit Mikita on the rear end and it bounced into the net past Gump Worsley. That was goal number one.

In his 22-year career, Mikita would add 926 assists for a total of 1,467 points. He also racked up 150 points in 155 post-season games. He won the Art Ross Trophy in 1964 and '65, and in 1967 he won the Ross as well as the Hart and Lady Byng trophies, becoming the first triple trophy winner in NHL history. If that weren't enough, he repeated the trifecta in 1968. By this time he was without a doubt the greatest offensive scoring threat in the NHL. In addition to the four scoring titles, he added a second-place finish to teammate Bobby Hull in 1966 and another four finishes in the top ten throughout his career. He was an eight-time all-star, named to the First Team six times and twice to the Second Team. Stan Mikita and Bobby Hull were the two offensive giants of the game in the 1960s. During that decade they combined for 756 goals, 857 assists and 1,613 points. They won seven Art Ross Trophies, four

Hart Trophies and three Lady Byng Trophies. Ironically, they rarely saw the ice at the same time. (Note: statistics tabulated from 1960–61; however, Hull's Art Ross Trophy win in 1959–60 was included in the tally.)

When Stan Mikita retired from hockey during the 1979–80 season, he was third in all-time scoring behind Gordie Howe and Phil Esposito. He was elected into the Hall of Fame in 1983, a deserving honour for a spectacular career.

True or false: Stan Mikita led the league in penalty minutes one season, only to win the Lady Byng Trophy the next year.

I often have to correct this, one of the greatest misconceptions about Stan Mikita. But although he was close to the penalty lead in 1964, when he picked up 146 minutes, he fell five penalty minutes short of tying Vic Hadfield of the Rangers, who spent 151 minutes in the box. It would be another three seasons before he won the first Lady Byng. His penalty minutes dropped from a career high of 154 in 1965 to 12—a career low—in 1966–67 and 14 in 1967–68, the two years in which he won the Lady Byng.

There were a number of reasons for the decline. For one thing, Mikita matured. And, as he grew more established in the league, he had created his space, if you will, and no longer needed to react to every single incident. The Black Hawks recognized his importance and simply did not want him engaged in every potentially volatile situation. The man himself said it best: "You need a heck of a long stick to score from the penalty box!"

1968–1975
BOBBY ORR

Robert Gordon Orr was born on March 20, 1948, in Parry Sound, Ontario. At the age of 12 he was put on the Bruins' protected list, and by 14 he was playing major junior hockey with the Oshawa Generals in the elite Ontario Hockey Association.

His junior career was phenomenal. At 15, he broke the OHA record for goals by a defenceman with 29. The mark had been 20, held by Jacques Laperriere of the Montreal Junior Canadiens. Orr played in the 1966 Memorial Cup finals against Edmonton, but was hampered by a groin injury and the Oil Kings claimed the national junior crown.

At 18, Orr attended his first Boston camp, and overwhelming accolades were immediately heaped on the young man. The Bruins had missed the playoffs in each of the past seven seasons. Orr would lead them to the promised land. Or so they hoped.

Although Orr won the Calder Trophy that season, the Bruins missed the playoffs for the eighth time in a row. In fact, they posted a poorer record in the regular season than they had in 1965–66. But when Boston acquired Phil Esposito in May 1967, the seeds of a winning team were sown. The Bruins were quarterfinalists in 1968, semifinalists in 1969, and Stanley Cup champions—for the first time in 29 years—in 1970. Orr scored the Cup-winning goal, which is regarded as the greatest NHL goal of all time.

Throughout the remainder of his all-too-brief career, Orr had many people convinced, and with justification, that he was not only the greatest defenceman of all time, but perhaps the greatest player of all time. His three Hart Trophy wins as MVP were overshadowed by Gordie Howe (six) and Eddie Shore (four), and equalled by Howie Morenz. But Orr did something no one had ever done before: he was the first defenceman to lead the league in scoring—an unbelievable feat that he accomplished in 1970 and 1975.

Orr had the best traits of all the greats rolled into one. He controlled a game like Doug Harvey; he could shoot—perhaps not like Hull, but he could fire it; he had great speed and manoeuvrability, like Hull and Morenz; he shared Shore and Richard's desire to win at all costs; and, like Howe, he was tough. Most of Orr's records have been surpassed, but those who saw him play will never forget the way he dominated the game in the late 1960s and early '70s. He was inducted into the Hall of Fame in 1979, the same year in which he officially retired.

Who wore number 4 for Chicago immediately prior to Bobby Orr's arrival in 1976 and immediately after his 1979 retirement from the team and the game?

Dave Logan wore number 4 before Orr, while Keith Brown wore it afterward. Although he's famous for the number 4, Orr wore number 2 throughout his minor-hockey days and into his tenure with the Oshawa Generals. However, that number had been retired, for Eddie Shore, long before Orr arrived on the scene in Boston. There are photos of Orr wearing a number 27 and numbers 30 and 31 in his inaugural Bruin training camp but he did in fact begin his NHL career as number 4 after the previous player to wear the number, Al "Junior" Langlois, suffered an eye injury during training camp in 1966. Langlois left the Bruins and ended up retiring after playing the 1966–67 season with the Los Angeles Blades of the Western Hockey League.

1965–1975

PHIL ESPOSITO

Phil Esposito was born on February 20, 1942, in Sault Ste. Marie, Ontario. Those of us who remember the NHL of the late 1960s and early '70s recall with wonder the scoring exploits of the big man from "the Soo."

Esposito played junior hockey with the St. Catharines Teepees, the same team that had produced Bobby Hull and Stan Mikita. His initial tryout with the Teepees' parent team, the Chicago Black Hawks, in 1962 was anything but successful, so his pro career began with the St. Louis Braves of the old Eastern Pro league. He turned in a solid 90-point effort in 1962–63, then split the '63–64 season between St. Louis and Chicago. In 43 games with the Braves, he racked up 80 points, while in 27 games with the Hawks he accumulated the grand total of 5 points. On many nights, his ice time was no more than one quick shift. It is doubtful that anyone in the hockey world could foresee what lay ahead.

Espo eventually worked his way into the lineup, becoming the team's number two centre. But a lack of scoring on the Hawks, particularly in the playoffs, paved the way for the biggest break of his career. Citing the big man's inability to produce in the post-season, Chicago GM Tommy Ivan traded him, along with Ken Hodge and Fred Stanfield to the last-place Boston Bruins for Gilles Marotte, Hubert "Pit" Martin and minor-league goalie Jack Norris. The date was May 15, 1967, and it's one of the most infamous in Chicago Black Hawks history.

There was no way of telling what a one-sided deal it would turn out to be. However, Bruins GM Milt Schmidt must have recognized some untapped potential in Esposito. He gave the centreman a new contract for more money, made him an alternate captain and had coach Harry Sinden put the big man between wingers who would feed him the puck. In Chicago, it had been the other way around. The payoff was immediate: Esposito would win five Art Ross Trophies over the next seven seasons, setting a record for points in a season with 126 in 1968–69, then breaking his own mark with the incredible total of 152 in 1970–71.

For eight straight seasons, Esposito finished no lower than second in the league in scoring.

Along the way he became the sixth player in NHL history to record 500 career goals, reaching the plateau on December 22, 1974, against Detroit goalie Jim Rutherford. The big goal came in his 803rd NHL game—meaning that he was 58 games faster to 500 goals than his one-time winger, Bobby Hull.

No player in hockey history dominated the scoring summaries the way Phil Esposito did between 1967 and 1975. Even though he had been in the top ten twice as a Hawk, his assault on the record books during his Bruin years was unprecedented, in my opinion ranking second only to the tremendous statistics generated by Wayne Gretzky in his prime.

Boston won the Cup twice during Esposito's tenure. Contrary to Tommy Ivan's assessment, the big pivot was a major playoff contributor, scoring 51 points in the 29 post-season games the Bruins played in their championship years of 1970 and '72. In an era when scoring 50 goals was equivalent to climbing Mount Everest, Phil Esposito rattled off five such seasons in a row. He followed his monstrous total of 76 with performances of 66, 55, 68 and 61 goals. In 1970–71, he also established a record for most shots on goal, with 550; equalled Joe Malone's mark of seven hat tricks in one season; and was part of a team that set a total of 35 other team and individual records. Of course, as we all know by now, the boys from Beantown ran into a tall, lanky goalie by the name of Ken Dryden in the first round of the post-season, and very quickly the pomp and pageantry of their record-setting 121-point season went down the drain.

Any bad feelings surrounding the team's early playoff demise in 1971 were erased by the Cup win in 1972, but the events of September 1972 represented what would arguably be the crowning glory of Phil Esposito's career. The "Summit Series" that pitted Canada against the Soviet Union was the most emotionally charged sporting event in Canadian history, and although history casts Paul Henderson as the hero, it was Esposito who carried that team. He absolutely refused to lose. The television interview he gave Johnny Esaw after Team Canada's loss in game four in Vancouver should be required viewing for all Canadians. Viewing it, you can see and feel the passion of a Canadian-born hockey player earning his living in the States but desperately wanting to win for his country. The emotional punch packed by the words that poured out of Espo's mouth was unmistakable.

The final years of Phil Esposito's playing career were spent in New York as a Ranger. In November 1975, another blockbuster deal saw Esposito, coming off a 61-goal season, traded to the Rangers with Carol Vadnais for Brad Park, Jean Ratelle and Joe Zanussi. Although devastated by the deal, he gathered himself together and played for the Broadway Blueshirts until 1980–81. In each of his four full seasons in New York, he scored 30 goals or more.

When Phil Esposito retired he was the second-leading scorer in NHL history with a total of 1,590 points. He was named to a total of eight All-Star teams—six times to the First Team, twice to the Second Team—and was inducted into the Hockey Hall of Fame in 1984.

What player recorded his 50th goal of the season on his birthday three times?

Phil Esposito. On February 20, 1972, he even scored number 50 against his brother Tony! The only other man to score number 50 on his birthday was Wayne Gretzky, who did it on his 24th birthday, January 26, 1985, against goalie Denis Herron and the Pittsburgh Penguins.

1974–1980
GUY LAFLEUR

Born on September 20, 1951, in Thurso, Quebec, Lafleur was destined to become the latest in the Montreal Canadiens' line of French-Canadian superstars. Like Bobby Orr, Lafleur was being watched closely as early as 12 years of age after his performance in the prestigious Quebec City Pee-Wee Tournament at the 1963 Winter Carnival. However, unlike the gregarious Bobby Hull or the aggressive Orr, Lafleur displayed an intense, almost brooding, attitude. Lafleur lived for the rink and channelled his full attention into developing his game. He left home and travelled to Quebec City to play junior hockey. Without the familiarity of his home, family, friends and teammates, his adjustment was difficult. This same sense of isolation would be evident four years later when he made the transition to the Montreal Canadiens.

The pressure was intense. It began with his sweater number. Lafleur had worn number 4 throughout his career to date. Now here he was, not only taking Jean Beliveau's spot on the roster, but being asked if he wanted the Hall of Famer's famous number. Undecided, Lafleur spoke to Beliveau, who advised him that he could take number 4 if he wanted, but it would be better to take a new number and make it his own. It was a saving grace in a season that would test management, fans and Lafleur himself.

Lafleur struggled during his first three years, although the team wrapped a couple of quarter-final defeats around a Stanley Cup win in 1973. With the beginning of the 1974–75 season, though, "the Flower" began to bloom. Some of the reasons for his emergence: he stopped wearing a helmet, signed a new contract and got married. He would string together six straight 50-goal seasons, earning a slot on the First All-Star Team in each of them. He also won three scoring titles, two Hart Trophies, a Conn Smythe Trophy and four more Stanley Cup championships. He was the game's dominant player and he played with flair: his blond hair flowed behind him as he streaked down the ice, firing that patented slap shot from the top of the face-off circle.

The circumstances that led to Lafleur's retirement from the Canadiens in 1984 are well documented. The dynasty of the '70s made a number of early playoff exits in the 1980s, and much of the pressure for success fell on Lafleur's shoulders. After suffering injuries both on and off the ice, and feeling the strain of constant scrutiny from the media and the Montreal fans, Lafleur could take no more and packed it in on November 26, 1984. Was it the right thing to do? Under those circumstances and in that situation, no question. Could he still play the game? Absolutely!

Hollywood could not have written a better script for Lafleur's comeback. In 1988, he signed with the New York Rangers. On February 4, 1989, he returned to the Forum and scored twice. On March 30, 1991, he was in a Quebec Nordiques uniform for his final game on Forum ice and he scored again as the crowd chanted his name, "Guy! Guy! Guy!"

Lafleur was inducted into the Hockey Hall of Fame in 1988. His comeback with the Rangers made him only the second man in hockey history to play in the NHL after becoming a Hall of Famer. Gordie Howe was the other at that time, Mario Lemieux followed later which has led the Hall of Fame to rescind the automatic inductions for superstar players after they retire. Everybody wait's three years now regardless.

How many seasons did Guy Lafleur wear a helmet in the NHL?

Three—his first three years, in fact, from 1971–72 until 1973–74. Here are some other statistical notes on Lafleur that you may find interesting. He never had a five-goal game in the NHL, although he did have one four-goal game, on January 26, 1975, in a 7–2 win over the Penguins. When he played in his first All-Star Game, he didn't wear his familiar number 10. Instead, he suited up in number 16. Carol Vadnais, who had seniority, wore number 10. A similar conflict affected Bobby Orr in 1969. Jean Beliveau had dibs on number 4, so Orr wore number 5.

1972–1986
MARCEL DIONNE

French Canada has always produced its share of superstars. In the late 1960s, three of the biggest names would all go on to spectacular NHL careers: Guy Lafleur, Gilbert Perreault and the man known as "the Little Beaver," Marcel Dionne.

Dionne was born in Drummondville, Quebec, on August 3, 1951, almost two months before Lafleur. These two men would meet on more than one occasion, whether it was in the rinks of small-town Quebec or the arenas of the NHL. Even at an early age, comparisons between the two players were inevitable, and were it not for a very gutsy move by Dionne at the age of 17 their head-to-head meetings would have been much more frequent.

In 1968, Dionne did the unthinkable. He left Drummondville to pursue what he thought—and he had been told—would be a better route to the NHL, joining the St. Catharines Black Hawks of the OHA. The decision did not sit well in la belle province, and the fallout carried over into the 1971 Memorial Cup semifinals between Dionne's Black Hawks and Lafleur's Quebec Remparts. The Hawks needed a police escort out of the rink after their first visit. Trailing in the series three games to two, the players' parents simply would not approve of the return visit, and the Black Hawks forfeited the series. When people talk about hockey violence today they have no idea what it was like a couple of generations ago.

In the NHL's 1971 amateur draft, Dionne was drafted second to Lafleur. He was selected by the Detroit Red Wings. His four years as a Wing could not have come at a more tumultuous stage in the team's history. As the team consistently missed the playoffs, Dionne locked horns with some of the coaches. Despite a huge season in 1974–75 that saw him record 121 points, he could not come to terms with the Red Wings during the off-season and his rights were transferred to Los Angeles in one of the biggest deals of the decade.

Bart Crashley accompanied Dionne in the deal, while Terry Harper, Dan Maloney and a second-round pick came the other way. It was without question the best deal of Los Angeles GM Jake Milford's career. It's a wonder Milford could ever complete a transaction, given that he was involved in one of the weirdest deals of all time. When he was a player, Milford was once traded by his owner, Eddie Shore, for two hockey nets. If that weren't bad enough, he later heard Shore complain about the condition of the nets.

Dionne played the next 12 seasons in L.A., recording 100 points seven more times and scoring 50 goals six times. He teamed up with Dave Taylor and Charlie Simmer to form the Triple Crown Line, which was the first forward unit in NHL history to have all three members break the 100-point barrier—that was in 1980–81. All he did was consistently score points. Dionne was the first player in history to record 100 or more points in a season with two different teams.

Dionne's consistent appearance on the scoresheet was truly remarkable, yet playoff success always eluded him. He never played on a team that went to the semifinals, let alone the finals, and he remains to date the highest scorer in NHL history not to win a Stanley Cup championship. Dionne represented Canada in international play on six occasions, including the 1976 and 1981 Canada Cup tournaments and four trips to the World Championships. He also was on Team NHL for the 1979 Challenge Cup series against the Soviet National Team.

With Dionne's offensive output dwindling, Phil Esposito, the New York Rangers GM and a long-time opponent on the ice, took a chance and acquired the 35-year-old veteran. Accompanying Dionne were Doug Crossman, a former standout defenceman in the junior ranks, and a third-round draft pick. Bob Carpenter, the first American-born player to score 50 goals in a season, and Tom Laidlaw went to the Kings. The deal did little for either club, as both were eliminated in the first round of the playoffs.

Marcel Dionne would hang up his skates in 1989 after putting up some astounding numbers: 731 goals and 1,040 assists for 1,771 points in 1,348 games. Only Gordie Howe had been more prolific on the ice. There is one assist in particular that stands out in my memory. On October 16, 1988, Phil Esposito and the Rangers, no doubt hoping to turn back the hands of time, signed Guy Lafleur to a free-agent tryout. Lafleur made the team and scored his first goal for the Rangers—for any NHL team other than the Montreal Canadiens—in the third game of the season against the Vancouver Canucks. At 7:22 of the first period, with the Canucks' Doug Lidster in the penalty box, Lafleur scored against Steve Weeks. The goal was assisted by Brian Mullen and Marcel Dionne, who set Lafleur up beautifully from behind the net. To see these long-time adversaries connect on such a graceful play, 17 years after their respective junior teams were ready to kill each other, was truly to witness hockey history.

Marcel Dionne won only one scoring championship in his career. It came in 1980, the year he tied Wayne Gretzky for the lead in points, with 137. Dionne got the nod because he'd scored two more goals, 53 to Gretzky's 51. What was unusual about Dionne's 52nd goal of the season, which in effect was the goal that gave Dionne his only Art Ross Trophy?

The oddity about this goal was that Dionne scored on Dion. Same name, different spelling. It was March 22, 1980, at 4:15 of the first period of a 4–1 win over the Quebec Nordiques and goalie Michel Dion. Goal number 53 came three nights later, in a 5–2 win over Don Cherry's Colorado Rockies. The goalie was Hardy Astrom.

1979–1997
WAYNE GRETZKY

Wayne Gretzky, a man who was destined to change forever the game of hockey, was born on January 26, 1961, in Brantford, Ontario. Gretzky was skating at two and snapping them upstairs when he was three. Well, that may be a slight exaggeration, but not by much. How many kids score 378 goals in one year as a 10-year-old? His accomplishments were overwhelming. He was the scoring leader in every single tournament he played in, from his very first up to and including the 1991 Canada Cup. Only during the 1996 World Cup and the 1998 Olympics in Nagano did he not lead the tournament point parade. At the time of his retirement, he held or shared 61 NHL records and he dominated the Art Ross and Hart Trophy races like no player before him. He led the league in scoring 10 times, and he was MVP nine times. Some feel that one day there will be a separate trophy for the most assists in one season: the Wayne Gretzky Award. If there had been one in his playing days he would have won it 13 times. That would have gone nicely with the 10 Art Ross Trophies and 9 Hart Trophies.

He enjoyed team success, too: four Stanley Cup championships in Edmonton and a trip to the finals with L.A. in 1993; Canada Cup triumphs in 1984, '87 and '91; second-place finishes in the 1981 Canada Cup and in the 1996 World Cup. Finally, at the age of 36, he led the Rangers to the semifinals in 1997.

Gretzky opened up roads for the game to follow where previously there were only dead ends. His individual success, his elevation of the Kings franchise on the ice and at the box office, and his marketable personality were instrumental in generating fan and media interest in hockey in the southwestern U.S., leading to expansion into San Jose and Anaheim and the move of the Winnipeg Jets to Phoenix.

Since his retirement, Gretzky has singled out two games as his all-time best. On the international front, there was game two of the 1987 Canada Cup finals, which was a best-of-three series between Canada and the Soviets. The series went the full three games, every one of them ending in a 6–5 score. Russia won the first game in overtime, while Canada won game two in double overtime. Mario Lemieux scored the winner, while Gretzky had five assists. Canada won the tournament in game three, with Lemieux again scoring the winner, assisted by Gretzky. There was 1:26 to play. Gretzky cites game seven of the 1993 semifinals against Toronto as his best NHL game. That was a 5–4 Los Angeles victory that sent the Kings on what remains to this day their only trip to the finals. In that game, Gretzky recorded his eighth playoff hat trick.

Gretzky retired in 1999 after a 20-year NHL career—he also played a year in the WHA. He was inducted into the Hockey Hall of Fame that same year, becoming the 10th and last person for whom the mandatory three-year waiting period for induction was waived. Simply put, Wayne Gretzky is the greatest offensive force in the history of sports.

Wayne Gretzky started playing hockey in 1967 and retired from the NHL in 1999. In all that time, 32 years, he tucked one side of his hockey sweater into the back of his hockey pants every single time—except once. Where, when and why?

January 2, 1979. It was game one of a three-game set between the WHA All-Stars and Moscow Dynamo. Not only was Gretzky going to play on the same team as the player he'd idolized when he was growing up, he was going to play on the same line. Gretzky centred a line with Gordie Howe on his right wing and Mark Howe on his left. The WHA would win all three games, played at Edmonton's Northlands Coliseum, by scores of 4–2, 4–2 and 4–3. The Gretzky–Howe–Howe threesome connected for a total of 11 points in the three games.

Prior to the first game of the series, Gordie noticed Gretzky tucking in his sweater. "Let me fix that for ya, kid," Howe said, proceeding to pull out the tail of Wayne's sweater. Grabbing some hockey tape, Howe taped the sweater to Gretzky's hockey pants. Not wanting to contradict the legend—his hero—Gretzky went out on the ice without the sweater tucked in for the only time in his entire hockey career. Ninety-five seconds into the game, Gretzky opened the scoring, assisted by Mark Howe and Paul Shmyr. The WHA All-Stars fell behind 2–1 before Gordie Howe tied the game in the second period, with an assist from son Mark. Mark Howe would score the winning goal in the third period, assisted by his linemates: Gordie Howe and Number 99, Wayne Gretzky.

1978–1987
MIKE BOSSY

Born in Montreal, Quebec, on January 22, 1957, Mike Bossy personified the term "natural goal scorer." Interestingly, Bossy never scored as many goals in a season—or over his career—as Wayne Gretzky or several others, but he did do something that none of them did: he recorded nine straight 50-goal seasons.

Hockey fans will always wonder why Bossy was chosen so late in the 1977 draft. Fourteen players were selected ahead of him, and two teams, the Toronto Maple Leafs and New York Rangers, had each passed him over twice. You can bet that New York Islanders GM Bill Torrey was one happy camper to find that Bossy was still available. Bossy had been a scoring machine with Laval in the Quebec Major Junior league, scoring 70 goals as a 17-year-old, followed by seasons of 84, 79 and 75 goals. Incredible numbers.

Bossy stood the hockey world on its ear during the 1977–78 season. While debate raged over who was the best player in the world, Montreal's Guy Lafleur or the Winnipeg Jets' Anders Hedberg, Bossy proceeded to rack up 53 goals, the most ever by a rookie in the NHL. The previous mark was 44, set by Rick Martin of the Buffalo Sabres in 1971–72.

The Islanders were fast becoming a team to be reckoned with, and their one-two punch on the scoresheet was provided by Mike Bossy and Bryan Trottier. Head coach Al Arbour played Billy Harris on their left wing for two-plus seasons and the line earned the moniker the Long Island Lighting Company or the LILCO Line. Harris was the team's first-ever selection in the amateur draft in 1972. After Harris was dealt with Dave Lewis to the L.A. Kings for Butch Goring, Arbour moved big Clark Gillies into Harris's slot on the left side and the combination was magical.

The line's new nickname was the Trio Grande and they had the perfect combination of skills. Trottier was a tough, talented two-way centre who could score, pass and take care of business in his own end. Gillies was a left winger who could put the fear of God into you with a look, yet he could also put the puck in the net. Bossy, the ultimate sniper, benefitted from the room Gillies created for him and from Trottier's playmaking.

Bossy followed up his 1978 Calder Trophy win with a season of 69 goals and 126 points, quickly and decisively dispelling any talk of a sophomore jinx. In 1979–80, he topped the magic 50 mark for the third straight time, making goal scoring look as automatic as Tiger Williams taking a trip to the penalty box. That season the Islanders won their first Stanley Cup, ending Montreal's reign as four-time champs.

Fans may wonder why I picked Bossy over his teammate, Bryan Trottier. Indeed, based on his accomplishments, a strong argument could be made for Trottier's inclusion, but in my opinion it was Bossy who was the go-to guy. In each of the next six years, he racked up 50-plus goals, including four seasons in which he topped 60. That gave him a total of nine 50-goal seasons and five 60-goal years. Both are NHL records—in the latter case he shares the record with Wayne Gretzky, while he owns the former distinction outright. As great a sniper as he was, he was also an accomplished playmaker. Seven times he broke the 100-point barrier, the third-highest total behind Gretzky (15), Mario Lemieux (10) and Marcel Dionne (eight). Peter Stastny also recorded seven 100-point seasons.

Bossy's finest hour came during the 1983 semifinals against Boston, which the Islanders won, four games to two. Two of his five playoff hat tricks were recorded in that series, and he scored the winning goal in all four Islander victories—a first in NHL history, and still an NHL record. Clark Gillies also recorded four straight winners in the playoffs, but his streak was spread over two playoff series. Bossy still holds seven club marks from that series and that particular playoff year.

Bossy maintained his torrid pace for two more seasons before succumbing to his second serious injury in four years. This time it was his back, and as a result the 1986–87 season saw him out of action for a total of 17 games, the most he ever missed in his NHL career. He managed 38 goals and 75 points, but he was only able to appear in six of the Isles' 14 playoff games. The pain of not being able to help his teammates was probably even more severe than what he was experiencing with his back.

Mike Bossy took off the entire 1987–88 season before deciding to find out whether, after the rest and treatment, his back would withstand the pounding of NHL action. It was not to be. He officially announced his retirement before the 1988–89 campaign began and hockey lost one of its all-time greats. Bossy was inducted into the Hockey Hall of Fame in 1991, his first year of eligibility, and his number, 22, has been retired by the New York Islanders. He was truly one of the greatest goal scorers the game has ever known.

Who are the only two players in NHL history to record back-to-back Stanley Cup–winning goals?

One of the purest goal scorers the game has ever known, Mike Bossy scored 50 goals or more in nine successive seasons. Bossy was the only NHLer to score four game winners in one playoff series, in the 1983 semifinals against Boston. He also as mentioned is one of only two players to score back-to-back Cup winners. Jack Darragh is the other. Bossy accomplished the feat in 1982 against Vancouver and 1983 against Edmonton. Jack Darragh did it with the Ottawa Senators in 1920 and 1921 in wins over the Seattle Metropolitans and the Vancouver Millionaires, respectively. The list of multiple Cup-winning goal scorers includes Howie Morenz with Montreal in 1924 and 1930; Toe Blake with Montreal in 1944 and '46; Jean Beliveau with Montreal in 1960 and '65; Henri Richard with Montreal in 1966 and 1971; Bobby Orr with Boston in 1970 and '72; and, finally, Jacques Lemaire with Montreal in 1977 and '79.

1984–1997

MARIO LEMIEUX

Born on October 5, 1965, in Montreal, Quebec, Mario Lemieux grew up idolizing Guy Lafleur. Raised in Laval, Mario would eclipse all of Lafleur's records in the Quebec Major Junior Hockey League and then leave everybody, but one, behind in his assault on the NHL record book. Throughout his career, the comparisons with Gretzky were numerous and inevitable. In most people's eyes, Lemieux came up short both on and off the ice. However, many in the hockey world also feel that the 1987 Canada Cup, where the two were not only teammates but linemates, had the most profound effect on Lemieux's career.

It's said that Gretzky showed Lemieux the way to prepare for a tournament such as this. In doing so, he assisted on nine of Lemieux's tournament-leading 11 goals. Lemieux exploded for his first 70-goal season in 1987–88, and the year after that he finally led the Pittsburgh Penguins into the post-season with a Gretzky-like 199 points.

The Penguins' championship seasons of 1991 and 1992 allowed Lemieux the opportunity to shine like the superstars before him. His back-to-back Conn Smythe Trophy wins elevated him to elite status, and the hockey world was primed for "Super Mario" to pick up where Number 99 had left off, reeling in the 200-point seasons. This is probably why the news of Lemieux's Hodgkin's disease was made even more startling. Coupled with Lemieux's nagging back injury, fans were very quickly forced to comprehend a league without big Number 66.

Lemieux fought his way past every obstacle, even missing the entire lockout season of 1995, in an attempt to get healthy. With all eyes watching his return in 1995–96 he picked up right where he left off. Two more years, two more 50-goal seasons, two more 100-point seasons, two more scoring titles, another Hart Trophy win and numerous other personal statistical accomplishments.

The Penguins rode the coattails of a rejuvenated Lemieux as far as the semifinals in 1996, losing to the Florida Panthers in a seven-game series that can only be described as smothering. After one more season, Mario Lemieux, at the age of 32, hung up the blades, stating that the hooking, holding and interference—and not cancer, a bad back or lack of will to play—was chasing him from the game.

Lemieux went out in 1997 just as he had come in 1984: with a flourish. He won his sixth Art Ross Trophy and had his tenth 100-point season. When the Penguins were beaten out by the Philadelphia Flyers in the first round of the playoffs, Lemieux gave the fans one last wave as he circled the rink. It was very emotional as all knew the game was losing one of its all-time best players. But on December 27, 2000, Mario Lemieux, now a Penguins owner, made a triumphant return as a player, picking up three points including a goal in a 5–0 Pittsburgh win over the Leafs. His first point in three years, eight months and one day came 33 seconds into the game. Lemieux drew one of the assists on Jagr's 20th goal of the season. What followed in the ensuing months was nothing short of remarkable.

Lemieux scored 35 goals and 76 points in only 43 games, and the Penguins—at home and on the road—became hockey's hottest ticket. Fans intent upon witnessing history packed NHL arenas. It may go down as one of the most compelling hockey stories of all time. Lemieux joins Guy Lafleur and Gordie Howe as a Hall of Fame inductee who came back to play. He was enshrined in the Hall in 1997, the ninth player at the time to have the mandatory waiting period waived. Mario Lemieux truly is "the Magnificent One."

The Pittsburgh Penguins hold the NHL record for the longest winning streak at 17 games. The last of those wins was recorded against the New York Rangers on April 9, 1993—the final score was 10–4. Who scored the winning goal in this record-setting game, and who assisted?

Mario Lemieux, assisted by Tom Barrasso. Lemieux had five goals that night. His third goal, netted at 16:05 of the second period, was the game winner. It was one of 47 shorthanded goals Lemieux scored in his NHL career. In 1989, Lemieux set a record that still stands for most shorthanded goals in one season, with 13. Wayne Gretzky, in 1983–84, scored 12. Getting back to the game in 1993, Lemieux scored his first three goals against Ranger goalie Corey Hirsch. His fourth and fifth goals of the game were scored on Mike Richter.

The Barrasso–Lemieux connection is interesting because Tom Barrasso is the highest-scoring NHL goalie of all time, with 49 career assists. He assisted on three of Lemieux's playoff goals, tying him for ninth in that category. Larry Murphy, with 16 assists, is first.

1981–1997
MARK MESSIER

The man who would be described as a "moose on the ice" made an auspicious pro-hockey debut in 1978, when he broke in with the Indianapolis

Racers of the WHA. After five games with them he was shipped to the Cincinnati Stingers, where he would see action in 47 games, tallying a goal and 10 assists for 11 points. He also racked up 58 penalty minutes. Bear in mind, he was just 17 years old when the 1978–79 season began.

Mark Messier was born on January 18, 1961, in Edmonton, Alberta. Although he'd already turned pro, the power forward was ruled eligible for the 1979 NHL entry draft, and was selected 48th overall by the Edmonton Oilers. The homecoming was brief; early in the season, on October 30, 1979, Oilers GM Larry Gordon assigned him to the Houston Apollos of the Central Hockey League. He returned to the parent club on November 8 and never played in the minors again.

Messier established himself as a force right from the get-go with 120 penalty minutes to go with his 33 points in that first season. The media spotlight was focused completely on teammate Wayne Gretzky, but Messier slammed his way to prominence on the team and in the NHL. Year two was substantially better than his rookie season, and in 1981–82, he exploded, emerging as the ultimate hockey player: he was aggressive, mean, downright nasty on the ice, yet he also had soft hands, as evidenced by his 50 goals and 88 points.

The 1982–83 season saw the "boys on the bus" really come together as they clawed their way to the Cup finals. Messier was a major player on offence, posting the first of his six 100-point seasons, and more importantly maintaining a goal-a-game pace in the playoffs: 15 markers in 15 games, the sign of a true champion. The following spring saw Messier and the Oilers win their first Stanley Cup championship, and Messier was also awarded the Conn Smythe Trophy. More Cup wins followed in 1985, '87, '88 and '90. The last one was accomplished without Wayne Gretzky—something many fans and members of the media thought impossible. A few weeks later, Messier won the Hart Trophy as league MVP.

On October 4, 1991, Messier would follow his friend and former teammate, Wayne Gretzky, south of the border—albeit to the east coast rather than the west. He was traded to the New York Rangers for Bernie Nicholls, Steven Rice and Louie DeBrusk. In his first season with the Rangers, he won the Hart Trophy for the second time, becoming only the second player to win the award with two different teams—the first was Gretzky. Messier also remains the only player to date to win the Lester B. Pearson Award as a member of two different teams. The Pearson Award holds a special significance for those who win it because the players themselves vote on which of their peers is the MVP. Messier won this trophy in the same years he won the Hart.

Of all Mark Messier's great games, perhaps none was bigger than game six of the 1994 Eastern Conference finals. The Rangers were down three games to two against the New Jersey Devils, who seemed poised for a trip to the ultimate showdown. Instead, Messier guaranteed a win for New York, then backed it up by scoring a hat trick to lead the Rangers to a 4–2 win and force a seventh game, which the Rangers won on Stephane Matteau's overtime goal. The Blueshirts advanced to the Stanley Cup finals, where they beat Vancouver in seven games.

Messier's play has been equally inspiring on the international scene. He was summoned to replace an injured Wayne Gretzky in the 1991 Canada Cup tournament and spearheaded Canada to a tough victory over the U.S. in the finals. In the most thrilling three-game series in hockey history, the 1987 Canada Cup finals, Messier's hit on the USSR's Vladimir Krutov further charged the bench as Canada stormed back from an early 3–0 deficit eight minutes into the third and deciding game. He was also a member of Team Canada when it won the 1984 Canada Cup tournament and when it lost to the U.S. in the 1996 World Cup.

Debate still rages over his exclusion from Canada's Olympic team in 1998. My own opinion is that he did not belong there. He showed in the World Cup tournament that he had clearly lost a step, and I believe the thinking was that it would be impossible to include Messier in a part-time role, so he was left off completely. I don't believe his absence was a factor in Canada's losing a shootout to the eventual gold medallists from the Czech Republic.

In 1997, Messier, a free agent, signed with Vancouver, where he spent three years. When his former coach and GM, Glen Sather, took over the Rangers' managerial reins in the summer of 2000, he wasted no time in reacquiring the man known as Moose. Messier played 25 years in the NHL. His games-played total of 1,756 sits only 11 games behind Gordie Howe's all-time total of 1767. Ironically, Messier's final NHL game was March 31, 2004, Gordie Howe's birthday. Messier is also second in career points to Wayne Gretzky with a total of 1887. He was inducted into the Hall of Fame in 2007.

To date, who is the only player to be captain of two Cup-winning teams?

Mark Messier, with the 1990 Oilers and 1994 Rangers. Also of note statistically, he holds the playoff records for career shorthanded goals, 14, and sits fourth in all-time playoff games played with 236. As of this writing, Chris Chelios sits first with 266 playoff games. Nick Lidstrom is second with 263; Patrick Roy is third with 247.

2005–present

SIDNEY CROSBY

Sidney Crosby was born on August 7, 1987, in Halifax, Nova Scotia. The date has always had a symbolic connection with him. He wears sweater number 87 and signed an $8.7 million contract in 2007 because of his birthdate, 7/8/87. Crosby was drafted first overall in 2005 by the Pittsburgh Penguins out of the Quebec Major Junior Hockey League (QMJHL). During his two-year major junior career with the Rimouski Océanic, he earned back-to-back CHL Player of the Year awards and led his club to the 2005 Memorial Cup final. Including those two years in Rimouski and his two years of hockey prior with Shattuck–St. Mary's and midget hockey in Dartmouth, Crosby recorded 658 points in 252 games. In his first NHL season, Crosby finished sixth in league scoring with 102 points (39 goals, 63 assists), becoming the youngest player to record 100 points in an NHL season. He was also runner-up for the Calder Memorial Trophy (won by Alexander Ovechkin). In his second season, he led the NHL with 120 points (36 goals, 84 assists) to capture the Art Ross Trophy, becoming the youngest player and the only teenager to win a scoring title in any major North American sports league. That same season, Crosby also won the Hart Memorial Trophy as the Professional Hockey Writers Association's choice for most valuable player and the Lester B. Pearson Award (renamed the Ted Lindsay Award as of 2010) as the NHL Players Association's choice for most outstanding player. With those, he became only the seventh player in NHL history to earn all three awards in one year. The others were Phil Esposito in 1974; Guy Lafleur in 1977 and 1978; Wayne Gretzky, who did it four years in a row, 1982–85; Mario Lemieux in 1988, 1993 and 1996; Jaromir Jagr in 1999; and Martin St. Louis in 2004.

Crosby started the 2007–08 season with the team's captaincy and subsequently led them to the 2008 Stanley Cup Finals, where they were defeated by the Detroit Red Wings in six games. The Penguins returned to the finals against Detroit the following year and won in seven games; Crosby became the youngest captain in NHL history to win the Stanley Cup and the second youngest in Stanley Cup history behind only Mike Grant with the Montreal Victorias in 1896. In the 2009–10 season, Crosby scored a career-high 51 goals, tying him with Steven Stamkos for the Rocket Richard Trophy as the league leader; add his 58 assists and Crosby totalled 109 points, second in the NHL. During the off-season, Crosby received the Mark Messier Leadership Award. In 2010–11, Crosby sustained a concussion as a result of hits to the head in back-to-back games. The injury left him sidelined for 10 and a half months. After he had played eight games in the 2011–12 season, Crosby's concussion-like symptoms returned in December 2011, and he did not return to the ice until mid-March 2012. Internationally, Crosby has represented Canada in numerous tournaments for the country's junior and men's teams. After competing in the 2003 U-18 Junior World Cup, he represented Canada in back-to-back IIHF World U20 Championships, winning silver in 2004 and gold in 2005. At the 2006 IIHF World Championship, he led the tournament in scoring, while also earning Top Forward and All-Star Team honours. Four years later, Crosby was named to Team Canada for the 2010 Winter Olympics in Vancouver. Playing the United States in the gold-medal game, he scored the game-winning goal in overtime, now known forever as the "Golden Goal." The historic marker came at 5:59 p.m. EST on February 28, 2010, against American goalie Ryan Miller. Jarome Iginla assisted. Crosby scored it 37 years and five months to the day after Paul Henderson's historic marker that won the Summit Series for Team Canada in 1972.

Crosby scored his first NHL regular season goal on October 8, 2005, in a 7–6 loss to the Boston Bruins. He recorded two assists to go along with the goal, which he scored against Boston goaltender Hannu Toivonen. In that same game, Mario Lemieux recorded two goals for the Penguins. Lemieux was selected first overall in the NHL draft of 1984. Who was selected by the Montreal Canadiens, Crosby's childhood favourite team, with their last pick in the same draft as Mario Lemieux?

Troy Crosby, Sidney's father. The senior Crosby played two years as a goaltender with the Verdun Juniors, later named the Verdun Junior Canadiens. Among his teammates were Claude Lemieux and Jimmy Carson, the latter being the fifth youngest to record a 100-point season in the NHL behind Sid the Kid, Dale Hawerchuk, Wayne Gretzky and Mario Lemieux.

2005–present

ALEX OVECHKIN

Alexander Ovechkin was born September 17, 1985, in Moscow, USSR. He's the current captain of the Washington Capitals. Prior to playing in the NHL, Ovechkin played for HC Dynamo Moscow of the Russian Superleague for four seasons, from 2001 until 2005. He was the first overall selection in the 2004 NHL Entry Draft, drafted from Dynamo after three seasons with the club. Since the 2004–05 NHL season was wiped out because of a lockout, Ovechkin remained with Dynamo for one more season before transferring to the NHL for the 2005–06 season, in which he won the Calder Memorial Trophy as rookie of the year, scoring 52 goals and 54 assists to lead all rookies with 106 points. During the 2007–08 season, he led the NHL with 65 goals and 112 points to capture the Rocket Richard and Art Ross Trophies. That season he also won the Lester B. Pearson Award as the top player voted by the NHL Players' Association and the Hart Memorial Trophy as the league's MVP. He is the only player to win all four awards in the same season since the Rocket Richard Trophy's inception in 1999. In 2009, he again won the Hart Memorial Trophy as league MVP, the Lester B. Pearson Award and the Rocket Richard Trophy. Ovechkin also led the Capitals to their second consecutive division title. He won the Ted Lindsay Award, which the Pearson Award had been renamed, for a third straight year in 2010, as well as being named to the First All-Star Team for a fifth consecutive season.

If there's one play that aptly describes Ovechkin, it's a goal he scored on January 16, 2006, against the Phoenix Coyotes. It has become known as "thee goal" in hockey circles. Knocked down by Coyote defenceman Paul Mara, Ovechkin slid on his back down the ice, yet still managed to reach his stick over his head and find the puck. With a flick of his stick, he got the puck by goaltender Brian Boucher, and his goal will go down in the annals of hockey history as one of the greatest ever scored.

If there's been one drawback to his game it's been his and his team's inability to achieve playoff success. While Ovechkin was surpassing his rival, Sidney Crosby, for individual awards, winning in the NHL playoffs or the global hockey stage has eluded him. Benefiting from Ovechkin's early playoff exits has been his home country. With the Washington captain a perennial addition to its roster, Russia has enjoyed success in the World Championships in recent years, most recently with a gold medal in 2012.

Ovechkin's five consecutive first-team all-star berths set an NHL record. What was it?

It broke the previous mark of four, set by a Montreal goalie named Bill Durnan for the most consecutive first team all-star selections from the start of an NHL career.

JEAN RATELLE split his twenty-two-year career between the New York Rangers and Boston Bruins. A member of Team Canada in the Summit Series, Ratelle is also the first NHL player to record a 100th point for two different teams. Glenn "Chico" Resch is the New York Islanders goaltender in this photo. A sixteen-year pro with four NHL teams, he twice got his name on the Stanley Cup as an Islander, in 1980 and 1981.

Bruce Bennett Studios/Getty Images

FIRSTS AND LASTS

BEING EITHER THE VERY FIRST or the absolute last to do something in sports automatically qualifies a player as a trivia answer. I filter out the obvious or ridiculous questions and focus on the great ones. Those that come under the latter category often have a hidden hook. For example, Radek Bonk scored the first Ottawa Senators goal in the Corel Centre. Many of you would think that's wrong. You'd say it was Steve Duchesne, on January 22, 1996, in a 7–3 Senators loss to Chicago. Well, that would be right if I had asked who scored the first Ottawa goal in the Palladium. The Palladium was the arena's original name, one that lasted only about six weeks. On February 28, 1996, the Corel Corporation became a major sponsor of the Senators and the arena, and so the Palladium became known as the Corel Centre. Therefore, the first Ottawa goal in the newly christened Corel Centre was netted by Radek Bonk on February 28, 1996, in a 3–2 loss to the Buffalo Sabres.

Following are some questions about firsts and lasts—and not just first and last goals!—that I think you'll find challenging and amazing. Read on and you'll find out why.

1) No period in hockey is more revered than the era of the "Original Six," from 1942 until 1967. Incidentally, that nickname is a complete misnomer. Four of the six franchises were not original NHL teams. Only the two Canadian teams, Toronto and Montreal, were in the NHL in its first season, 1917–18. The four American teams—Boston, Chicago, Detroit and New York—all joined during the 1920s. But for 25 years there were indeed only six NHL teams, and the Boston Garden, Chicago Stadium, Detroit Olympia and Madison Square Garden were every bit as important to hockey lore as were the Montreal Forum and Maple Leaf Gardens. When were the first and last games played in the buildings that housed the Original Six teams for the longest period of time, and who scored the first and last goals in those buildings?

MONTREAL FORUM

First game: November 29, 1924
Score: Montreal Canadiens 7, Toronto St. Patricks 1
First goal scored by: Billy Boucher, Canadiens
Last game: March 11, 1996
Score: Montreal Canadiens 4, Dallas Stars 1
Last goal scored by: Andrei Kovalenko, Canadiens

The Forum was the Montreal Canadiens' fourth home in the NHL. The others were the Montreal Arena in Westmount—commonly and incorrectly referred to as the Westmount Arena—the Jubilee Rink and the Mount Royal Arena. Although it came to be associated with the Habs, the Forum had been built primarily to house the Montreal Maroons. Ice conditions could be problematic in any building that did not have artificial ice, and the Mount Royal Arena did not. So, the Canadiens were forced to open the 1924–25 season against the Toronto St. Pats at the Forum—before the Maroons had even had a chance to break in their new home! The Canadiens played the rest of their home games that season and the next at the Mount Royal Arena before joining the Maroons as full-time tenants of the Forum for the 1926–27 season.

MAPLE LEAF GARDENS

First game: November 12, 1931
Score: Chicago Black Hawks 2, Toronto Maple Leafs 1
First goal scored by: Harold "Mush" March, Black Hawks
Last game: February 13, 1999
Score: Chicago Blackhawks 6, Toronto Maple Leafs 2
Last goal scored by: Bob Probert, Blackhawks

The Maple Leafs franchise, formerly known as the St. Patricks and the Arenas, played its first NHL games at the Mutual Street Arena. The team became the Maple Leafs when a group led by Conn Smythe bought the team in February 1927. The construction of Maple Leaf Gardens was one of the greatest building feats in history. In 1931, as the Depression was in full swing, the arena went up at an incredible pace, and was completed in five months, 11 days.

I highly recommend that anyone who has even the remotest interest in hockey history read the memoirs of the late Conn Smythe, *If You Can't Beat 'Em in the Alley*, co-written with Scott Young. I believe Conn Smythe is one of the greatest Canadians ever to live, both for his service in the two world wars and his career as a sportsman.

I also found it a nice touch that, when it was made known that the Leafs would be leaving the Gardens, the NHL and Chicago Blackhawks agreed that the Hawks would provide the opposition for the last game, played 67 years, three months and a day after they helped open the building.

MADISON SQUARE GARDEN

First game: December 15, 1925
Score: Montreal Canadiens 3, New York Americans 1
First goal scored by: Wilf Green, Americans
Last game: February 11, 1968
Score: New York Rangers 3, Detroit Red Wings 3
Last goal scored by: Jean Ratelle, Rangers

Just as the Forum was originally built for the Montreal Maroons, Madison Square Garden's original tenant was a team called the New York Americans. You'll read more about them, and the Maroons, in Chapter 5. The current Madison Square Garden—the fourth building to bear that name—opened for NHL hockey on February 18, 1968. Both the "old" and "new" buildings have been home to the Rangers since their inception in 1926.

OLYMPIA STADIUM

First game: November 22, 1927
Score: Ottawa Senators 2, Detroit Cougars 1
First goal: John Sheppard, Cougars
Last game: December 15, 1979

Score: Detroit Red Wings 4, Quebec Nordiques 4
Last goal: Greg Joly, Red Wings

Two more teams that you can read about in the next chapter are the Detroit Cougars and Falcons. These were the forerunners to the Detroit Red Wings. In its first year, 1926–27, the Detroit franchise played its home games at the Border City Arena in Windsor while the Olympia was being built.

BOSTON GARDEN

First game: November 20, 1928
Score: Montreal Canadiens 1, Boston Bruins 0
First goal: Sylvio Mantha, Canadiens
Last game: May 1, 1995 (regular season)
Score: Boston Bruins 5, Ottawa Senators 4
Last goal: Pavol Demitra, Senators
Last game (playoffs): May 14, 1995
Score: New Jersey Devils 3, Boston Bruins 2
Last goal: Adam Oates, Bruins

The Bruins were the first American team to join the NHL, in 1924. The Boston Arena was their home for the first four years. The dates and details listed above for the last games played in the Garden represent the official final games. Prior to the 1995–96 season, an exhibition contest was played between the Bruins and the Montreal Canadiens. As was the case a few years later with the Chicago Blackhawks and Maple Leaf Gardens, this match was a closing of the circle: the Habs had been the first and, albeit unofficially, last opponents to play at the Garden. The Habs had helped opened the building almost 67 years earlier.

Boston won the preseason contest, but it's what happened after the game that had fans talking for a long time. Boston Bruins great Ray Bourque brought Normand Leveille, a former Bruin and a teammate of Bourque's whose career was cut short by a brain aneurysm, out onto the ice for a last skate. Leveille suffered the aneurysm nine games into his second season, on October 23, 1982. The doctors said that, were it not for his incredible physical condition, he surely would have died. He's still alive at the time of this writing. I would have to say that, next to the ovation given Rocket Richard on the final night at the Montreal Forum, this was the most amazing and touching scene I have ever witnessed in the sport.

CHICAGO STADIUM

First game: November 21, 1929
Score: Ottawa Senators 6, Chicago Black Hawks 5
First goal: Harold "Mush" March, Black Hawks
Last game: April 14, 1994 (regular season)
Score: Toronto Maple Leafs 6, Chicago Blackhawks 4
Last goal: John Cullen, Maple Leafs
Last game (playoffs): April 28, 1994
Score: Toronto Maple Leafs 1, Chicago Blackhawks 0
Last goal: Mike Gartner, Maple Leafs

The Chicago Black Hawks were one of three teams to join the NHL in 1926. For their first three years they called the Chicago Coliseum home, and they played several home games in Fort Erie, Ontario, while the finishing touches were put on the Chicago Stadium.

I doubt that any building, at any time in the history of hockey, was as loud as the old Stadium. Much of the electric atmosphere in the building was generated by a massive Barton pipe organ that was actually built into the walls of the arena. There was also a very loud horn that went off every time the Hawks scored. But nothing could prepare the uninitiated for the roar of the crowd during Wayne Messmer's performances of "The Star-Spangled Banner."

If you ever have a chance to see videotape of the 1991 NHL All-Star Game, pay particular attention to the singing of the anthem. The United States had just entered the Gulf War against Iraq, and patriotism was running high. Various signs hung around the Stadium reflected the mood of the day—at least inside that building. I challenge anybody to submit to me an example of a national anthem being sung with more emotion—and to a more enthusiastic crowd response—than that day in Chicago Stadium.

2) When was the first NHL game played in the United States?

December 1, 1924, at the Boston Arena. The Boston Bruins beat the Montreal Maroons, 2–1. At the time, these were the league's two newest expansion teams.

3) Who scored the first goals in franchise history for the 30 teams that were in the NHL at the start of the 2012–13 season?

MONTREAL CANADIENS

Scored by: Joe Malone

Date: December 19, 1917

Malone would be the NHL's inaugural scoring leader with 44 goals in 20 games. He got a great start on opening night, with a five-goal performance in Montreal's 7–4 win over the Senators in Ottawa.

TORONTO MAPLE LEAFS

Scored by: George "Paddy" Patterson

Date: February 17, 1927

George Patterson scored the first Leafs goal in their first game, a 4–1 victory over the New York Americans. Conn Smythe had purchased the team in midseason and changed the name from the Toronto St. Patricks, more commonly referred to as the St. Pats, to the Toronto Maple Leafs. Patterson was dealt to the Montreal Canadiens for cash the following season, making him the second player in NHL history to have played for the Canadiens and the Maple Leafs. Bert Corbeau was the first.

BOSTON BRUINS

Scored by: Thomas "Smokey" Harris

Date: December 1, 1924

Boston won its first game, 2–1, over the Montreal Maroons. Smokey Harris played only six games in his NHL career, toward the end of a very successful pro career. He'd played in several Stanley Cup playoffs representing teams in the PCHA. In game four of the 1916 finals, his hat trick for the Portland Rosebuds forced a fifth and deciding game against the Montreal Canadiens. Montreal won 2–1 to clinch its first Cup victory. Harris scored three goals in those six NHL games, and none was bigger from a historical perspective than that first one. Smokey's brother Henry played for the Bruins in 1930–31.

DETROIT RED WINGS

Scored by: Frank Carson

Date: November 10, 1932

Carson scored two goals, including the first in Red Wing history and the first game winner in their history, in a 3–1 win over the Chicago Black Hawks. The time of the goal was 12:59 of the first period.

CHICAGO BLACK HAWKS

Scored by: George Hay

Date: November 17, 1926

George Hay is a Hockey Hall of Famer, inducted in 1958, something difficult to fathom if you review his statistics, but his was a different era. Hay was a four-time first-team all-star in the Western Canada and Western hockey leagues. Chicago beat the Toronto Maple Leafs, 4–1, in their first game.

NEW YORK RANGERS

Scored by: Bill Cook

Date: November 16, 1926

Bill Cook was named to the Hockey Hall of Fame in 1952. In this, the Rangers' first NHL season, he led the NHL in scoring. He played on one of hockey's most famous lines of all time, the "A" Line, with his brother Fred "Bun" Cook and Frank Boucher. New York's first game was a 1–0 win over the Montreal Maroons.

PHILADELPHIA FLYERS

Scored by: Bill Sutherland

Date: October 11, 1967

Sutherland scored the franchise's first goal in a 5–1 loss to the Oakland Seals. He would also later score the first Flyers goal at the Spectrum, their home rink, in a 1–0 win over the Pittsburgh Penguins. After retiring from the Winnipeg Jets of the WHA in 1974, Sutherland became the second man to coach the team after it joined the NHL, when he took the helm for three games in 1979–80.

LOS ANGELES KINGS

Scored by: Brian Kilrea

Date: October 14, 1967

Brian Kilrea scored two goals in this game, including an empty-net tally, to help Los Angeles to a 4–2 win over the Philadelphia Flyers. Kilrea would score only three goals in a 26-game NHL career. However, he had a stellar career in the minor pro leagues and is currently the all-time winningest coach in Canadian major junior hockey with over 900 victories. Every one of those wins has come behind the bench of the Ottawa 67s. Kilrea retired from coaching in 2009.

PITTSBURGH PENGUINS

Scored by: Andy Bathgate

Date: October 11, 1967

Better known for his exploits with the Rangers and Maple Leafs, Bathgate scored the Penguins' only goal in a 2–1 loss to the Montreal Canadiens in the team's first game. Jean Beliveau recorded career goal number 400 in the contest. Ten days later, Pittsburgh became the first expansion team to beat an Original Six team when they doubled Chicago by a score of 4–2.

ST. LOUIS BLUES

Scored by: Larry Keenan

Date: October 11, 1967

Larry Keenan scored the Blues' first-ever goal in their first game, a 2–2 tie with the Minnesota North Stars. Keenan also scored the first playoff overtime goal in Blues history on April 10, 1968. St. Louis beat the Philadelphia Flyers 3–2 in game three of a best-of-seven quarterfinal series on Keenan's goal at 4:10 of the second overtime period. The Blues went on to win the series in seven games, making it all the way to the finals. By the way, Larry Keenan and Mike Keenan are not related.

VANCOUVER CANUCKS

Scored by: Barry Wilkins

Date: October 9, 1970

Wilkins, a defenceman, scored the first Canucks goal in their first game, a 3–1 loss to the Los Angeles Kings. Wilkins was a former teammate of Bobby Orr's, both in junior hockey with the Oshawa Generals and briefly with the Boston Bruins. He played 418 games in the NHL with three teams, Boston, Vancouver and Pittsburgh, scoring 27 goals and 152 points.

BUFFALO SABRES

Scored by: Jim A. Watson

Date: October 10, 1970

Buffalo won its first-ever game, 2–1, over the Pittsburgh Penguins. This was not only the Sabres' first franchise goal, it was Watson's first NHL goal after 77 career games. He would go on to score a total of four goals in 221 games played. I included his middle initial to avoid confusion with Jimmy Watson, the Philadelphia Flyers defenceman who began his NHL career in 1972–73.

NEW YORK ISLANDERS

Scored by: Eddie Westfall

Date: October 7, 1972

Former Bruin Eddie Westfall scored the Islanders' first goal in their first-ever game, a 3–2 loss to their expansion cousins the Atlanta Flames. Westfall was the Islanders' first captain, wearing the "C" through four full seasons and part of a fifth. He also led the team in assists in their debut season, with 31. It was two weeks into the season before the Islanders drew their first fighting major, and oddly enough it was goaltender Billy Smith who dropped the gloves. Smith fought with New York Rangers winger Rod Gilbert on October 21, 1972.

WASHINGTON CAPITALS

Scored by: Jim Hrycuik

Date: October 9, 1974

Jim Hrycuik scored the Capitals' first goal in their first game, a 6–3 loss to the New York Rangers. Hrycuik was two days past his 25th birthday. Twenty games and four goals later, Hrycuik was out of the NHL, never to return. He finished his pro career by playing parts of two seasons with the Richmond Robins of the AHL.

EDMONTON OILERS

Scored by: Kevin Lowe

Date: October 10, 1979

Kevin Lowe, the Oilers' first-ever selection in the NHL amateur draft, scored their first goal in a 4–2 loss to the Chicago Black Hawks. Wayne Gretzky drew one of the assists, while Brett Callighen got the other. Lowe's goal was scored with the man advantage, so it was also the team's first power-play goal. Lowe also received Edmonton's first fighting major after taking on Chicago's Grant Mulvey late in the third period.

CALGARY FLAMES

Scored by: Guy Chouinard

Date: October 9, 1980

Guy Chouinard scored two of the Flames' first three goals in their first game, a 5–5 tie with the Quebec Nordiques. He would play three seasons in Calgary after having spent four years, plus brief trials in a couple of other seasons, in Atlanta. His son Eric has played 90 games in the NHL as of 2011–12, for Montreal, Philadelphia and the Minnesota Wild.

NEW JERSEY DEVILS

Scored by: Don Lever

Date: October 5, 1982

Lever scored New Jersey's first-ever goal in a 3–3 tie with the Pittsburgh Penguins. He was also the first captain of the Devils, and he finished second in team scoring in their first year. Aaron Broten was the team's high scorer. Lever stayed a New Jersey Devil for three seasons before being dealt to the Buffalo Sabres.

SAN JOSE SHARKS

Scored by: Craig Coxe

Date: October 4, 1991

The Sharks were trailing 3–0 in their first-ever game, against the Vancouver Canucks, when Craig Coxe scored to ignite a three-goal rally in the third period. The Sharks tied the game, only to watch Vancouver's Trevor Linden score the winner with 19 seconds remaining. Coxe played nine more games for the Sharks, scoring one more goal, then was sent down to their farm team in the IHL. He never played in the NHL again. San Jose was his fourth NHL team, including two stops in Vancouver.

OTTAWA SENATORS

Scored by: Neil Brady

Date: October 8, 1992

Neil Brady scored the Senators' first preseason goal, in a 1–1 tie with the Hartford Whalers, then recorded their first regular-season marker in a 5–3 victory over the Montreal Canadiens. Brady's goal was scored on the power play, so of course he was also the first Senator to score with the man advantage. This game marked the return of NHL hockey to the nation's capital after an absence of more than 58 years.

TAMPA BAY LIGHTNING

Scored by: Chris Kontos

Date: October 7, 1992

Chris Kontos scored four goals in Tampa Bay's first game, a 7–3 win over the Chicago Blackhawks. His first goal was also the first power-play goal, and Kontos became the first Lightning player to record a hat trick and a four-goal game. Three years earlier, in 1989, Kontos became the first player in NHL history to record six power-play goals in one playoff series. He was a member of the Los Angeles Kings at the time, and he scored the six goals in a seven-game L.A. victory over the Edmonton Oilers. No one has equalled this mark.

FLORIDA PANTHERS

Scored by: Scott Mellanby

Date: October 6, 1993

Scott Mellanby scored the first franchise goal in a 4–4 tie with the Chicago Blackhawks. He was a Panther for eight seasons before being dealt to St. Louis in February 2001. There was another unique first concerning the Panthers' inaugural game: for the first time ever, a hockey game was broadcast in Spanish. Arley Londono and Manolo Alvarez called the game for radio station WCMQ in Florida.

MIGHTY DUCKS OF ANAHEIM

Scored by: Sean Hill

Date: October 8, 1993

In addition to their first goal, Sean Hill also recorded the first shot and took the first penalty in Anaheim's history. The Mighty Ducks lost their first game, 7–2, to the Detroit Red Wings. This was the only season Hill played for the Ducks. He finished his NHL career with 876 games played for eight NHL teams, including the Carolina Hurricanes; he went to the finals with them in 2002.

DALLAS STARS

Scored by: Neal Broten

Date: October 5, 1993

Neal Broten scored two goals, including the first in Dallas history, in their first game, a 6–4 victory over the Detroit Red Wings. Broten's number, 7, was the first to be retired by the Stars after their move from Minnesota to Dallas. During the 1994–95 season, Broten was traded to New Jersey, where he scored the Cup-winning goal for the Devils. He also had a brief 19-game stint as a Los

Angeles King before returning to Dallas at the conclusion of the 1996–97 season.

COLORADO AVALANCHE

Scored by: Valeri Kamensky

Date: October 6, 1995

Kamensky scored the first and third goals of a 3–2 Colorado win over the Detroit Red Wings. Kamensky was player of the year in the Soviet Union in 1991. He played eight seasons with the Quebec/Colorado franchise before signing as a free agent with the New York Rangers in 1999.

PHOENIX COYOTES

Scored by: Mike Gartner

Date: October 7, 1996

Mike Gartner scored Phoenix's first goal in their first win, 5–2 in Boston. The Coyotes had been shut out, 1–0, in their inaugural game in Hartford. Gartner's goal was one of three he scored that night, making him the first Coyote to record a hat trick. Gartner would score 32 goals for Phoenix in 1996–97, becoming the first player in NHL history to score 30 or more goals in one season for five different teams. Washington, Minnesota, the New York Rangers and Toronto were the other four.

CAROLINA HURRICANES

Scored by: Kevin Dineen

Date: October 1, 1997

Kevin Dineen scored the Hurricanes' first goal in a 4–2 loss to Tampa Bay. He had also scored the last goal in Hartford Whalers history (the Hurricanes had moved from Hartford). Dineen broke into the NHL with the Whalers in 1984–85 and has played 12 of his 17 NHL seasons to date with the Hartford/Carolina franchise, so it is fitting that he would score Hartford's last goal and Carolina's first.

NASHVILLE PREDATORS

Scored by: Andrew Brunette

Date: October 13, 1998

Andrew Brunette scored the Predators' first goal in their second game, a 3–2 win over the Carolina Hurricanes. Nashville's first game was a 1–0 shutout at the hands of the Florida Panthers. Brunette was dealt to the Atlanta Thrashers on June 21, 1999, for a draft pick.

COLUMBUS BLUE JACKETS

Scored by: Bruce Gardiner

Date: October 7, 2000

Bruce Gardiner scored the first of three straight Columbus goals as they stormed to a 3–0 lead, only to have the Hawks roar back and take the game, 5–3.

MINNESOTA WILD

Scored by: Marian Gaborik

Date: October 6, 2000

Marian Gaborik scored the Wild's first goal in regular-season play in their first game, which was a 3–1 loss to the Mighty Ducks of Anaheim. Gaborik was also the Wild's first-ever draft selection, taken third overall in the 2000 entry draft.

WINNIPEG JETS

Scored by: Nik Antropov

Date: October 9, 2011

The 15,004 people crammed into the MTS Center were no doubt disappointed in the 5–1 loss but at least had a goal to cheer for. Antropov scored the first goal for the new Jets franchise in the third period on Montreal goalie Carey Price. Brad Stuart and Alex Burmistrov assisted. Antropov also assisted the final goal ever in Atlanta Thrasher history, scored by Tim Stapleton on April 10, 2011. Ron Hainsey also drew an assist on the historic goal as the Thrashers lost 5–2 to the Pittsburgh Penguins. The goal was scored on goaltender Brent Johnson, whose father, Bob Johnson, played his final NHL game 36 years and four days earlier, also for the Pittsburgh Penguins, although in a losing cause to the Washington Capitals, 8–4.

4) Who scored the last regular-season goal of the Original Six era?

Wayne Rivers of the Boston Bruins, on Saturday, April 1, 1967. Rivers scored at 19:18 of the third period of a 5–2 loss to Toronto. Wayne Connelly assisted. It was the latest goal scored in the three NHL games played that final day of the schedule. Chicago beat the New York Rangers 8–0 in an afternoon matchup, while Montreal beat the Red Wings, 4–2, in Detroit.

5) Who is the last player to lead his team in goals, assists, points and penalty minutes in the same season?

Joe Thornton of the Boston Bruins, in 1999–2000. Thornton had 23 goals, 37 assists and 60 points to lead the Bruins in all three offensive categories. What is surprising is that his 82 PIMs were enough to lead a team once known as the Big Bad Bruins. Marty McSorley had logged 62 minutes in the penalty box in just 27 games, but his famous run-in with Donald Brashear in Vancouver brought his season to an end, enabling Thornton to overtake him.

The second-last player to lead his team in all four categories was Darcy Tucker with Tampa Bay in 1998–99. His numbers were 21–22–43–176 in 82 games. Chris Gratton actually had four more assists than Tucker that season, but he'd recorded seven of them as a member of the Philadelphia Flyers. Prior to Tucker, Theo Fleury of the Calgary Flames accomplished this unusual feat. He scored 27 goals and 51 assists for 78 points to go with his 197 penalty minutes in 1997–98. Cory Stillman tied Fleury for the team lead in goals.

6) Who was the first American-born player to play 1,000 regular-season games in the NHL?

Gordie Roberts, born in Detroit, Michigan, on October 2, 1957. Roberts played his 1000th game on December 9, 1992, in a 5–2 loss to the Buffalo Sabres. He did get on the scoreboard that night with an assist on an Adam Oates goal and two minor penalties. In fact, Roberts was named after Detroit Red Wings superstar Gordie Howe. Roberts played for six NHL teams over 15 years. In 1979–80, he broke in with the Hartford Whalers, where one of his teammates was his legendary namesake, the aforementioned Howe. On April 6, 1980, Howe scored his final regular-season goal at 11:25 of the second period against Detroit and goaltender Rogie Vachon. Assisting on the play were Ray Allison and Gordie Roberts.

7) Who was the first European-born, -raised and -trained player to play 1,000 games in the NHL?

Borje Salming. On January 4, 1988, Salming played in career game number 1,000 against the Vancouver Canucks. It was a 7–7 tie. In the twilight of a tremendous career, the Leafs' Number 21 recorded an assist on Toronto's fifth goal of the game, scored by Mark Osborne. In keeping with his reputation, owner Harold Ballard did nothing to acknowledge one of the greatest Leafs of all time. Ballard had flown out on a pre-planned vacation and was not present at the game. The evening did, however, hold some significance for Salming, as his brother Stig had flown in from Sweden to be in attendance for the historic game.

8) When was the first time in NHL history that two brothers opposed each other as coaches?

On December 16, 1934, the Patrick brothers, Frank and Lester, stood behind opposing benches. Frank was in charge of the Boston Bruins, who prevailed 2–1 on this night over Lester's New York Rangers. Lester Patrick's sons, Lynn and Murray, were the next set of brothers to coach against each other. They were followed by the Wilsons, Johnny and Larry; the Murrays, Terry and Bryan; and finally the Sutters, Brian, Darryl, Duane and Brent—the only set of four brothers to have coached in the NHL. Duane was the third brother to become a bench boss when he co-coached a game with Joe Cirella on November 4, 1997, replacing the suspended Doug MacLean of the Florida Panthers.

9) When were the first tie game, the first scoreless game, and the first penalty-free game in NHL history?

The first tie game was played February 11, 1922, between the Toronto St. Pats and the Ottawa Senators in Ottawa. The final score was 4–4 after 20 minutes of overtime failed to break the deadlock. The first penalty-free game was played on January 31, 1923, in Montreal. The Canadiens beat the Hamilton Tigers, 5–4. The referees would not be so fortunate in the next two meetings between these clubs. On February 14, 1923, Hamilton's Bert Corbeau attacked Montreal goalie Georges Vezina with his stick, cuffing the netminder's scalp and breaking his nose. Another brawl broke out in the rematch on February 21, 1923. Among the many combatants was referee Lou Marsh, who duked it out with several fans. The first 0–0 game was played December 17, 1924, between the Hamilton Tigers and Ottawa Senators. Once again, this was after a 20-minute overtime period. Jake Forbes for Hamilton and Alex Connell for Ottawa were the goaltenders.

10) Regular-season overtime was discontinued on December 21, 1942, because of wartime restrictions on travel. Who scored what would be the last regular-season overtime goal for a period of almost 41 years?

Lynn Patrick. The last regular-season game to feature overtime was played in New York on November 10, 1942, as the Rangers beat the Chicago Black Hawks, 5–3. It's interesting to note that teams didn't play sudden-death overtime. The extra period was played in its entirety, regardless of how many goals were scored. In this case the Rangers broke a 3–3 tie with two goals, scored by Bryan Hextall and Lynn Patrick. The next regular-season game to go into overtime would not take place until October 8, 1983.

11) Who scored the first regular-season overtime goal when overtime was reinstated in 1983?

Bob Bourne of the New York Islanders, on October 8, 1983. He scored 24 seconds into overtime in a game played in Washington. New York won, 8–7. Quite the shootout.

12) The rules governing regular-season overtime were changed for the 1999–2000 season. Under the new scheme, each team would remove a skater from the ice, so that teams at full strength would play four-on-four rather than five-on-five. Also, instead of walking away empty-handed, the losing team would be rewarded with a point in the standings. Who scored the first "four-on-four" overtime goal?

The Calgary Flames' Valeri Bure. He scored at 3:05 of overtime in a 4–3 win over the Vancouver Canucks on Wednesday, October 13, 1999. Marc Savard and Phil Housley assisted. This was actually the second overtime goal that season—on October 7, 1999, San Jose's Mike Ricci scored a power-play goal at 3:44 of overtime. Assists went to Nicklas Sundstrom and Gary Suter and the Sharks beat Edmonton, 3–2. The difference is, this was scored during a four-on-three situation rather than four on four. Edmonton's Josef Beranek was in the penalty box, having received a five-minute major for checking from behind with two seconds left in the third period.

13) Wayne Bonney, a linesman in the San Jose–Edmonton game mentioned above, was the first in NHL history to do what?

Wayne Bonney was the first official in NHL history to wear a helmet. He would subsequently also become the first to attach a visor to his helmet. The long-serving linesman, an Ottawa native, officiated in the 1,500th game of his career in 2000–01.

14) Who scored the first power-play goal in NHL history after which the penalized player was allowed to leave the penalty box?

Maurice "Rocket" Richard. The goal was scored during the 1956 All-Star Game between the defending Cup champs, the Montreal Canadiens, and an assortment of all-stars from throughout the league. The date was October 9, 1956, and it was the first contest using the new rule that allowed players to leave the penalty box if a power-play goal was scored during a minor penalty. The goal was scored at 14:58 of the second period, Bert Olmstead and Doug Harvey assisted, and the penalized player was George "Red" Sullivan.

The game ended in a 1–1 tie, thanks to Ted Lindsay's goal for the All-Stars four minutes after the Rocket's tally. Sullivan later would become the first coach in Pittsburgh Penguins history.

There were two power-play goals scored on the first night of the regular season that year. Not knowing the exact time the games started, I'm going by game time to name the first players to score a regular-season power-play goal after which the penalized player came out of the box.

- Hank Ciesla of the Chicago Black Hawks scored a power-play goal on October 11, 1956, at 2:29 of the first period in a game against Detroit. It was the only Hawks goal in their 3-1 loss. Ted Lindsay was serving the Detroit penalty. Glenn Hall was the Detroit goalie. Wally Hergesheimer assisted. Ciesla was previously a Memorial Cup winner with St. Catharines in 1954. Hergesheimer was the AHL's top rookie in 1951, the year after Terry Sawchuk. Hergesheimer, uniquely, was missing part of two fingers on his right hand due to a punch-press accident years before.
- Allan Stanley, a defenceman with the Boston Bruins, scored a power-play goal that same night at 8:11 of the first period against Toronto and goalie Ed Chadwick. Jim Morrison was in the box for the Leafs. The goal was assisted by Doug Mohns and Cal Gardner. Ironically, Stanley would later win one of the most significant face-offs in Toronto history on May 2, 1967, near the end of game six of the Cup finals. Stanley was a defenceman for Toronto by this time, and he beat Jean Beliveau on the draw that would eventually lead to George Armstrong's empty-net goal cementing the Stanley Cup victory for Toronto, their last to date.

Doug Mohns would later be traded from Boston to Chicago in a deal for Ab McDonald. The Hawks employed Mohns on the wing with Stan Mikita and Kenny Wharram, basically becoming Scooter Line 2, so named after the original

Scooter Line, which included Mikita and Wharram with McDonald. Mohns was also the first captain in Washington Capitals history.

Cal Gardner, like Allan Stanley, also played for the Maple Leafs in his career, although unlike Stanley, whose time with the Leafs came after his historic Boston goal, Gardner played for the Leafs prior to joining Boston. Gardner scored the Cup-winning goal for the Leafs in 1949. Later, his sons Dave and Paul played in the NHL as well.

Jim Morrison was a much-respected defenceman in pro hockey for 22 years, following a Memorial Cup win with Barrie in 1951. Morrison would later win the Eddie Shore award as the AHL's top defenceman in 1966, with the Quebec Aces.

15) Who was the first player to be selected to the NHL's end-of-season All-Star teams at two different positions?

Aubrey "Dit" Clapper of the Boston Bruins. Clapper was the Second Team's right winger in the very first year the NHL announced its All-Star teams, 1931. Eight years later, Clapper was a First-Team defenceman—again representing the Boston Bruins. Clapper would earn three more nominations in total—to the First Team in 1940 and '41, and to the Second Team in 1944.

Alex Delvecchio of Detroit was the second player to merit this rare distinction. Delvecchio was a Second-Team centre for Detroit in 1953 and the Second Team's left winger in 1959.

Three men, each of whom came between Clapper and Delvecchio, earned all-star nominations as players and then as coaches. Ralph "Cooney" Weiland was the Second Team's centre as a Detroit Red Wing in 1935 and was coach of the First Team—and the Boston Bruins—in 1941. The New York Rangers' Frank Boucher was the centre on the Second Team in 1931 and a three-time First-Team centre in 1933, '34 and '35. His work as the Rangers' bench boss in 1941–42 was rewarded with a nomination to the First Team as coach. Finally, Johnny Gottselig was a Second Team left winger for the Chicago Black Hawks in 1939 and the coach of the Second Team, again representing the Hawks, in 1946.

16) What was the last year in which coaches were named to the end-of-season NHL All-Star teams?

That would be 1946. As mentioned above, Johnny Gottselig of Chicago earned the slot on the Second Team, while Dick Irvin of the Montreal Canadiens was the First Team coach. Irvin was voted to one of the All-Star teams nine times in the 16 seasons that coaches were considered for the honour. His three First Team nominations came in 1944, '45 and '46. Irvin coached in the NHL for 26 seasons and reached the Stanley Cup finals an incredible 16 times—with three different teams: Chicago, Toronto and Montreal. He won the Cup four times—including the Leafs' first-ever title, which capped off their first season at Maple Leaf Gardens in 1931–32.

17) What was the first year in which each of the teams in the annual All-Star Game featured three goalies?

It was 1992, on January 18, in Philadelphia. San Jose had joined the NHL this season, 1991–92, and two more expansion teams, in Ottawa and Tampa Bay, were on the horizon, so it was decided to expand the All-Star Game rosters at all positions. An extra goaltender was added to each side, thereby allowing each goaltender to play one period. In this first year, the Campbell Conference team featured Eddie Belfour, Tim Cheveldae and Kirk McLean, while Patrick Roy, Don Beaupre and Mike Richter represented the

Prince of Wales Conference. Belfour was the goals-against leader in this game. He allowed only one goal, to Kevin Stevens, in his 20 minutes of action. Remarkable, considering the Campbell Conference won the game, 10–6. It should be noted that Toe Blake used three goalies in the All-Star Game in Toronto in 1968: Terry Sawchuk, Eddie Giacomin and Glenn Hall each played a period. This was just Blake's preference as the visiting coach at that time.

18) Who was the first player to wear number 13 in the NHL?

Much like the number 99 question in Chapter 7, the answer to this one depends on your source. For years it was thought that Billy Boucher of the Montreal Canadiens had worn number 13, but that is now considered incorrect. The latest Montreal media guide has Boucher wearing number 5 for the Canadiens. If that's indeed the case, then the distinction belongs to Wilfred "Gizzy" Hart of the Detroit Cougars in 1926. He wore number 13 for two games before being dealt to the Montreal Canadiens, where he finished the season wearing number 11.

19) Who was the first goaltender to record two assists in one NHL game?

Eddie Giacomin of the New York Rangers, on March 19, 1972. Giacomin assisted Bill Fairbairn and Pete Stemkowski in a 5–3 win over the Toronto Maple Leafs at Madison Square Garden. Over the course of that season, two goalies—Eddie Johnston of Boston and Al Smith of Detroit—each recorded four assists, together breaking the record for most assists in one season by a goalie. Bernie Parent of the Philadelphia Flyers had three assists in 1969–70.

In 1974–75, Gilles Meloche of the California Golden Seals recorded six assists, and that record stood until Mike Palmateer of the Washington Capitals chalked up eight helpers in 1980–81. The current record-holder is Grant Fuhr, with 14 assists in 1983–84. Curtis Joseph of the 1991–92 St. Louis Blues recorded nine assists to slip past Palmateer into second place on this list.

20) Who was the first goaltender to record a point in an NHL All-Star Game?

Arturs Irbe of the Carolina Hurricanes. At 2:02 of the second period of the 1999 All-Star Game in Tampa Bay, Irbe assisted on Teemu Selanne's goal. Alexei Yashin also drew an assist. This was the second All-Star Game to follow the current "North America vs. the World" format. The North American All-Stars won, 8–6.

21) Who was the last NHL goaltender to play without a facemask?

Andy Brown of the Pittsburgh Penguins. The date was April 7, 1974, and the Penguins lost 6–3 to the Atlanta Flames. After this season, Brown went on to play three seasons in the WHA, for the Indianapolis Racers, and he never wore a mask in that league, either. He retired from pro hockey after playing 10 games in the 1976–77 season.

Brown broke into the NHL with Detroit in 1971–72, and missed out on playing with Gordie Howe by one season. (He would, however, suit up against Howe many times in the WHA.) Brown's father, Adam, drew an assist on Howe's first NHL goal, scored on October 16, 1946. Sid Abel was credited with the other assist. Abel's assist was one of four he recorded on Howe goals that season. Gordie Howe finished his rookie year in the NHL with seven goals, and besides Abel, he was assisted by Ted Lindsay (twice), Jack Stewart, Lloyd Doran, Pat Lundy and Adam Brown.

22) Which two goalies were the first father–son combination in NHL history to each record shutouts?

On February 8, 1975, Pete LoPresti of the Minnesota North Stars blanked the Philadelphia Flyers, 5–0. Pete's father, Sam, recorded four shutouts for the Chicago Black Hawks over a two-season period, 1940–41 and 1941–42. Sam shut out the Detroit Red Wings, Toronto Maple Leafs, Brooklyn Americans and Boston Bruins. The Bruins' shutout, on February 15, 1942, came a little less than a year after Boston set an all-time record for most shots on goal by one team in one 60-minute game. On March 4, 1941, the Bruins took 83 shots in a 3–2 win over the Hawks—and goaltender Sam LoPresti.

The LoPrestis were the first father–son combination to play in the NHL and both be goaltenders. They have since been followed by the Riggins, Pat and Dennis; the Grahames, Ron and John; the Johnsons, Bob and Brent; and the Sauvés, Bob and Philippe.

23) Which was the last NHL team to embark on a 10-game road trip?

Between February 4 and 20, 1999, the San Jose Sharks went 4–5–1 on the longest uninterrupted road trip in NHL history. The Sharks travelled through four time zones and played on back-to-back nights twice. In 1987–88, the Calgary Flames had an 11-game stretch away from the Saddledome, but it was interrupted by the All-Star Game. Three games were played before the break, and eight came afterward. The Philadelphia Flyers had an 11-game road trip in 2005–06 that was interrupted by the Christmas holidays. On the mother of all road trips, the Vancouver Canucks in 2010 played 14 straight on the road, but were interrupted by the Olympic break. So the Sharks maintain that mark for continuous games played away from home.

24) Who were the first set of twins to be drafted into the NHL?

Patrik and Peter Sundstrom. The Sundstroms are one of seven sets of twins that have been drafted by NHL teams to date. Coincidentally, they are also the only set of twins not to be selected in the same draft. Patrik was picked 175th by Vancouver in 1980. Peter went 50th to the New York Rangers in 1981. Ron and Rich Sutter were both first-round selections in 1982. Peter and Chris Ferraro both went in the 1992 draft. Daniel and Henrik Sedin made quite a splash going two and three in the 1999 entry draft. Three sets of twins were chosen in the 2000 draft, an incredible coincidence: Matt and Mark McRae, 147th and 288th, both by the Atlanta Thrashers; Paul and Peter Flache, who were chosen 152nd and 262nd by Edmonton and Chicago respectively; and the Lundqvists, Henrik by the Rangers, 205th, and Joel by Dallas, 68th overall.

25) Who was the last goaltender to record a victory at Maple Leaf Gardens? What about the Montreal Forum?

Ironically, it was the same goalie: Jocelyn Thibault. He was in the Chicago net on February 13, 1999, when the Blackhawks beat Toronto, 6–2, in the final game at Maple Leaf Gardens. On March 11, 1996, he was the winning goaltender for the Montreal Canadiens in their 4–1 victory over the Dallas Stars, which closed the Forum.

The victory at Maple Leaf Gardens was also the 100th of Thibault's career, making him just the fifth NHL goaltender to reach the century mark before his 25th birthday. Tom Barrasso, Martin Brodeur, Grant Fuhr and Patrick Roy are the other four.

26) Who was the first player to take two penalty shots in the same season—with two different teams?

Mark Recchi. Recchi was stopped by Buffalo's Dominik Hasek on March 8, 1995, as a member of the Montreal Canadiens. On February 6, 1995, while a member of the Philadelphia Flyers, Recchi missed against Ottawa's Don Beaupre.

27) Who was the last player to be traded who had scored his 30th goal of the season by the time of the deal?

On February 28, 1999, Theo Fleury, was dealt from Calgary to Colorado and he had scored exactly 30 goals on the season for the Flames. Fleury was the eighth player who had scored 30 goals by the time of a trade. Here are the others:

Player	G	Traded from	Traded to	Year
Mark Recchi	33	Pittsburgh Penguins	Philadelphia Flyers	1992
John Cullen	31	Pittsburgh Penguins	Hartford Whalers	1991
Mike Gartner	34	Minnesota North Stars	New York Rangers	1990
Dino Ciccarelli	32	Minnesota North Stars	Washington Capitals	1990
Geoff Courtnall	32	Boston Bruins	Edmonton Oilers	1988
Doug Shedden	32	Pittsburgh Penguins	Detroit Red Wings	1986
Norm Ullman	30	Detroit Red Wings	Toronto Maple Leafs	1968

28) Doug Jarvis holds the NHL record for most consecutive games played, with 964. What was the last team he played against before the streak ended?

Game number 964 of this incredible string was against the New York Rangers on October 10, 1987. Going into the 1987–88 season, Jarvis had not missed a regular-season game in his 12-year NHL career. He played the first two games of 1987–88 before Hartford coach Jack "Tex" Evans sat Jarvis down and dressed Brent Peterson in his place. Jarvis would not play another game in the NHL. The only "blemish" on Jarvis's career came during the 1979 playoffs, when he missed four games due to injury.

29) What was the last team that the Philadelphia Flyers beat in their NHL record-setting streak of 35 games without a loss in 1979–80?

On January 6, 1980, the Flyers beat the Buffalo Sabres by a score of 4–2 to run their record during the streak to 25–0–10. The league's previous best had been a 28-game undefeated streak by the 1977–78 Montreal Canadiens.

30) Who was the first player in NHL history to appear in 500 consecutive games?

Murray Murdoch of the New York Rangers. The left winger played his 500th game in a row on February 23, 1937, in a 2–1 victory over the Toronto Maple Leafs. He also appeared in the remaining eight games of the schedule, giving him 508 straight games over 11 seasons. Murdoch is the only NHL player never to miss a game in his entire career. On top of the 508 playoff games, he played in 55 consecutive playoff games, helping New York to two Stanley Cup championships. Murdoch finished his pro career with the Philadelphia Ramblers of the International-American Hockey League in 1937–38, playing—what else?—a full season of 44 games.

31) Who was the last player to score the first goal of his NHL career on a penalty shot?

Jay McClement of the St. Louis Blues on October 11, 2005, against Chicago Blackhawks goaltender Nikolai Khabibulin, was the most recent to record his first NHL goal on a penalty shot. Ralph Bowman was the first, on November 13, 1934, for the St. Louis Eagles against Montreal Maroons goaltender Alex Connell. Phil Hoene of the Los Angeles Kings did it on December 11, 1973, against the Minnesota North Stars and goaltender Cesare Maniago. On October 11, 1981, Ilkka Sinisalo of the Philadelphia Flyers scored his first goal on a penalty shot against Pittsburgh Penguins goaltender Paul Harrison. Reggie Savage of the Washington Capitals, on November 18, 1992, against the Minnesota North Stars and goaltender Jon Casey, became the fourth player to accomplish this oddity.

32) Who was the last player to retire without scoring a single playoff goal despite having played at least 100 playoff games?

That "honour" belongs to defenceman Craig Muni, who appeared in 113 playoff games over 12 playoff seasons without once igniting the red goal light. He did play for three Stanley Cup–winning teams in Edmonton in 1987, '88 and '90, and he racked up 17 assists in post-season play. He scored 28 times in 819 regular-season games, including a career high of 7 in 1986–87. Still, he is on record as being the player with the most playoff games played without a goal.

33) Who was the first unanimous choice in Hart Trophy voting (for most valuable player in the NHL)?

Wayne Gretzky. In 1982, he received 65 of a possible 65 first-place votes. Seems like an obvious enough answer, but when you think of some of the names among the Hart Trophy winners—Bobby Orr and Gordie Howe, in particular—it's kind of surprising that there hadn't been a unanimous vote before.

34) Who was the first coach to be the undisputed choice for the Jack Adams Award (coach of the year)?

This answer might surprise some people. Gordon "Red" Berenson was the first coach to win this award with a unanimous vote. In 1980–81, Berenson led the St. Louis Blues to a 45–18–17 record, good for 107 points—a 27-point improvement in the standings over the year before. The Jack Adams Award is voted on by the league's general managers. Hard to believe you could ever get a bunch of GMs to agree completely on anything.

35) New Jersey Devils goaltender Martin Brodeur holds the career mark for shutouts. As of 2011–12, his total is 119 in the regular season, and he set the post-season mark with his 24th career shutout against the Florida Panthers on April 19, 2012, in game four of their first-round matchup. When did Brodeur record his first regular-season shutout?

Number one came on October 20, 1993, in a 4–0 win over Anaheim. Brodeur made 17 saves; the opposition goalie was Ron Tugnutt, who holds the modern-day record for saves in one game with 70 in a 3–3 tie between his team at the time, the Quebec Nordiques, and the Boston Bruins on March 12, 1991. In Brodeur's first shutout, Devils forward Corey Millen scored the winning goal. Brodeur became the all-time shutout leader with number 104, passing Terry Sawchuk's 103 on December 21, 2009, in a 35-save performance against the Pittsburgh Penguins, which curiously was the last team that Terry Sawchuk shut out, on February 1, 1970. Scoring the winning goal in Brodeur's record-setting game was Bryce Salvador.

36) Against which team did goaltender Tom Barrasso record his final two assists, making him the career leader for points by a goaltender?
Tom Barrasso notched the 47th and 48th assists of his career on January 5, 1999, in Pittsburgh's 5–1 win over the Calgary Flames. The goal scorers were Kevin Hatcher and Martin Straka. Both goals came in the third period. Barrasso passed Grant Fuhr for the career lead in points by a goalie.

The win was number 336 of Barrasso's career, moving him at that time into 10th spot on the all-time list. Barrasso was also just the third goaltender ever to win both the Calder and Vezina trophies in the same year (1984). Frank Brimsek with Boston in 1939 and Tony Esposito with Chicago in 1970 were the first two, and Eddie Belfour with Chicago in 1991 was the fourth.

37) Who was the last player to play for four teams in one season?
Dave McLlwain, in 1990–91. He started the season with Winnipeg, where he played three games before being traded to Buffalo. Two weeks later, he was shipped to the New York Islanders. (The principals in that deal were Pierre Turgeon, who also joined the Islanders, and Pat LaFontaine, who was bound for Buffalo.) Finally, in March, he was traded to Toronto. McLlwain is also the only player to play for teams in four different divisions in one season: Winnipeg was in the Smythe Division, Buffalo in the Adams, the Islanders in the Patrick and the Maple Leafs in the Norris Division.

Dennis O'Brien is the only other player to play for four teams in one season. He played for the Minnesota North Stars, Colorado Rockies, Cleveland Barons and Boston Bruins in 1977–78. Roman Vopat played for three teams in three divisions in 1998–99. He was with Los Angeles in the Pacific Division, Chicago in the Central and Philadelphia in the Atlantic.

38) What was the date of the first game Scotty Bowman coached in the NHL?
The all-time winningest coach in NHL history first stepped behind the bench on November 22, 1967—two days after he had been named coach of the St. Louis Blues, replacing Lynn Patrick. St. Louis lost to the Montreal Canadiens, 3–1, and behind the Habs bench was the legendary Toe Blake, who was in his last season as an NHL coach. Blake is one of only three men who have an overall winning record against Bowman. Michel Bergeron and Ken Hitchcock are the other two.

39) Who was the last goaltender to record playoff shutouts with three different teams?
Curtis Joseph. On May 2, 1999, he blanked the Toronto Maple Leafs' first-round opponent, the Philadelphia Flyers, in game six. St. Louis and Edmonton were the other two teams for whom he'd recorded shutouts in the playoffs. In game one of that same series, played on April 22, the Flyers' John Vanbiesbrouck joined the group, shutting out the Leafs. Vanbiesbrouck had previously recorded shutouts in post-season action with the New York Rangers and Florida Panthers.

Four other goalies belong to this elite circle: Mike Vernon, with Calgary, Detroit and San Jose; Grant Fuhr, with Edmonton, Buffalo and St. Louis; John Ross Roach, with the Toronto St. Patricks, New York Rangers and Detroit Red Wings; and Lorne Chabot, with the Rangers, Maple Leafs and Red Wings.

40) Which NHL team was the last to lead the league in goals scored during the regular season without having a single player average a point a game?

The Montreal Canadiens. In 1961–62, the Habs led the NHL with 259 goals scored in 70 games played. Their leading scorer that year was Ralph Backstrom, with 65 points in 66 games.

41) Who was the first defenceman to score a goal on a penalty shot in the NHL?

Francis "King" Clancy. Clancy was a member of the Toronto Maple Leafs when he scored against the Chicago Black Hawks and goaltender Mike Karakas on November 14, 1936. This was also the last of 136 goals that Clancy would score in his career, making him the only player in NHL history to score his last goal on a penalty shot. Pat Egan of the Brooklyn Americans was the second defenceman to score on a penalty shot, doing so on November 16, 1941, in a 3–2 win over the Montreal Canadiens and goalie Bert Gardiner.

42) Who was the last player to score a goal in four periods of a regular-season game?

Sergei Fedorov of the Detroit Red Wings. In a 5–4 win over the Washington Capitals on December 26, 1996, Fedorov scored all five goals, including the game winner in overtime. He also scored at least once in each of the three periods of regulation time. The only other player to accomplish this feat in the NHL was Bernie Nicholls. On November 13, 1984, in a 5–4 Los Angeles victory over Quebec, Nicholls scored in all three periods, then netted the winner in overtime.

43) What is the last tie-breaking criterion to determine the NHL's point-scoring champion?

When there is a tie among scoring leaders, the NHL awards the title to the player who scored the most goals. If there's still a tie, the player who played in the fewest games gets the nod. If there's still no winner, the last resort is to give top spot to the player whose first goal of the season was the earliest.

There have been three ties to date in the history of the NHL, and in each case the first condition was enough to break the deadlock. In 1962, Bobby Hull and Andy Bathgate each registered 84 points, but Bobby Hull won the Art Ross Trophy because he'd scored 50 goals to Bathgate's 28. The same situation came up in 1980, when Marcel Dionne and Wayne Gretzky were tied at 137 points. Since Dionne had scored 53 goals to Gretzky's 51, he was declared the scoring champ. And finally, in the lockout-shortened year of 1995, Jaromir Jagr and Eric Lindros tied at 70 points. Jagr's 32 goals secured him the Art Ross over Lindros's 29, scored in two fewer games.

44) Who was the last player to be drafted first overall, yet never play a single NHL game?

Rick Pagnutti, a defenceman drafted by the Los Angeles Kings in 1967, played 10 years of pro hockey but never made it to the NHL. He joined Andre Veilleux, chosen with the number one pick by the New York Rangers in 1965, and Claude Gauthier, selected first overall by the Detroit Red Wings in 1964. Neither Veilleux nor Gauthier played professional hockey at any level.

Prior to 1969, the NHL amateur draft was completely different than the version we know today. Question 24 in Chapter 7 will shed a little more light on that. It will suffice to say that these were not necessarily blue-chip prospects.

45) When was the last time that Rule 19(a) of the NHL rule book was applied to a goaltender?

To my knowledge it's only been called once. Minutes prior to game one of the 1996 Stanley

Cup finals, Colorado Avalanche coach Marc Crawford asked for this rule to be applied to Florida goaltender John Vanbiesbrouck. The rule states that only white tape, or a knob of some other protective material approved by the NHL's rules committee, may be used at the top of a goalie stick. The reason being, of course, that black tape could be mistaken for the puck if a goalie is flopping around. It certainly makes sense; it's just interesting that nobody thought to call for the rule to be applied at any previous point along the playoff trail. Anyway, there's no penalty for violating the rule, but Vanbiesbrouck was forced to change the tape on his sticks. Florida lost the game, 3–1, and lost the series in four straight. Knowing how superstitious hockey players—and especially goalies—can be, who knows if this made a difference to the outcome of the series?

46) Who was the last player in NHL history to play a full season and not draw a single penalty?

Craig Ramsay of the Buffalo Sabres. In 1973–74, Ramsay played all 78 games, recording 20 goals, 46 points—and zero PIMs. He'd also played 57 penalty-free games in the NHL in his rookie season, 1971–72. In the 1973 playoffs, Ramsay scored the first post-season goal in Sabres history, against the Montreal Canadiens.

47) Who was the first player to be drafted in three successive expansion drafts?

Jim Thomson. In 1991, the Minnesota North Stars drafted him off the Los Angeles Kings' roster. A month later, the Stars dealt him back to L.A. In 1992, he was selected by the Ottawa Senators. Thomson played 15 games for Ottawa before they, too, dealt him back to the Kings, in a four-player deal. Finally, in 1993, Anaheim selected him from those same Los Angeles Kings. He played six games for the Ducks before calling it a career.

48) Who was the goalie on the night that Bobby Orr scored his final point in the NHL?

Rogie Vachon of the Detroit Red Wings. On October 28, 1978, Orr, playing for the Chicago Black Hawks, scored a goal at 14:42 of the third period. Ivan Boldirev and Alan Daigle assisted. The Hawks lost to the Wings, 7–2.

49) Who scored the goal on which Bobby Orr registered his first regular-season point in the NHL?

Wayne Connelly. The date was October 19, 1966, and it was Orr's first game. Orr drew an assist on Connelly's power-play goal, scored at 5:44 of the second period. The Boston Bruins beat the Detroit Red Wings, 6–2.

50) Who scored the last playoff goal at the Montreal Forum?

Al Iafrate of the Boston Bruins, on April 27, 1994. It was game six of a first-round series between the Bruins and Canadiens. Iafrate scored the game-winning goal, an unassisted marker, at 7:51 of the third period. Nearly five minutes earlier, at 2:57 of the third, Kirk Muller had scored the Habs' last playoff goal in the Forum. It was also unassisted. With this 3–2 win, Boston tied the series at three games each and won game seven in Boston, 5–3, to take the series.

DINO CICCARELLI played for five NHL teams, including the Minnesota North Stars, where as a rookie in 1981, he scored a record 14 goals during their run to the Stanley Cup final. He recorded 608 goals and 1200 points during a twenty-year pro hockey career.

Bruce Bennett Studios/Getty Images

5

DEFUNCT TEAM TRIVIA

WITHIN ANY LEAGUE THAT IS more than 90 years old, it stands to reason that there will be some significant changes. Of course, player movements through trades and free-agent signings are commonplace, but teams moving or changing their names are not. To date in the NHL, there have been 53 different team names. Two names, the Ottawa Senators and the Winnipeg Jets have been used twice. Counting the original Senators and the Jets, 26 of those 53 names have been thrown onto the hockey scrap heap. Some of the greatest trivia questions of all time can be found within the history of those teams. Here are some of the best ones.

MONTREAL WANDERERS

1) When did the Montreal Wanderers play in the NHL?

The Wanderers were an original NHL franchise that lasted only four games. Their rink, the Westmount Arena, burned down on January 2, 1918, and the team folded. Prior to their brief NHL existence the Wanderers had been one of the most successful franchises in hockey history. They won four Stanley Cup championships in a five-season stretch: in 1906, March 1907, 1908 and 1910.

2) Who was their captain for those four games in 1917–18?

Art Ross, who was also the Wanderers' playing coach. Ross had been a Cup winner as a player with the Kenora Thistles, who represented the smallest town ever to win the Stanley Cup. They were victorious in January 1907. After his playing career, Ross went on to coach the Hamilton Tigers for a season, then took the reins for the Boston Bruins for 16 years. He was also their general manager for 30 years, from their inception until 1954. The Art Ross Trophy is awarded annually in his honour to the NHL's scoring leader.

3) A member of the Wanderers scored the first-ever goal in NHL history. The team also boasted the first American-born player in the NHL, and their goaltender was the first player in NHL history to later have a son play in the league. Who were these three men?

Dave Ritchie scored the first goal in NHL history on December 19, 1917 when the Montreal Wanderers beat the Toronto Arenas, 10–9. That same night, the Montreal Canadiens were beating the Ottawa Senators 7–4, but Ritchie's goal was scored the earliest in the two games. Ritchie is also the only player to have played for each of the five original franchises in the NHL. His career started with the Montreal Wanderers. After the fire and subsequent folding of the Wanderer franchise, Ritchie finished the season as a member of the Ottawa Senators.

The Toronto Arenas signed Ritchie as a free agent in the 1918–19 season. He was returned to the Quebec Bulldogs for the 1919–20 season, as he was originally their property prior to the NHL's formation. The Bulldogs did not have money to operate until 1919–20, the league's third season. Ritchie, along with the rest of the Bulldog players, had been dispersed throughout the league. In 1919, all of the players were returned.

Ritchie's rights were transferred to Hamilton along with the rest of the players after the 1920 season. But before he could suit up for them he was dealt to the Montreal Canadiens. By playing for the Canadiens in 1920–21 he became the first and only player to suit up for all five original NHL franchises.

The first American-born player was Gerry Geran. He was born in Holyoke, Massachusetts, on August 3, 1896. Geran played only four games for the Wanderers (who forfeited two games before withdrawing from the league with a 1–5 record), but he would resurface eight years later and play most of the 1925–26 season with the Boston Bruins.

The player whose son later played was goaltender Bert Lindsay. His son was none other than Ted Lindsay, a Hall of Famer and a four-time Stanley Cup winner with Detroit.

TORONTO ARENAS

1) Who scored the first goal in Toronto Arenas history?

Reg Noble at 1:45 of the first period of a game played against the Montreal Wanderers on December 19, 1917—the score was 10–9 for the Wanderers. Noble is on record as having the longest career from the inception of the NHL in 1917. His final NHL season was 1932–33, when he was a member of the Montreal Maroons.

2) The Toronto Arenas were the first team to use two goalies in one game. Who were they?

Arthur Brooks and Sammy Hebert. In the second period of that very first opening-night loss to the Wanderers, Toronto coach Dick Carroll pulled a Mike Keenan–style goalie switch. Brooks was yanked in favour of Hebert, but in the third period Brooks would return to finish the game.

3) The Toronto Arenas were the first NHL team to be shut out. Which team were they playing against, and who was the goalie who registered the shutout?

The Montreal Canadiens beat Toronto 9–0 on February 18, 1918. Legendary goaltender Georges Vezina held the Arenas scoreless.

4) What Toronto Arenas defenceman became the first blueliner to record four goals in a game?

Harry Cameron. Cameron popped four goals in a 7–5 Toronto win over the Montreal Canadiens on December 26, 1917. He would later score four in a game as a member of the Montreal Canadiens in 1920.

5) How long did the Toronto Arenas play in the NHL?

The franchise used the Arenas name for only two seasons in the NHL, but they made their mark in

1918, becoming the first NHL club to win the Stanley Cup. More information on that Cup win can be found in Chapter 2.

OTTAWA SENATORS

1) How long was the original version of the Ottawa Senators part of the NHL?

The Ottawa Senators were an original NHL franchise in 1917. They played until 1931, then took a one-year hiatus from the league, returning in 1932. They played two more seasons before folding. That made for a total of 16 NHL seasons. Prior to their demise, the Senators were the most successful franchise in hockey history, having won the Stanley Cup nine times—five times prior to the formation of the NHL. Included in that total was a stretch of three straight wins in 1903, '04 and '05.

2) Who scored the first goal in the Senators' NHL history?

Eddie Gerard scored Ottawa's first goal in a 7–4 loss to the Montreal Canadiens on December 19, 1917. Ottawa would get its revenge nearly 75 years later when the modern version of the Senators beat the Habs 5–3 on October 8, 1992.

3) Which Ottawa goaltender holds the NHL record for the longest shutout streak in NHL history?

Alex Connell blanked the opposition for six consecutive games and parts of two others for a total of 460 minutes and 49 seconds. The streak began on January 28, 1928, with the final 25 minutes and 39 seconds of a 2–1 victory over the Montreal Canadiens. It continued with shutout wins over the Toronto Maple Leafs and Montreal Maroons, a pair of scoreless ties against the New York Rangers and another against the Pittsburgh Pirates—bear in mind that in those days teams played 10 minutes of overtime if a game was tied, so the scoreless draws actually lasted 70 minutes—and a 1–0 win over the Canadiens. Finally, Connell managed to hold the fort for the first 35:50 of a game against Chicago before Duke Keats finally scored on him, breaking the streak.

4) One of the first brother combinations to play on the same NHL team played for the Ottawa Senators in 1922. Who were they?

Two of the four Bouchers, Frank and George. Their other two brothers, Bill and Bob, were teammates on the 1924 Cup-winning Montreal Canadiens. Also in 1922, Sprague and Odie Cleghorn were teammates on the Montreal Canadiens.

5) A former Ottawa Senator holds the NHL record for scoring at least one goal in the most consecutive games. Who is he and what are his statistics during the streak?

Harry "Punch" Broadbent scored at least one goal in 16 straight games in 1921–22. He scored a total of 27 goals during the streak. Punch was also the NHL's scoring champ that season, finishing seven points ahead of teammate Cy Denneny, 46–39. This was the second time that teammates had finished one-two in NHL scoring, something that has happened 32 times in league history. Unfortunately, Broadbent was shut down in the Sens' two-game, total-goals playoff series against Toronto, and Ottawa lost by an aggregate score of 5–4.

6) The first Swedish-born player to play in the NHL was a member of the Ottawa Senators. Who was he?

Gustav Forslund. He was born in Umea, Sweden, on April 25, 1908. He grew up in Canada and played one year in the NHL, with Ottawa in

1932–33. In 48 games, he recorded 4 goals and 9 assists for 13 points, while drawing only 2 minutes in penalties.

7) The first winner of both the Hart Trophy and the Lady Byng Trophy was a member of the Ottawa Senators. Who was he?

Frank Nighbor of Pembroke, Ontario. The "Pembroke Peach" won the inaugural Hart Trophy in 1924, and he was a recipient of the Lady Byng Trophy in its first two years, 1925 and '26.

8) The Ottawa Senators hold the NHL record for fewest goals allowed in one season. When was it and how many goals did they allow?

The 1925–26 version of the Ottawa Senators allowed only 42 goals in 36 games. The 1928–29 Montreal Canadiens allowed 43 goals in 44 games, giving them a better goals-against average, but Ottawa's total is still the lowest of all time.

9) Who scored the last goal in club history?

Des Roche. The date was March 17, 1934, and the Senators tied the Montreal Maroons 2–2. The goal was scored at 16:35 of the third period and assisted by his brother, Earl Roche, and Syd Howe. The Maroons' goalie was Dave Kerr.

TORONTO ST. PATRICKS

The Toronto St. Patricks, more commonly referred to as the St. Pats, were a continuation of the Toronto Arenas franchise under new ownership. They played from 1919–20 until February 15, 1927, when Conn Smythe took over the team and renamed it the Maple Leafs.

1) The first coach fired in NHL history lost his job as bench boss of the St. Pats. What was his name and who replaced him?

Frank Heffernan was the playing coach of the Toronto St. Pats when he was released as coach 12 games into the season, having posted a record of 5–7–0. He stayed on as a player for seven more games. Heffernan was replaced by Harry Sproule, who finished the season. There was a revolving door at the helm of the St. Pats over the next few seasons. Dick Carroll and Eddie Powers coached a season each before Charlie Querrie took over for the 1922–23 season. He lasted six games, then gave way to another playing coach, Jack Adams. This was the second midseason coaching change in NHL history.

2) The first St. Pats player to lead an NHL statistical category did so in the team's first year, 1919–20. Who was he, and what category was he the leader of?

Cully Wilson was his name and he was the penalty leader with 79 minutes.

3) The St. Pats had one player who was a two-time NHL scoring leader. Who was he?

Cecil "Babe" Dye. He led the league in 1923 and 1925 with 37 and 46 points respectively.

4) The first goaltender to be a captain in the NHL was with the St. Pats when he wore the "C." Who was he?

John Ross Roach. He captained the St. Pats in 1925. Six other goalies followed him as captains: George Hainsworth with the Montreal Canadiens, Roy Worters with the New York Americans, Alex Connell with the Ottawa Senators, all in 1932–33, Charlie Gardiner with Chicago in 1933–34, Bill Durnan with the Canadiens in 1947–48 and Roberto Luongo with the Vancouver Canucks in 2008, though he could technically not wear the "C."

5) In what year were the Toronto St. Pats the Stanley Cup champions?

1922. See Chapter 2 for more information.

QUEBEC BULLDOGS

1) How long did the Quebec Bulldogs last in the NHL?

They played only one season, 1919–20. Some sources report that the team was actually chartered as the Quebec Athletics. Prior to joining the NHL they were a two-time Cup champion, in 1912 and 1913.

2) The league scoring leader in 1919–20 was with the Bulldogs. Who was he?

Joe Malone, who as a Montreal Canadien won the scoring title in the NHL's first season, 1917–18. Malone was originally Quebec property, but the Bulldogs, a charter member of the league, didn't have the financial backing to play until 1919–20. A special dispersal draft of Quebec's players was held, and the Habs picked him up. In 1919–20, Malone scored a record-setting 49 points, a mark that stood until 1928, when Howie Morenz accumulated 51 points for the Canadiens. Malone scored the first goal in Quebec team history on December 24, 1919, in a 12–5 loss to the Montreal Canadiens and goalie Georges Vezina. He also scored the last goal in team history on March 10, 1920, in a 10–4 win over Ottawa and goalie Clint Benedict. He scored six goals in all that night. Malone also had a seven-goal game on January 31, 1920, when the Bulldogs beat the Toronto St. Pats, 10–6. The shell-shocked Toronto goalie was Ivan Mitchell.

3) Quebec shares the record for fewest wins in one NHL season. How many did they win, and with whom do they share the record?

The Quebec Bulldogs' record in their lone NHL season was 4–20–0. The four wins represent an all-time low in NHL history. The dubious standard was matched by the Philadelphia Quakers in 1930–31. Quebec defeated the Toronto St. Pats twice, the Montreal Canadiens once and the Ottawa Senators once. That same year, Quebec set the all-time record for the highest goals-against average in one season: 7.38. They allowed 177 goals in only 24 games.

HAMILTON TIGERS

1) How many seasons did the Hamilton Tigers play in the NHL?

Five, from 1920–21 until 1924–25.

2) What was the name of their rink?

The Barton Street Arena.

3) Who scored the first goal in team history?

Cecil "Babe" Dye, who would later have some big years with the Toronto St. Pats, scored the first goal in team history on December 22, 1920, in a 5–0 win over the Montreal Canadiens. Dye scored twice that night, the first goal coming at 12:30 of the first period.

4) Who was the first former professional goalie to coach in the NHL?

Percy LeSueur, with the Hamilton Tigers in 1923–24. He led the team to a 9–15–0 record.

5) Who is the only goalie in NHL history to give up six-goal games to a set of brothers?

Howard Lockhart of the Hamilton Tigers. On January 26, 1921, he gave up six goals to Corb Denneny of the Toronto St. Pats in a 10–3 Toronto victory. Roughly six weeks later, Cy Denneny of the Ottawa Senators scored six times on Lockhart in a 12–5 Ottawa victory. In between, Lockhart was victimized for five goals by the Montreal Canadiens' Newsy Lalonde. This came in a 10–5 Montreal win on February 16, 1921. A tough couple of months—then again, his nickname was "Holes."

6) Which was the only NHL hockey team ever to go on strike?

Those same Hamilton Tigers, at the conclusion of the 1924–25 season. It seems that several members of the team felt that, with the league's schedule increased from 24 games to 30, their pay should also be increased. Leading the charge was Christopher Redvers Green, known as Red, and the brother of Wilfred Thomas "Shorty" Green. The Greens argued that the players had signed contracts to play a 24-game schedule and felt that they were each owed an additional $200 for the extra games. League president Frank Calder threatened to suspend and fine the boys, but they did not budge. They also did not play any more games. It was the death of hockey in Hamilton, right then and there. During the off-season the franchise was sold to Bill Dwyer, who promptly moved them lock, stock and barrel to Manhattan and renamed them the New York Americans.

7) Who scored the last goal in Hamilton Tigers history?

Appropriately, it was Red Green in a 4–1 loss to the Montreal Canadiens on March 9, 1925.

MONTREAL MAROONS

1) How long were the Montreal Maroons in the NHL?

Fourteen seasons. I wish I had a dollar for every person who has asked me, or tried to tell me, that this franchise was associated in any way, shape or form with the Montreal Canadiens. Nothing doing. The Maroons were a separate franchise that began play in 1924–25 under the ownership of James Strachan and Donat Raymond. They paid the NHL $15,000 for the right to enter an expansion team. The Maroons twice won the Stanley Cup: in their second season, 1926, which at the time set a record for the fastest Cup win by an expansion team, and in 1935. The New York Rangers matched the Maroons' speed record, beginning play in 1926–27 and winning their first championship in 1927–28. More on these Cup wins can be found in Chapter 2.

2) Who scored the first goal in Montreal Maroons history?

The Maroons played their expansion cousins, the Boston Bruins, in their first game. The date was December 1, 1924. Montreal lost 2–1. Scoring their first goal was Charlie Dinsmore, at the nine-minute mark of the first period.

3) What's the most impressive individual statistic in Maroons history?

This is just my opinion, but I believe that 23-year-old Nels Stewart winning the scoring championship in his first year in the league, 1925–26, was amazing. Then again, Stewart was an amazing player. More about him can be found in Chapter 3.

4) Who were the three members of the "S" Line?

Nels Stewart, Reginald "Hooley" Smith and Albert "Babe" Siebert. All three could put the puck in the net and rack up the points, but they were just as likely to be near the top in penalty minutes. The trio played together for five seasons. Years later, there would be another "S" Line in the NHL, when Ken Schinkel, Eddie Shack and Ron Schock played together for the Pittsburgh Penguins in the early 1970s.

5) The first NHL goaltender to wear a mask was a member of the Montreal Maroons. Who was he?
Clint Benedict. Benedict donned the facial protection to protect a broken nose suffered when he was hit by a shot from Howie Morenz. He wore it for several games throughout February and early March of 1930. When the nose healed, he took the mask off—and promptly had his nose broken again. That was the third time he'd suffered a broken nose, and Benedict said enough was enough. He retired after that game. He finished the season with a 6–6–1 record and a 3.13 goals-against average, plus the distinction of being the first goalie ever to wear a mask in the NHL.

My research indicates that Charlie Rayner with the New York Rangers was the second goalie to don a face shield to protect an injury, although I have never seen a photo of him wearing one. Of course, Jacques Plante is the first to wear a mask on a permanent basis, beginning on November 1, 1959, after a hard shot from Andy Bathgate hit him in the face in the second period of a Montreal Canadiens–New York Rangers contest.

6) The Stanley Cup–winning Montreal Maroons of 1934–35 featured three very strong lines, and they were identified by the sweaters they wore in practice—one line wore all blue sweaters, one all green and one all red. They became known as the blue, green and red lines. Who were the nine forwards?
The Blue Line was composed of Dave Trottier, Russ Blinco and Earl Robinson. Trottier was one of Eddie Shore's opponents the night he fought five guys, an NHL record for the most fights in one game. Blinco was the first player in NHL history to wear glasses.

The Green Line's three players were Herbie Cain, Bob Gracie and Gus Marker. Cain would later lead the NHL in points, in 1944 with Boston. He set an NHL record that year with 82 points.

The Red Line was made up of Hooley Smith, the last of the "S" Line still with the Maroons, Lawrence "Baldy" Northcott and Jimmy Ward. Northcott and Ward scored two of the Maroons' goals in their Cup-clinching game in 1935 against the Toronto Maple Leafs. Northcott's was the Cup winner.

7) The Montreal Maroons were involved in the longest hockey game ever played. Who was the opposition?
The eventual Stanley Cup champions, the Detroit Red Wings. The Maroons and Wings played the second game in NHL history to go into a sixth overtime period in March 1936. The game started at 8:25 p.m. on the 24th and ended at 2:24 a.m. on the 25th. By the time Modere "Mud" Bruneteau scored the winning goal—the only goal of the game—the teams had played 176 minutes and 30 seconds of hockey. Hec Kilrea assisted the goal. The goaltenders were Lorne Chabot on the losing side and Normie Smith for Detroit. Smith stopped somewhere in the neighbourhood of 85 shots—the number varies depending on the source of information—while Detroit fired somewhere in the range of 90 shots at Chabot. There were nine minor penalties in the entire game. The Red Wings won the next two games, sweeping the best-of-five series.

8) Who scored the last goal in Montreal Maroons history?
Jimmy Ward. In fact, Ward scored the team's last two goals. The Maroons lost 6–3 to their arch-rivals, the Montreal Canadiens, on March 17, 1938. It meant that the Kennedy Cup would be awarded, for the last time, to the Canadiens. The trophy—named after George Kennedy, the

manager of the Habs when they won their first Stanley Cup championship in 1916—was awarded to whichever of the Montreal teams had the best record in games between the two. The time of Ward's last goal was 19:46 of the third period, and it was assisted by Paul Runge and Baldy Northcott. Wilf Cude of the Canadiens and Bill Beveridge of the Maroons were the goaltenders.

NEW YORK AMERICANS

1) How many years were the New York Americans in the NHL?

The New York Americans were in the NHL for 16 seasons in all, from 1925–26 until 1940–41. At that point, they changed the franchise's name to the Brooklyn Americans and played one more year. More on Brooklyn a little later.

2) Who scored the first goal in New York Americans franchise history?

Appropriately, it was an American-born player—and a New Yorker to boot. Billy Burch, from Yonkers, New York, scored the team's first goal in a 2–1 road victory over their expansion cousins, the Pittsburgh Pirates. The date was December 2, 1925. Burch scored at 6:12 of the second period. Charlie Langlois got the winner for New York in overtime. It was a shorthanded goal scored at 3:10. Burch was one of the many New York players who had been on the Hamilton Tigers' roster the year before. In fact, he was the Hart Trophy recipient in 1925 as the NHL's most valuable player. He would win the Lady Byng Trophy in 1927, making him New York's first trophy winner.

3) Who scored the first NHL regular-season goal in New York City?

Given the significance of the New York area to the NHL over the years, I felt this was a pertinent question. The New York Americans played their first home game on December 15, 1925, against the Montreal Canadiens. They lost 3–1, but not before opening the scoring at the 11:55 mark of the first period on a goal by Shorty Green, one of the leaders of the Hamilton strike the year before. Billy Boucher scored twice for Montreal, while Howie Morenz had the single. This was Montreal's fifth game since their legendary goaltender, Georges Vezina, collapsed on the ice in the season opener against Pittsburgh. He was suffering from tuberculosis, and he lost his fight against the disease on March 27, 1926. Playing for Montreal that night at the old Madison Square Garden was goalie Herb Rheaume.

4) Besides Billy Burch's Lady Byng Trophy win, members of the New York Americans won five other individual awards. What were they, and who won them?

Roy "Shrimp" Worters, the shortest goalie in NHL history at five foot three, won the Hart Trophy in 1929. He also won the Vezina Trophy as top goalie in 1931. Dave "Sweeney" Schriner won the other three trophies. He was the Calder Award winner in 1935 as rookie of the year and he was a two-time scoring champ, in 1936 and 1937. Schriner also owns the distinction of being the first player born in Russia to be inducted into the Hockey Hall of Fame. I had a conversation with his sister several years ago, and she told me that Sweeney was born in a town called Kraft, Russia. The family moved to Calgary soon afterward.

In those early years with the Americans, the team would inevitably be delayed—thanks to Schriner—when crossing the Canada–U.S. border. Schriner would always give Russia as his birthplace, prompting border guards to check into his background thoroughly. Eventually, his teammates asked him just to say he was born in Canada;

he did, and they never experienced another delay. He was inducted into the Hall in 1962.

With regard to the scoring championships, it's not known what award or trophy was given to the winners in the years prior to 1948, when the Art Ross Trophy became a permanent award for the scoring champ. For several years before that, an Art Ross Award was given to the player deemed to be the most outstanding, and it usually went to the scoring leader. Confusion with the Hart Trophy became a problem, so it was decided in 1948 to make the Ross the permanent trophy for the scoring leader. Suffice it to say that Schriner received some sort of recognition for his scoring exploits in 1936 and '37.

5) How many times did the Americans make the playoffs?

Five: 1929, '36, '38, '39 and '40. They made it to the second round twice but never got as far as the Stanley Cup finals.

6) The Americans had three other statistical leaders not yet mentioned. Who were they and what were the categories?

Mervyn "Red" Dutton led the league in penalty minutes in 1931–32. Dutton might be better known to some as the NHL's second president, a job he took on under emergency circumstances after the sudden death of Frank Calder in 1943. He kept the job for three years before giving way to Clarence Campbell. Dutton also uttered one of the best lines in hockey history. Growing impatient while waiting for a referee to drop the puck to start a game, Dutton hollered, "Forget about the puck, just start the game!"

Art Chapman led the NHL in assists two years in a row, 1935 and 1936. Chapman was Sweeney Schriner's centreman. Nels Stewart, the former Montreal Maroons star, tied Larry Aurie of Detroit for the league's goal-scoring lead in 1936–37, with 23. Stewart had been purchased that year from the Boston Bruins. He scored three goals with Boston and 20 with the Amerks.

7) What division did the New York Americans play in?

At one point, in the late 1920s and early '30s, the NHL was a thriving 10-team circuit split into two divisions, the Canadian Division and the American Division, with five teams in each. There were six American teams, so one of them had to play in the Canadian Division. Given that the Americans had moved from Hamilton, Ontario, they were tagged for the Canadian Division.

BROOKLYN AMERICANS

1) In a desperate attempt to save the franchise, the owners of the New York Americans—trying to piggyback on the popularity of the Brooklyn Dodgers—changed the team's name to the Brooklyn Americans for the 1941–42 season. It didn't work. Red Dutton and company folded operations after that season, although there was hope for several years afterward that they would resurface. There is one significant piece of trivia associated with the Brooklyn Americans. What is it?

No question, Tommy Anderson's Hart Trophy win in 1941–42. Anderson, who was born in Edinburgh, Scotland, in 1910, was tied for 10th in scoring that season with 41 points. He became the first of only two winners of the Hart Trophy to play on a last-place team. Al Rollins, a goaltender with Chicago in 1954, was the other. Anderson never played in the NHL again.

2) What was the other notable individual statistic involving Brooklyn?

Pat Egan, a defenceman nicknamed "Boxcar," led the league in penalty minutes that year, with 124.

3) Who scored the last goal in New York/Brooklyn franchise history?

Harry Watson. Watson was an 18-year-old rookie who would go on to win five Stanley Cup championships with Detroit and Toronto, score a Cup-winning goal, and be inducted into the Hockey Hall of Fame. Watson's 10th goal of the season in an 8–3 loss to the Boston Bruins was the franchise's last goal. It was scored on March 17, 1942, at 10:09 of the third period and assisted by Norm Larson and Tommy Anderson. Frank Brimsek of Boston and Charlie Rayner of Brooklyn were the goaltenders. King Clancy refereed the game.

PITTSBURGH PIRATES

1) How long did the Pittsburgh Pirates play in the NHL?

Five seasons, from 1925–26 until 1929–30.

2) Who scored the first goal in Pirates history?

Lionel Conacher. The future Hall of Famer, Canadian athlete of the first half of the 20th century and member of Parliament scored in their first game, a 2–1 win over the Boston Bruins on November 26, 1925. Harold Darragh scored the winner for Pittsburgh that night. His brother was Jack Darragh, the first man to score two Stanley Cup–winning goals and the first to do it in back-to-back years. Harold finished second in voting to Frank Boucher for the Lady Byng Trophy in 1929.

3) Two defunct franchises combined for an incredible outburst of shots on goal one night. Who were the teams and what was the total?

On December 26, 1925, the Pittsburgh Pirates were in New York to play the Americans. The teams combined for a total of 141 shots. The Americans had 73, the Pirates 68. It's still the all-time NHL record. The busy goaltenders were Jake Forbes for New York and Roy Worters for Pittsburgh.

4) What is Pittsburgh's playing coach, Odie Cleghorn, credited as being the first to do?

Cleghorn is believed to be the first coach to change players while the play was still going on—or, as the expression goes, "on the fly." He coached the Pirates for their first four years.

5) Who scored the last goal in Pittsburgh Pirates history?

Herb Drury scored both Pittsburgh goals in a 4–2 loss to the Detroit Falcons on March 18, 1930. The time of the last goal was 17:45 of the second period.

PHILADELPHIA QUAKERS

1) How long were the Philadelphia Quakers in the NHL?

The Quakers were formerly the Pittsburgh Pirates. They played their one and only season in the NHL in 1930–31.

2) Who scored their first goal?

Wally Kilrea. It was a while in coming. The Quakers were shut out on home ice in their first game at the Philadelphia Arena. The score was 3–0 for the New York Rangers. Then they were shut out in their second game, a 4–0 loss to the Toronto Maple Leafs. They also lost their third game, but at least they got on the scoreboard.

Kilrea scored in the third period, beating Detroit Falcons goalie Dolly Dolson. The date was November 16, 1930, and the final score was 5–1 Detroit. Wally's nephew, Brian Kilrea, would score the first goal in Los Angeles Kings history 37 years later.

3) Unfortunately, as mentioned earlier in the section on the Quebec Bulldogs, the Quakers won only four games, tying the all-time mark for fewest wins in a season. Who did they beat in those four games?

The Detroit Falcons twice, the Toronto Maple Leafs and Montreal Maroons once each.

4) There wasn't much in the way of positive statistics for the Quakers in their only season, but at least they didn't get pushed around. They had the third- and fourth-most-penalized players that year. Who were they?

D'arcy Coulson racked up 103 penalty minutes for third place, while Allan Shields was fourth with 98. Detroit's Harvey Rockburn led the league with 118, while Boston's Eddie Shore was second with 105.

5) Who scored the last goal in Philadelphia Quakers history?

Gerry Lowrey scored in their last game on March 22, 1931. His goal came at 15:30 of the third period in a 4–4 tie with the Montreal Canadiens. It was assisted by Wally Kilrea.

ST. LOUIS EAGLES

1) How long did the St. Louis Eagles play in the NHL?

Only one season, 1934–35. The Eagles were formerly the Ottawa Senators franchise.

2) Who scored the first goal in St. Louis Eagles history?

Earl Roche on November 8, 1934, in a 3–1 loss to the Chicago Black Hawks. The time of the goal was 14:35 of the second period. Ralph "Scotty" Bowman assisted.

3) Statistically, there wasn't much to remember about the Eagles. However, they can lay partial claim to the man who finished second in the scoring race that year, and full claim to the player who was second in penalty minutes. Who were these players?

Syd Howe and Irv Frew. Howe began the season as a St. Louis Eagle but was traded along with Ralph Bowman to Detroit on February 11, 1935, for Ted Graham and $50,000. Howe had accumulated 27 points with the Eagles and recorded another 20 in Detroit. His total of 47 was good for second spot behind Charlie Conacher of Toronto, who had 57.

Irv Frew totalled 89 PIMs, second to Toronto's Red Horner, who had 125 and was in the midst of leading the NHL for eight straight seasons.

4) Who scored the last goal in St. Louis Eagles history?

Carl Voss, who had been the NHL's rookie of the year two years before as a Detroit Red Wing. Voss scored early in the third period of a 5–3 loss to the Toronto Maple Leafs on March 19, 1935. The goalies were Bill Beveridge for St. Louis and George Hainsworth for Toronto.

DETROIT COUGARS

1) How long did the Detroit Cougars play in the NHL?

The Detroit franchise was awarded in 1926, but it operated under the Cougars name for only four seasons. At that point, they became the Detroit Falcons. The Falcons name lasted for two seasons before James Norris bought the team and changed the name to the Detroit Red Wings.

2) Who scored the first goal in Detroit Cougars history?

Detroit lost its first game, 2–0 to the Boston Bruins, and its second game, 4–1 to the Pittsburgh Pirates. Scoring their first franchise goal was Harold "Slim" Halderson. The goal was assisted by Frank Fredrickson. The date was November 20, 1926, and the goalie he scored on was Roy Worters.

3) The Cougars' first captain was also their first coach and their first general manager. Who was he?

Art Duncan handled all three roles that first year, then was traded to the Toronto Maple Leafs the following season. How does a general manager get traded, you ask. Keep in mind, things were different in those days. Charles Hughes, the Detroit governor, wanted to hire Jack Adams to coach and manage the team. Rather than keep Duncan as a player—and he was a very good defenceman—Hughes traded him to Toronto for Bill Brydge. Brydge was also a defenceman, but nowhere near Duncan's quality. Toronto coach and general manager Conn Smythe won that deal.

4) Where did Detroit play their home games in their first year?

In Windsor, Ontario, at the Border Cities Arena.

5) Did the Cougars ever make the playoffs?

Once, in 1928–29. They were beaten 7–2 in a two-game, total-goals series by the Toronto Maple Leafs.

DETROIT FALCONS

1) Who scored the first goal in Detroit Falcons history?

Ebbie Goodfellow, on November 13, 1930. The Falcons beat the New York Rangers, 1–0. The time of the goal was 19:45 of the second period. Clarence "Dolly" Dolson and John Ross Roach were the goalies for Detroit and New York respectively.

2) The Detroit Falcons had two notable players. Who were they and what were they known for?

Harvey Rockburn, whom you read about briefly in Question 4 of the Philadelphia Quakers section, was the NHL's penalty leader in 1930–31 with 118 minutes. That same season, Ebbie Goodfellow was second in points with 48. The Canadiens' Howie Morenz led the way with 51.

3) Who scored the last regular-season goal in Detroit Falcons history?

The same man who scored their first goal, Ebbie Goodfellow. The date was March 20, 1932. Detroit lost 3–2 to Toronto. Goodfellow scored at 1:35 of the third period, with an assist from Wally Kilrea. Lorne Chabot for Toronto and Alex Connell of Detroit were the goalies.

OAKLAND SEALS/CALIFORNIA SEALS/ CALIFORNIA GOLDEN SEALS

1) This franchise had a very unusual history. How long did the Seals play in the NHL?

The Seals franchise played nine seasons, from 1967–68 until 1975–76. They were part of what the NHL calls the "modern expansion." Six teams joined the loop in 1967, doubling its size. Along with Oakland there were the Los Angeles Kings, Minnesota North Stars, Philadelphia Flyers, Pittsburgh Penguins and St. Louis Blues. They joined the six existing teams, the Boston Bruins,

Chicago Black Hawks, Detroit Red Wings, Montreal Canadiens, New York Rangers and Toronto Maple Leafs.

2) Who was the first owner of the Seals, and what was his connection to Hollywood?
Twenty-eight-year-old Barry Van Gerbig was a former varsity goaltender for the Princeton Tigers. That gave him a connection to the sport of hockey. His Hollywood connections? Well, Bing Crosby was his godfather, and his father-in-law was Douglas Fairbanks Jr.

3) What was the name of the Seals' home rink?
The Oakland–Alameda County Coliseum.

4) Who scored the first goal in franchise history?
Defenceman Kent Douglas, who'd been named rookie of the year in 1963 as a Toronto Maple Leaf. Douglas scored at 3:23 of the first period on October 11, 1967, in a 5–1 victory over the Philadelphia Flyers. The goal was assisted by ex-Leaf Bobby Baun, the Seals' first captain, and George Swarbrick, the Western Hockey League rookie of the year in 1965 with the San Francisco Seals.

5) When did Van Gerbig sell the team, and how is this franchise sale connected to one that transpired in the NHL in 2001?
The team was sold in August 1968. Van Gerbig sold his interests to three men who at that time also owned the Harlem Globetrotters. One of them was George Gillett, who on January 31, 2001, announced that he was purchasing the Montreal Canadiens. He would own the team for eight and a half years before selling his interest to the Molson family on June 20, 2009.

6) When did they become the California Golden Seals?
Almost exactly two years later, in August 1970. Charlie O. Finley, the flamboyant owner of the Oakland A's of Major League Baseball, bought the team and changed the name. He also changed the team colours to the green, gold and white of the A's and, in one of hockey's more bizarre moves, he had the players' skates painted white. I've talked to Marshall Johnston, a former Golden Seal as both a player and a coach, about those days, and he maintains that their skates were a couple of pounds heavier by the end of the season because the trainers were painting over all of the scuffs after each game. Quite the gimmick.

7) When did the NHL salvage the Golden Seals and attempt to keep the franchise afloat?
The NHL took over the troubled franchise in February 1974 and for the 1974–75 campaign they were renamed the California Seals, the name they kept until they bowed out of the league two years later.

8) Who was the Seals' only major award winner? Who were some of the other notable players in the history of the franchise?
Ted Hampson had a solid year for the California Seals in 1968–69 and he won the Bill Masterton Trophy for "dedication, perseverance and sportsmanship." He was also runner-up to Detroit's Alex Delvecchio for the Lady Byng Trophy. That same season, the Seals' Norm Ferguson showed lots of promise as a rookie, finishing second in the voting for the Calder Trophy to Danny Grant of the Minnesota North Stars. Unfortunately, he was never able to equal those first-year numbers of 34 goals and 54 points. Ferguson ended up having some very solid seasons in the WHA with San Diego, and his son Craig has had trials

in the NHL with Montreal, Calgary and Florida.

Gerry Ehman recorded the first three-goal game in Seals history on January 7, 1968, in a 6–0 win over Los Angeles. Terry Sawchuk was the Kings' goaltender. Carol Vadnais and Dennis Hextall tried to maintain a level of security for their teammates in those early days. Vadnais tied Reggie Fleming of Philadelphia for the most fighting majors in 1969–70. They had 12 each. Dennis Hextall was second in penalty minutes in 1970–71 to Keith Magnuson of Chicago. Magnuson had 291, Hextall 217.

The record shows that Oakland's scouts and management had somewhat of an eye for talent. Three players who would go on to record 50-goal seasons played for the franchise at one time. Reggie Leach scored 50 for Philadelphia on two occasions, Charlie Simmer did the same for Los Angeles, and Dennis Maruk had a pair of 50-goal seasons for Washington.

9) What California Golden Seals goaltender holds the NHL record for most losses in one season by a goalie?

Gary Smith. Through no fault of his own, Smith faced quite the onslaught of rubber in 1970–71. He played in 71 games, which was tops in the league that season, and registered 48 defeats. Smith picked up the nickname "Suitcase" after he played for 13 pro franchises in his 16-year career. However, in his hometown of Ottawa and to his close friends, he will always be known as "Axe." Definitely not a goalie to be trifled with in front of the net.

10) The Seals do own one neat distinction: they were the first franchise to draft a European in the first round of the amateur draft. Who was he?

Bjorn Johansson was his name. He was selected fifth overall by the Seals in 1976, but by the time the defenceman suited up for the start of the NHL season the team had moved to Cleveland and become the Barons. Johansson did not last long in the NHL. He played 15 games, scoring one goal and adding an assist.

11) The Montreal Canadiens and Oakland Seals made a trade on May 22, 1970. Who was involved, and why did it become the most significant deal in Canadiens history?

Montreal traded Ernie Hicke and their first-round pick in the 1970 amateur draft for Francois Lacombe and Oakland's first-round pick in 1971. The Seals drafted Chris Oddleifson with the 1970 pick. Unfortunately for them, they finished last the following season, meaning the Canadiens ended up with the first choice overall. They chose Guy Lafleur.

12) Who scored the last goal in Seals history?

Jim Moxey, on April 4, 1976, in a 5–2 win over Los Angeles. Rick Hampton assisted. The goal came with two seconds to play in the game.

CLEVELAND BARONS

1) How long did the Cleveland Barons last in the NHL?

Two seasons. Cleveland inherited the Seals franchise—and, unfortunately, all of its headaches. They were unable to make any headway on the ice or at the box office and disappeared after the 1977–78 season.

2) What former Stanley Cup–winning defenceman was the coach of the team for both seasons?

Jack "Tex" Evans. Evans was with the Chicago Black Hawks when they won the Stanley Cup in 1961. He coached the Barons to almost identical records of 25–42–13 in 1976–77 and 22–45–13 in 1977–78.

3) Who scored the first goal in Cleveland Barons history?

Fred Ahern, on October 6, 1976. The time of the goal was 8:41 of the third period of a 2–2 tie with Los Angeles. Jim Moxey, who had scored the last Seals goal, assisted the first Baron goal.

4) What was the name of the rink the Barons played in?

The Richfield Coliseum. It had a seating capacity of 18,544, which was the biggest in the NHL at the time.

5) The Barons placed only two players among the league's statistical leaders, both for their penalty totals. Who were they?

Randy Holt and Len Frig. Holt was fourth in penalty minutes in 1977–78 with 249 minutes, 20 of which were picked up with the Chicago Black Hawks. Holt was dealt from Chicago to Cleveland on November 23, 1977. Randy and his older brother Gary are the only brother combination to play for the Barons in their brief history. Gary played two games in Cleveland in 1976–77.

Randy Holt holds the NHL record for most penalty minutes in one game, 67, which is quite an accomplishment given that hockey is a 60-minute game. He accumulated this incredible total on March 11, 1979, as a member of the Los Angeles Kings in a game against the Philadelphia Flyers. Holt registered one minor, three majors, two misconducts and three game misconducts. Frig led the NHL in misconduct penalties in 1976–77 with 10.

6) The Barons were the Philadelphia Flyers' opposition on the night that an unofficial NHL record that has yet to be broken was set. What was the mark and who set it?

It was one of those nights for Tom Bladon on December 11, 1977, as his Flyers beat Cleveland 11–1. Bladon was a plus-10 that night and nobody has broken—or tied—that record since. Theo Fleury of the Calgary Flames was plus-9 in a game against San Jose. This is an unofficial record because plus-minus statistics were not kept in the early years of the NHL. Bladon also recorded eight points that night, which broke Bobby Orr's record for most points in one game by a defenceman. Paul Coffey of Edmonton also had an eight-point game in 1986.

7) Who scored the last goal in Cleveland Barons history?

Dennis Maruk, on April 9, 1978, in a 3–2 loss to Pittsburgh. Maruk scored at 15:28 of the third period, with assists going to Kris Manery and Mike Fidler. Denis Herron for the Penguins and Gilles Meloche for the Barons were the goaltenders.

MINNESOTA NORTH STARS

1) How long did the North Stars play in the NHL?

Twenty-six seasons, from 1967–68 until 1992–93. They made the playoffs 17 times in that span.

2) Who scored the first goal in Minnesota North Stars history?

Bill Masterton, on October 11, 1967, in a 2–2 tie with the St. Louis Blues. Masterton's goal was unassisted. It was scored at 15:20 of the second period.

3) Who was the highest-scoring winger in the NHL in 1969–70?

Jean-Paul Parise. Known everywhere as J.P., Parise tied for seventh in scoring in 1969–70 as a member of the Minnesota North Stars. However, his 72 points represented the most of any winger in the league that year. Parise was tied with centreman Red Berenson of St. Louis, and they both trailed defenceman Bobby Orr of Boston and five other centres: Phil Esposito, Stan Mikita, Phil Goyette, Walt Tkaczuk and Jean Ratelle.

4) Who was the only Minnesota North Star to record a five-goal game in the NHL?

Former Ottawa 67s junior Tim Young. Young scored five goals for Minnesota in an 8–1 win over the New York Rangers on January 15, 1979. Doug Soetaert and Wayne Thomas were the Ranger goalies. Young was tied for third in assists in 1976–77 with Larry Robinson and Borje Salming. All three had 66. Guy Lafleur with 80 and Marcel Dionne with 69 were one-two in this category.

5) Former North Star Bill Masterton is the only NHL player to pass away due to an injury suffered during a game. Masterton was with Minnesota when, in a game against the Oakland Seals on January 12, 1968, he hit his head on the ice after being checked by Ron Harris and Larry Cahan. He died on January 15. Following his death, the NHL Writers' Association commissioned a trophy called the Bill Masterton Trophy, to be awarded each season to the player "who best exemplifies to a high degree the qualities of perseverance, sportsmanship and dedication to hockey." Only one member of the Minnesota North Stars ever won the award. Who was it?

Al MacAdam in 1979–80. MacAdam had a tremendous season, registering 42 goals and 93 points, plus an additional 16 points in 15 playoff games.

6) Who were the Minnesota North Stars' other trophy winners?

Danny Grant and Bobby Smith each won the Calder Trophy, in 1969 and 1979 respectively. Grant tied with Oakland's Norm Ferguson for the rookie goal-scoring lead. Each had 34, which was an NHL record at the time. Grant would become the second Detroit Red Wing to score 50 goals in a season. Smith was the first Minnesota player to record a 100-point season, in 1981–82. He later would score the Montreal Canadiens' Cup-winning goal in 1986 and, after a deal that sent him back to Minnesota, he tied the playoff record for most game-winning goals in one playoff year with five in 1991. The current record for playoff game winners is seven, by Brad Richards with Tampa Bay in 2004.

Gump Worsley and Cesare Maniago were runners-up for the Vezina Trophy in 1972. Tony Esposito and Gary Smith of Chicago were the winners.

7) In what years did the North Stars reach the Stanley Cup finals?

In 1981 and 1991. In '81, they were beaten by the New York Islanders, who won their second of four straight Stanley Cup championships. Ten years later the Stars lost to the Pittsburgh Penguins, who won their first of two straight Cups.

8) Minnesota was the first modern expansion team to beat an Original Six team in a playoff game. Whom did they beat, and when?

Minnesota beat the Montreal Canadiens in game two of the 1971 semifinals on April 22. The score was 6–3. Montreal would eventually win the series in six games.

9) Which Minnesota North Star still holds the NHL records for most goals and most points in one playoff year by a rookie?

Dino Ciccarelli. In the 1981 playoffs, Ciccarelli scored 14 goals and added 7 assists for 21 points in 19 games.

10) Who was the first American-born player to record 100 points in one season?

Neal Broten of the Minnesota North Stars. Broten achieved this distinction with two assists in a 6–1 win over the Toronto Maple Leafs on March 26, 1986. He would finish the season with 105 points.

11) Which was the first team in NHL history to have four rookies score 20 goals or more in one season?

The Minnesota North Stars in 1976–77. Roland Eriksson and Glen Sharpley each had 25 goals, Steve Jensen had 22 and Alex Pirus scored 20. The only other team to match this feat were the Winnipeg Jets. You'll find the list of Jets players later in this chapter.

12) Which two numbers did the North Stars retire?

Number 19, for the aforementioned Bill Masterton, and number 8 for Bill Goldsworthy. Goldsworthy was a 10-year member of the North Stars and a former captain. He was an extremely popular player with his teammates and the fans. His trademark celebration after scoring a goal became known as the "Goldy shuffle."

13) Who scored the last goal in Minnesota North Stars history?

Ulf Dahlen. Dahlen scored at 19:11 of the third period on April 15, 1993. The North Stars lost 5–3 to Detroit. Russ Courtnall and Dave Gagner assisted. Jon Casey for Minnesota and Tim Cheveldae for Detroit were the goaltenders. The last penalty ever in Minnesota North Star history was taken by Mike Modano at the 20:00 minute mark of the second period for high sticking.

ATLANTA FLAMES

1) How long were the Atlanta Flames in the NHL?

Eight seasons. They joined the NHL in 1972, along with the New York Islanders, and moved to Calgary in 1980.

2) Who scored the first goal in franchise history?

Morris Stefaniw, on October 7, 1972, in a 3–2 win over the Flames' expansion cousins, the New York Islanders. Stefaniw scored at 12:48 of the first period, assisted by Lew Morrison. Phil Myre for Atlanta and Gerry Desjardins for the Islanders were the goaltenders. It was the only NHL goal Stefaniw ever scored. After 13 games he went back to the minors, where he posted some good numbers but never made it back to the NHL.

3) What was the name of the rink the Flames played in?

It was called the Omni in honour of the Omni group, the club's original owners.

4) Who were the Atlanta Flames' trophy winners?

Eric Vail and Willi Plett won the Calder Trophy as rookies of the year in 1975 and 1977 respectively. Both players were second in the league in shooting percentage in their rookie seasons. Vail scored 39 goals on 177 shots, a success rate of 22 percent. Chicago's Jim Pappin led the category that year with 22.8 percent. Plett scored on 33 of 156 shots—21.2 percent of the time, second to the 21.7 registered by Philadelphia's Gary Dornhoefer. In 1978–79, Plett was third in the league in penalty minutes with 213. Toronto's duo of Dave "Tiger" Williams and Dave Hutchison were one-two with 298 and 235 minutes respectively. Tom Lysiak was second to Denis Potvin in the Calder Trophy voting in 1974. Bob MacMillan won the Lady Byng Trophy in 1979.

5) Atlanta had three other noteworthy performers in their eight-year history. Who were they?
The 1978–79 season was a big one for the franchise. Bob MacMillan and Guy Chouinard formed a line with Eric Vail and combined for 298 points. MacMillan tallied 108, Chouinard 107 and Vail 83. Goaltender Dan Bouchard led the league in wins that same season with 32.

6) Who was the Atlanta Flames' first coach?
Bernie "Boom Boom" Geoffrion, the second man in NHL history to record a 50-goal season. Geoffrion led the Flames into the playoffs in their second year; however, they were swept by the Philadelphia Flyers in four straight. The Atlanta Flames missed the playoffs only twice in their eight seasons.

7) Who scored the last regular-season goal in Atlanta Flames history?
Ken Houston, on April 5, 1980, against Washington. Houston's goal at 17:34 of the third period tied the game at four. Don Lever and Kent Nilsson assisted. Pat Riggin for Atlanta and Wayne Stephenson for Washington were the goalies.

8) Who drew the last penalty ever in regular-season play for the Atlanta Flames?
Paul Henderson. Yes, the Paul Henderson of 1972 Summit Series fame. He was sent to the penalty box at 8:04 of the third period in that final game against Washington.

KANSAS CITY SCOUTS

1) How long was Kansas City in the NHL?
The Scouts, an expansion franchise that was admitted to the league in 1974 along with the Washington Capitals, were in the league for two seasons, 1974–75 and 1975–76.

2) What was the name of the rink where they played their home games?
The Crosby Kemper Memorial Arena.

3) Who scored the Scouts' first regular-season goal?
Simon Nolet, 56 seconds into the second period on October 9, 1974. The goal was assisted by Dave Hudson and Jim McElmury. The Scouts lost to the Toronto Maple Leafs.

4) Kansas City had one of the first players in NHL history to wear number 13 on its roster. Who was the player?
Robin Burns. Burns played in both seasons that the team was based in Kansas City. Depending on which sources you consult, he was the third player known to wear number 13. Gizzy Hart with the Detroit Cougars in 1927 and Jack Stoddard with the New York Rangers in 1952 were the others.

5) Who were the three coaches in Kansas City's short history?
Bep Guidolin, Sid Abel and Eddie Bush. Guidolin was the Scouts' first coach. He was the youngest NHL player of all time when he made his 1942 debut with the Boston Bruins. He was 16 years old. Sid Abel took over the coaching reins 46 games into Kansas City's second season. Acting as both their coach and general manager, Abel remained behind the bench for three games only. Eddie Bush replaced Abel for the remainder of the 1975–76 season. As a player, Bush was the first defenceman in NHL history to record five points in a playoff game. He did it on April 9, 1942, in a 5–2 Detroit victory over Toronto.

6) Who scored the last goal in Kansas City Scouts history?

Craig Patrick, in a 6–2 loss to Vancouver on April 4, 1976. That's the same Craig Patrick who was the assistant coach to Herb Brooks for the "Miracle on Ice," Team USA's gold medal win at the 1980 Olympics. Patrick's goal was scored at 5:42 of the third period. He was assisted by Dave Hudson, who also assisted on the first goal in franchise history, and Henry Boucha. Patrick was also a coach and GM for the New York Rangers and the Pittsburgh Penguins; he won two Stanley Cups as the Penguins GM in 1991 and 1992.

COLORADO ROCKIES

1) How long did the Colorado Rockies last in the NHL?

The Rockies played six seasons, from 1976–77 until 1981–82.

2) Where did they play their home games?

The McNichols Sports Arena.

3) Who scored the first goal in Rockies history?

Larry Skinner, on October 5, 1976, in a 4–2 win over the Toronto Maple Leafs. The goal was scored at 3:16 of the first period and assisted by Chuck Arnason and Wilf Paiement. The Leaf goalie was Wayne Thomas. A couple of other notes from this game: Dave Hudson, who assisted on the Kansas City Scouts' first and last goals, scored the second goal in Rockies history; and Dave "Tiger" Williams of the Leafs picked up a triple minor penalty in an altercation with Colorado goalie Doug Favell and defenceman Tracy Pratt.

4) Who recorded the first three-goal game in Colorado history, and what connection did this player's father have to the team he recorded the three goals against?

Paul Gardner was the first Rockies player to have a three-goal game. The date was January 5, 1977, and the opposition was the Toronto Maple Leafs. Gardner's father, Cal, scored the Cup-winning goal for the Leafs in game four of the 1949 finals.

5) What first-overall draft pick of the Colorado Rockies figured prominently in the first goal ever credited to an NHL goaltender?

Rob Ramage was Colorado's first pick, and the first pick overall, in the 1979 amateur draft. In a game between the Rockies and the New York Islanders on November 28, 1979, the Islanders were being called on a delayed penalty. Rockies goalie Bill McKenzie raced to the bench for an extra attacker. Ramage, a defenceman, went into the corner after the puck and fired it back to the point position—unfortunately, where he would normally be stationed. The puck went the length of the ice and into the empty net for an Islanders goal. It was determined that the last Islander player to touch the puck was goaltender Billy Smith, so he was credited with the goal. The final score was 7–4 for New York.

6) Flamboyant coach Don Cherry was the bench boss in Colorado for one season, 1979–80. What was the coincidence associated with the man Cherry replaced?

Cherry took over for Aldo Guidolin. In 1974, when Cherry became coach of the Bruins, he took the place of another Guidolin—Armand, better known as Bep.

7) Who was the only Colorado Rockie to win a major award?

Goaltender Glenn "Chico" Resch won the Bill Masterton Trophy in 1982, becoming the first goaltender to win that award. Of Colorado's 18 wins in 1981–82, Resch was the winning goalie in 16 of them. He was fourth in the league in games played, 61, and he received votes for both the Vezina and Hart Trophies.

Barry Beck receives honourable mention for being the runner-up to Mike Bossy for the Calder Trophy in 1977–78. Beck set a record that season for most goals in one season by a rookie defenceman with 22. The mark stood for 11 seasons until it was broken by Brian Leetch, who currently holds the record with 23 goals.

8) In 1980–81, the NHL had yet another rookie finish second in shooting percentage. This player was drafted by the Colorado Rockies. Who was he, what was his percentage and who was ahead of him?

Paul Gagne scored 25 goals on 99 shots for a percentage of 25.3. He was second to Charlie Simmer of Los Angeles, who connected on 32.7 percent of his shots.

9) Who scored the last goal in Colorado Rockies history?

John Wensink, on April 3, 1982, in a 3–1 win over the Calgary Flames. He scored at 16:22 of the third period and was assisted by Kevin Maxwell and Stan Weir. Chico Resch for Colorado and Pat Riggin for Calgary were the goaltenders.

HARTFORD WHALERS

1) How long did the Hartford Whalers play in the NHL?

Hartford was in the NHL for 18 seasons, from 1979–80 until 1996–97. Prior to that they were a charter member of the WHA. Known originally as the New England Whalers, they played in all seven seasons of the WHA's existence.

2) What was the name of the rink they played their home games in?

This is a bit of a trick question. The Whalers played their first 22 NHL home games in Springfield, Massachusetts, the home of their minor-league affiliate, the Springfield Indians. The roof of their home arena, the Hartford Civic Center, had collapsed under the weight of snow and ice on January 18, 1978, displacing the Whalers while the roof was repaired and the seating capacity increased.

3) Who scored the Hartford Whalers' first NHL goal?

Gord Roberts on October 11, 1979. It was their only goal in a 4–1 loss to the Minnesota North Stars. Mike Rogers drew the only assist. Gary Edwards was the Minnesota goalie, while John Garrett was in the Hartford net.

4) What three hockey legends skated on the same line during that first season, comprising the oldest line in hockey history?

That distinction belongs to 51-year-old Gordie Howe on right wing, 39-year-old Dave Keon at centre and 41-year-old Bobby Hull at left wing. Hull was acquired from Winnipeg on February 27, 1980. He played nine games for the Whalers, scoring seven points. Hull scored his last NHL goal on March 12, 1980, in a 4–4 tie with Detroit.

Hull was used primarily on Hartford's third line, and Howe on their fourth, but the two did see a few shifts together with Keon, making them the oldest line in NHL history. The trio boasted 75 years of major pro hockey experience. Also playing as a line late that season were Gordie Howe and his two sons, Mark and Marty. The date of this historic event was March 9, 1980, in a 1–1 tie with the Boston Bruins. They played one shift together in the second period.

5) Gordie Howe scored goal number 800 of his NHL career as a Hartford Whaler. He also scored the last goal of his career as a Whaler. When were these two goals and who were they against?

Howe scored his 800th on February 29, 1980, in a 3–0 win against St. Louis. It was Hartford's second goal of the game, scored at 1:27 of the third period. Greg Carroll and Bernie Johnston drew the assists, and the Blues' goalie was Mike Liut. Howe's last goal ever came against the Montreal Canadiens in the playoffs on April 9, 1980. The Whalers lost that game 8–4. It was the second game of a best-of-five series, which the Canadiens swept. Howe's goal was Hartford's fourth of the game, scored at 13:59 of the third period. Appropriately, his son Mark drew the only assist. The Montreal goalie was Denis Herron.

6) Who is the only Hartford Whaler to win a major NHL trophy?

Doug Jarvis, who won the Bill Masterton Trophy in 1987. While a member of the Whalers, Jarvis also became the NHL's all-time iron man on December 26, 1986, in a 1–1 tie against the team Jarvis played his first NHL game for, the Montreal Canadiens. It was game number 915 in a row for Jarvis, passing the mark of 914 set by Gary Unger. He would finish his career having played in 964 consecutive games, still the all-time record.

The 1986–87 season was a good one for the Whalers. Mike Liut was runner-up to Ron Hextall for the Vezina Trophy, and coach Jack "Tex" Evans finished second to Jacques Demers for the Jack Adams Award, given to the league's top coach.

7) What Hartford defenceman became the first rearguard in NHL history to score two shorthanded goals in the same game?

Mark Howe. On October 9, 1980, in an 8–6 Hartford loss to St. Louis, Howe scored two shorthanded goals in the second period.

8) What Hartford Whaler tied for the NHL goal-scoring lead in 1980?

Blaine Stoughton. Stoughton played on a very effective Whalers line called "Stash, Dash and Bash." Stoughton was Stash, Pat Boutette was Bash and Mike Rogers was Dash. In 1979–80, Stoughton scored 56 goals, the same number as Buffalo's Danny Gare and Charlie Simmer of the Los Angeles Kings, and tops in the league.

Rogers was also a prolific scorer. He recorded back-to-back 105-point seasons in 1979–80 and 1980–81, was traded to the New York Rangers and rolled up another 103 points with them in 1981–82.

9) Only two players in NHL history have worn the number zero. One was Paul Bibeault, a goaltender in the 1940s with the Toronto Maple Leafs, Montreal Canadiens, Boston Bruins and Chicago Black Hawks. He wore zero with Toronto. The other was a Hartford Whaler. Who was he?

Neil Sheehy wore 0 during the 26 games he played for Hartford in 1988. He was traded to Washington that summer. Sheehy did this to honour his Irish roots. He said it made his last name look like O'Sheehy, which was comical more than anything but makes a great trivia question.

10) What were the three retired numbers in Hartford history?

Gordie Howe's number 9, Johnny McKenzie's number 19 and Rick Ley's number 2. McKenzie's was the first to be retired. It happened on the same day that the Whalers acquired Bobby Hull from Winnipeg: February 27, 1980. Although I can't confirm this, I'd hazard a guess that the Whalers were kicking a little dirt at the Boston Bruins by retiring McKenzie's sweater. He had been a long-time Bruin, spending almost seven seasons in the black and gold and winning the Stanley Cup twice. His tenure with the Whalers was much shorter, only two and a half seasons, but the New England teams had a bitter rivalry. McKenzie's play was steady enough, but it hardly warranted such an honour.

When Howe's number was retired on February 18, 1981, it made him the first player to have sweaters retired in two cities. The Detroit Red Wings officially took number 9 out of circulation on March 12, 1972. Five other players to date have had their sweater retired by two teams: Bobby Hull, Wayne Gretzky, Ray Bourque, Mark Messier and Patrick Roy.

Rick Ley's number 2 was retired on December 26, 1982. He was called the "heart and soul" of the Whalers during his tenure with them. Ley succeeded Ted Green as captain of the Whalers when they were in the WHA and he wore the "C" for six years. He later coached the Whalers for two seasons.

11) Who scored the last goal in Hartford Whalers history?

Kevin Dineen, on April 13, 1997. Dineen's goal was the game winner in a 2–1 victory over the Tampa Bay Lightning. The time of the goal was 0:24 of the third period. The Whalers coaching staff made a classy move near the very end of the game. Knowing it was the last game ever in Hartford, they allowed backup goalie Jason Muzzatti to play the final second of the contest so that he would also get his name on the final gamesheet. Sean Burke had played the first 59:59 of the game. Dineen's goal was assisted by Geoff Sanderson and Andrew Cassels.

WINNIPEG JETS (ORIGINAL VERSION)

1) How long did the first Winnipeg Jets team last in the NHL?

Seventeen seasons. From 1979–80 until 1995–96.

2) Who scored their first regular-season goal in the NHL?

Morris Lukowich, assisted by Peter Marsh and Barry Melrose. The time of the goal was 13:24 of the third period in a game that the Jets lost 4–2 to the Pittsburgh Penguins. Gary Smith for Winnipeg and Greg Millen for Pittsburgh were the goaltenders.

3) Who were the five Winnipeg Jets who won trophies?

Dale Hawerchuk won the Calder Trophy in 1982 and was runner-up for the Hart Trophy as league MVP in 1985. The winner of the Hart that year was Wayne Gretzky. Teemu Selanne won the Calder Trophy in 1993 for his record-setting rookie efforts. He scored a staggering 76 goals and 56 assists for 132 points in his first season, breaking Mike Bossy's rookie record of 53 goals and Peter Stastny's mark of 109 points.

Winnipeg coach Tom Watt was the winner of the Jack Adams Award as coach of the year in 1982. Bob Murdoch won the Jack Adams Award in 1990, and honourable mention should go to Barry Long, who was runner-up for the trophy in 1985.

Kris King was the King Clancy Trophy winner in the Jets' last season, 1995–96. The Clancy award is relatively new. It was first awarded in 1988 to Lanny McDonald. It goes each year to the player who best exemplifies leadership qualities on and off the ice and who has made a noteworthy humanitarian contribution in his community.

4) Who assisted on Teemu Selanne's record-breaking 54th goal in 1993?

Phil Housley and Tie Domi. The date was March 2, 1993. The Jets lost 7–4 to the Quebec Nordiques.

5) The Winnipeg Jets are the only NHL team to use four goaltenders in a three-game playoff series. When was the series played and who were the goaltenders?

Winnipeg was swept by the Calgary Flames in the best-of-five first round in 1986. Their four goaltenders were Dan Bouchard and Brian Hayward, who played in a 5–1 series-opening loss. Hayward and Marc Behrend shared duties in a 6–4 loss in game two. Daniel Berthiaume went the distance in the third game, losing 4–3 in overtime. Lanny McDonald got the series winner for Calgary.

6) The Winnipeg Jets were the first team in NHL history to have a European-born and -raised captain. What was his name?

Lars-Erik Sjoberg was the captain of the Jets in their first NHL season, 1979–80. Sjoberg had been named player of the year in Sweden in 1969. The high point of his five-year WHA career came in 1978, when he was named the league's top defenceman and the Jets won their second Avco Cup championship in three years (they would also win in the league's final season, 1979).

Captains Johnny Gottselig and Stan Mikita of Chicago were both born overseas. Gottselig was born in Odessa, Russia, and was captain of the Hawks from 1935 to 1940. Mikita was born in Sokolce, Czechoslovakia, and was captain for parts of two seasons, 1975–76 and 1976–77. Both players moved to Canada as children.

7) Who was the only other player besides Bobby Hull to wear number 9 for the Jets?

Doug Smail wore the number from 1980 until 1988. The number was retired in Hull's honour on February 19, 1989. Smail also holds a share of the NHL record for the fastest goal from the start of a game. The mark is currently five seconds, set by Smail on December 20, 1981, in a 5–4 Winnipeg win over St. Louis. Bryan Trottier of the New York Islanders equalled it in 1984, as did Alexander Mogilny with Buffalo in 1991.

Thomas Steen's number, 25, was the only other number retired in Winnipeg history. Steen played 14 seasons for the Jets, from 1981 until 1995.

8) The Jets own the second-best one-season improvement in NHL history in terms of points. How big was the increase, and when was it?

The arrival of Dale Hawerchuk in 1981–82 helped spark Winnipeg to a 48-point improvement over the previous year. The Jets accumulated 80 points, compared with 32 in 1980–81. The biggest improvement in NHL history is 58 points by the San Jose Sharks in 1993–94.

9) Who are the two Winnipeg Jets who recorded five-goal games?

The first was Willy Lidstrom, in a 7–6 win over the Philadelphia Flyers and goalie Pete Peeters on March 2, 1982. The other was Alexei Zhamnov, on April 1, 1995, in a 7–7 tie with the Los Angeles Kings. Zhamnov victimized Kelly Hrudey for three goals and Grant Fuhr for two.

10) The Winnipeg Jets share an NHL record with the New York Islanders and the Buffalo Sabres for most 30-goal scorers in one season: six. When did Winnipeg accomplish this and who were the 30-goal scorers?

The season was 1984–85. Dale Hawerchuk led the way with 53 goals. Rounding out the list were Paul MacLean with 41, Laurie Boschman and Brian Mullen with 32 each, Doug Smail with 31 and Thomas Steen with 30.

11) What goaltender, who played only one full game in the NHL during his career, has the highest goals-against average of all time?

Ron Loustel. Loustel faced a 51-shot barrage in the only NHL game he ever played. He gave up all 10 goals in the Jets' home game of March 27, a 10–2 loss to the Vancouver Canucks. The Canucks fired 20 shots at Loustel in the third period. His one and only NHL contest came 20 days after his 19th birthday. Loustel was a Jets draft pick from 1980. His NHL game was one of only three pro games he played in. The other two were in the minors, one each in the Central Hockey League and the International Hockey League.

12) Who scored the last regular-season goal in Jets history?

Darrin Shannon, on April 14, 1996. The Jets lost 5–2 to Anaheim. Shannon's goal was scored at 19:48 of the third period, with assists going to Mike Eastwood and Oleg Tverdovsky. Nikolai Khabibulin and Dominic Roussel shared the Winnipeg netminding duties, while Guy Hebert was the goaltender for the Ducks.

QUEBEC NORDIQUES

1) How long did the Quebec Nordiques play in the NHL?

Sixteen seasons, from 1979–80 until 1994–95.

2) Who scored their first NHL regular-season goal?

Real Cloutier, at 9:51 of the third period on October 10, 1979. What's amazing about this is that it was his first of three consecutive goals as he almost singlehandedly brought the Nordiques back in their first game against the Atlanta Flames. The final score was 5–3 for Atlanta. Cloutier's hat trick was accomplished in his first NHL game, making him one of only four players to score three times in his first game. Alex Smart with the Montreal Canadiens was the first to accomplish this rarity, on January 14, 1943, in a 5–1 Montreal win over Chicago. Fabian Brunnstrum recorded his hat trick on October 15, 2008, for the Dallas Stars in a 6–4 win over the Nashville Predators. Brunnstrum had a fourth goal disallowed in that contest. Derek Stepan scored his three on October 9, 2010, in a 6–3 victory for his New York Rangers over the Buffalo Sabres.

3) Who were the three Quebec Nordiques trophy winners?

Peter Stastny won the Calder Trophy in 1981 after scoring 109 points—which was then a record for first-year players. Stastny finished second to Wayne Gretzky in the scoring race of 1982–83—a distant second, mind you: he was 72 points behind the Great One. Fourteen years later, in 1995, Peter Forsberg won the Calder Trophy. Marc Crawford was the Jack Adams Award winner in 1995, and honourable mention goes to Joe Sakic, who was runner-up to Gretzky in 1992 for the Lady Byng Trophy.

4) Who are the only two men to coach both the Quebec Nordiques and the Montreal Canadiens in the NHL?

Jacques Demers and Jean Perron. Demers was the Nordiques' first coach in the NHL and he was with the Montreal Canadiens for three full seasons and part of a fourth. His resumé includes the Canadiens' Cup win of 1993. Jean Perron won a Cup championship with Montreal in 1986, but was gone by 1988. He coached Quebec's last 47 games of the 1988–89 season.

5) Quebec once had three players record hat tricks in one game. Who were the players, when was the game, and what NHL records did two of them set?

Peter Stastny, Anton Stastny and Jacques Richard are the three players. The date was February 22, 1981, and the Nordiques beat the Washington Capitals, 11–7. The Caps used two goaltenders in that game, Mike Palmateer and Wayne Stephenson. Both Stastny brothers were coming off three-goal games in a 9–3 win over Vancouver and goalie Gary Bromley two nights earlier.

The Stastnys each recorded five points on the strength of hat tricks and two assists each, giving them both a total of 14 points in two consecutive games. (This unusual stat remains a record to this day that was most recently challenged by Sam Gagner of the Edmonton Oilers in back-to-back games against Chicago and Detroit, on February 2 and 4, 2012. Gagner recorded eight points in Edmonton's 8–0 victory over the Blackhawks, tying the Oilers' existing club record, and then picked up three more points in Edmonton's 5–4 win in Detroit.)

They kept their hot hands in the Washington game, each recording eight points. Peter recorded four goals and four assists, Anton had three goals and five assists. The eight points in one game is the record for the most points in one game by a rookie and it still stands today. Imagine, a record set by two brothers, in the same season, in the same game, following a game in which they both had hat tricks.

Peter Stastny's 70 assists that season set the rookie record for the most assists in one season. It has since been tied by Joe Juneau of the Boston Bruins in 1992–93.

6) The most famous Number 88, Eric Lindros, refused to play for Quebec. Which two members of the Quebec Nordiques wore number 88?

Owen Nolan and Joe Sakic. Both of them started with the number before switching to numbers 11 and 19 respectively.

7) Who scored the last regular-season goal in Quebec Nordiques history?

Sylvain Lefebvre, on May 3, 1995. The goal was scored at 9:25 of the third period in a 4–1 win over the Hartford Whalers. Owen Nolan and Craig Wolanin assisted.

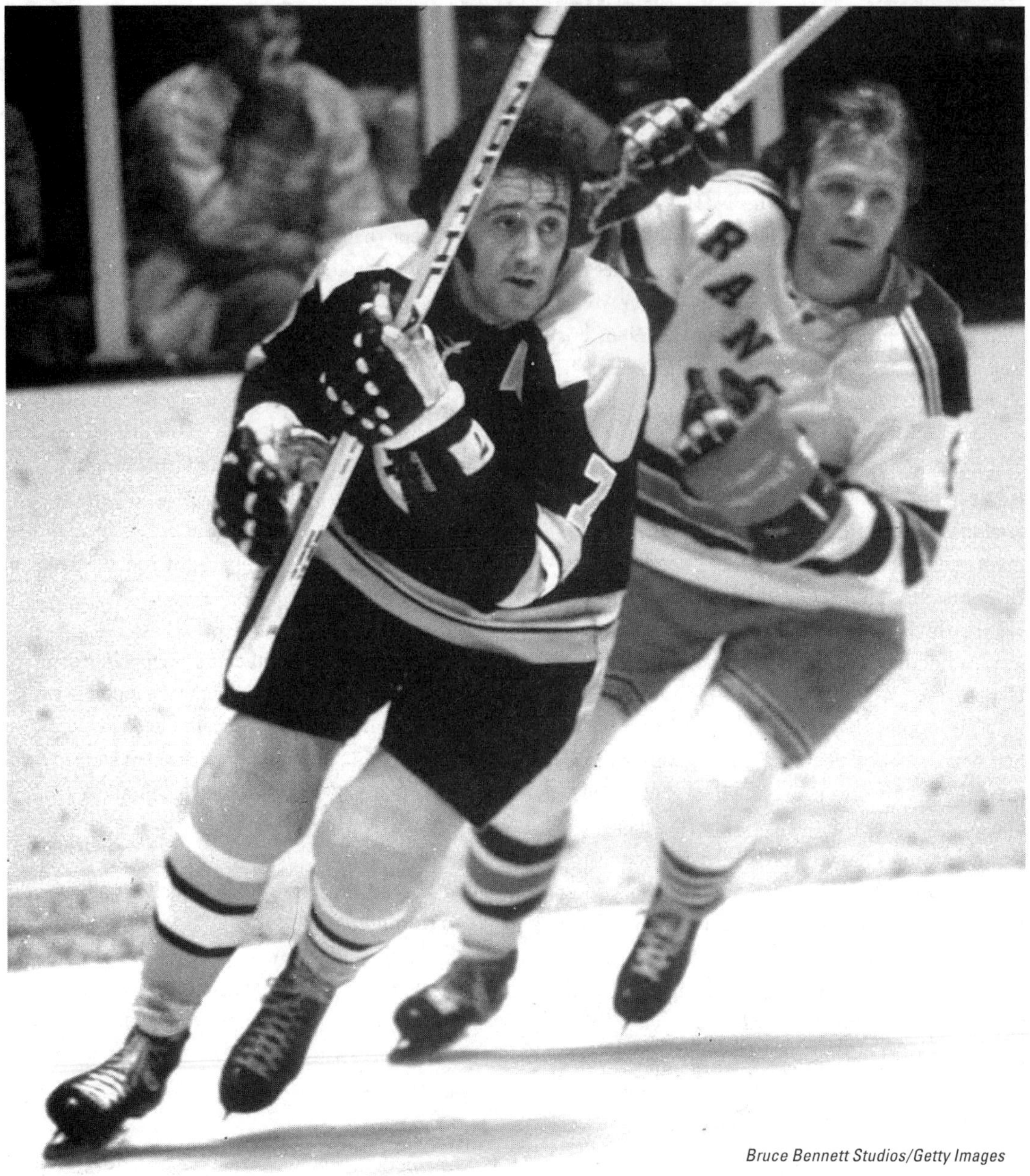

Bruce Bennett Studios/Getty Images

PHIL ESPOSITO was hockey's greatest goal scorer from close in front of the net. He also played the sport's best twenty minutes to help Team Canada come back in the third period of game eight in the 1972 Summit Series. Pursuing him is Glen Sather, current general manager of the New York Rangers. Sather played for six NHL teams, including New York. His long association with the Edmonton Oilers began in 1976–77, when he played his final pro season with Edmonton in the WHA.

6

THE MEN AT THE TOP

FIFTY GOALS. ONE HUNDRED POINTS. Five hundred goals. A thousand points. To fans and media alike, these are the benchmarks that define a season or a career as excellent. The first 50-goal season was in 1945. The first player to score 500 career goals reached that plateau in 1957. The first to reach 1,000 points in a career did it in 1960 and the first 100-point season was posted in 1969. In the years since, many of the great names, and some still currently playing, have met or exceeded those achievements. What I'm going to do in this chapter is look at each of these four offensive categories and offer up the best trivia questions and statistics from each.

50-GOAL SCORERS

Entering the 2012–13 season, there have been 91 players who have recorded 50 or more goals in one regular season in the NHL. These 91 players have combined for a total of 191 50-goal seasons, and their 50th goals were scored against a total of 119 different goaltenders. People ask me all the time about what memory techniques I use as I do my trivia gigs and my talks on the NHL across the country. Well, here's a perfect example, which of course will change, but for now just look at the "91" in those numbers for 50 goal scorers; a number can provide a cue to recalling facts, as in the case of the two lockouts we've had in NHL history—the first one was 103 days, the second 301 days. Sometimes it's easier to remember things than you might think.

1) How many players under the age of 20 have recorded a 50-goal season?

Two. Wayne Gretzky with Edmonton and Jimmy Carson with Los Angeles. Gretzky was two months past his 19th birthday when he scored his 50th goal on April 2, 1980, while Carson was 19 years eight months when he did it on March 26, 1988. Gretzky scored his goal against Gary Edwards of the Minnesota North Stars; the final score of the game was 1–1. Carson scored his goal against Chicago's Darren Pang in a 9–5 L.A. win. Ironically, they were traded for each other in the first Gretzky deal on August 9, 1988. Accompanying Gretzky to L.A. were Mike Krushelnyski and Marty McSorley. Along with Carson, the Edmonton Oilers got Martin Gelinas, three draft picks and $15 million. Here's a remarkable coincidence connected to the trade: Martin Gelinas was still playing in the junior ranks, for the Hull Olympiques. One of the owners of that team: none other than Wayne Gretzky.

After Gretzky and Carson, the next youngest to score 50 in a season was Steven Stamkos of the Tampa Bay Lightning in 2009–10. Stamkos was 20 years two months old when he recorded his first 50- goal season. Next was Pierre Larouche, who reached 50 with the Pittsburgh Penguins in 1975–76. Larouche was 20 years 5 months old when he became the second Penguin in history to reach the plateau and the fourth youngest in NHL history. Teammate Jean Pronovost was the first Penguin to score 50, reaching it ahead of Larouche by 10 days. Pronovost was one of the oldest 50-goal scorers, which leads us to the next question.

2) Who were the oldest players to score 50 goals in a season for the first time?

Johnny Bucyk of the Boston Bruins was two months shy of his 36th birthday when he popped number 50 on March 16, 1971, in an 11–4 Boston win over Detroit. The goaltender was Roy Edwards. Next on the list of golden oldies is 2000 Hall of Fame inductee, Joe Mullen. Mullen was 32 years 1 month old on March 31, 1989, when he scored number 50 for the Calgary Flames in a 4–1 win over the Winnipeg Jets. The Jets' goaltender that night was Bob Essensa. Rounding out the list of greybeards are Vic Hadfield with the Rangers in 1972, who was 31 years 6 months; Jean Pronovost of Pittsburgh was 30 years 3 months in 1976; Montreal's Bernie Geoffrion, 30 years 1 month in 1961; and Lanny McDonald, with the Calgary Flames in 1983, was 30.

3) Guy Lafleur scored 50 goals in a season six times. Three times he scored his 50th goal against the same goalie. Who was the goalie?

Denis Herron. Lafleur scored number 50 for the first time on March 29, 1975, in a 4–1 victory over the Kansas City Scouts. Herron was the goaltender. Lafleur also scored on Herron and the Pittsburgh Penguins in 1976—his second 50-goal season—and 1979, his fifth. Herron would become a teammate of Lafleur's in Montreal in 1979–80.

4) Only two players to date have scored their 50th goal of the season on their birthday. Who are they?

Phil Esposito and Wayne Gretzky. Gretzky scored goal number 50 for the sixth time on January 26, 1985, his 24th birthday. Gretzky was an Edmonton Oiler and he scored the goal against the Pittsburgh Penguins and goaltender Denis Herron. Gretzky scored 50 goals in a season nine times, an NHL record he shares with Mike Bossy.

Gretzky accomplished this unusual feat only once, but Esposito, who enjoyed five 50-goal seasons in all, did it three times. His birthday is February 20 and he celebrated in style on February 20, 1971, when he turned 29 and scored number 50 for the first time against the Los Angeles Kings and goalie Denis DeJordy. A year later, he scored his 50th goal against his brother Tony, who was with the Chicago Black Hawks. And on February 20, 1974, he scored number 50 against the Minnesota North Stars and goalie Cesare Maniago. Espo was a member of the Boston Bruins for all five of his 50-goal years.

5) Who was the first player born outside of Canada to score 50 goals in one NHL season?

Many readers would hazard a guess that it was one of the Europeans who came to NHL prominence in the 1980s. But it was Ken Hodge of the Boston Bruins. Hodge was born in Birmingham, England, in 1944. His one and only 50-goal season was in 1974. He scored the 50th on April 6 of that year in a 6–2 loss to the Montreal Canadiens. The goaltender was Michel "Bunny" Larocque.

6) Who was the only player to score 50 goals in a season for a last-place team?

Mike Bullard with the Pittsburgh Penguins in 1984. March 14 was the date of Bullard's 50th goal of the season, which came in a 7–6 loss to the Los Angeles Kings. The goalie he scored on was Markus Mattsson. The Penguins finished 21st in a 21-team league in 1983–84 with a total of 38 points.

7) How many players have scored 50 goals or more with two different NHL teams?

Eight—although in one case it's two different teams but the same franchise. I'm thinking of Keith Tkachuk, who scored 50 with the Winnipeg Jets in 1995–96. The Jets moved to Phoenix the following season, and Tkachuk scored 52 times. The other seven members of this club are as follows: Pierre Larouche, Pittsburgh Penguins, 1975–76, and Montreal Canadiens, 1979–80; Wayne Gretzky, eight times with the Edmonton Oilers and once with Los Angeles, in 1988–89; Pat LaFontaine, New York Islanders, 1989–90, and Buffalo Sabres, 1992–93; Alexander Mogilny, Buffalo, 1992–93, and Vancouver Canucks, 1995–96; Teemu Selanne, Winnipeg, 1992–93, and Mighty Ducks of Anaheim, 1996–97, Pavel Bure, three times with the Canucks and in 1999–2000 and 2000–01 with the Florida Panthers. The most recent member of this club is Jaromir Jagr, who had two 50-goal seasons with Pittsburgh and one with the New York Rangers. Jagr's 54 goals with the Rangers in 2005–06 is the current club record. He passed the Rangers' previous record holder, Adam Graves, with goal number 52 on March 27, 2006, in a 5–4 win over Buffalo and goalie Ryan Miller. Jagr's goal was the game winner.

8) To date, the Montreal Canadiens, Detroit Red Wings, Philadelphia Flyers, Calgary Flames and Los Angeles Kings have all had six players in their history score 50 goals or more in a season. One team has had nine. Which team?

The Pittsburgh Penguins. Evgeni Malkin's 50-goal season in 2011–12 made him the ninth Penguin to reach that plateau. His teammate Sidney Crosby was number eight with his 50-goal season in 2010. Jaromir Jagr's 50-goal season in 1995–96 made him the seventh Penguin to reach the plateau. The others were Jean Pronovost and Pierre Larouche in 1975–76, Rick Kehoe in 1980–81, Mike Bullard in 1983–84, Mario Lemieux, who did it six times, the first in 1986–87, and Kevin Stevens in 1991–92.

9) What season produced the most 50-goal scorers in NHL history?

A record 14 players scored at least 50 goals in 1992–93. Buffalo's Alexander Mogilny and Teemu Selanne of Winnipeg led the way with 76 goals each. The other 12 were, in order: Mario Lemieux, Pittsburgh, 69; Luc Robitaille, Los Angeles, 63; Pavel Bure, Vancouver, 60; Pierre Turgeon, New York Islanders, and Steve Yzerman, Detroit, 58 each; Kevin Stevens, Pittsburgh, 55; Brett Hull, St. Louis, and Dave Andreychuk, Buffalo/Toronto, 54 each; Pat LaFontaine, Buffalo, and Mark Recchi, Philadelphia, 53 each; Brendan Shanahan, St. Louis, 51; and Jeremy Roenick, Chicago, 50.

10) How many players have scored 50 goals in 50 games or less?

Seven. However, the NHL only recognizes five of them. To be officially credited with a "fifty-in-fifty" campaign, you have to score 50 times in your team's first 50 games. In other words, if you miss games due to an injury, yet still score 50 within your first 50 games, it won't be officially recognized by the league because your team has played more than 50 games. It's a little weird, but that's the way the league looks at it.

Maurice Richard with the Montreal Canadiens in 1944–45 was the first fifty-in-fifty man. It would be 46 years before there was a second: Mike Bossy with the New York Islanders in 1980–81. Only a year later, Wayne Gretzky would demolish the record, scoring goal number 50 in game number 39. He would break the barrier twice more: in 1983–84, he scored his 50th goal in game number 42, and in 1984–85, he did it in his 49th game.

Mario Lemieux joined the club in 1989. He scored his 50th in his 44th game, which was the Penguins' 46th of the season. In 1992–93, Lemieux scored number 50 in his 48th game, but it was the Penguins' 72nd, so it's not officially recognized. The same goes for 1995–96, when he scored number 50 in game number 50, which was the team's 59th.

To date, Brett Hull is the last official fifty-in-fifty marksman. In 1990–91, as a St. Louis Blue, he scored number 50 in his, and the team's, 49th game. A year later, Hull hit the mark in exactly 50 games. Brett and his father Bobby Hull are the only father-son combination to score 50 goals in a season.

Two other players have unofficial status in this elite group. Cam Neely of the Boston Bruins rocked the hockey world in 1993–94 when he came back from injury to score 50 goals in 44 games. But his 44th game was Boston's 66th of the season. A year earlier, in 1992–93, Alexander Mogilny of Buffalo scored goal number 50 in game number 46. Again, though, it was the Sabres' 53rd contest of the season. Mogilny had missed seven games due to injury.

11) Which two goaltenders have given up the most 50th goals?

Denis Herron and Grant Fuhr. Herron is the leader in this dubious category. Six times an opposing forward scored number 50 against him. Grant Fuhr is close behind, with five.

12) Nine of the 119 goaltenders who have had a 50th goal scored on them have played 35 games or fewer in their NHL career. One goaltender had a total of 35 minutes of ice time in the NHL, yet in that brief career he allowed a historic 50th goal. Who is he?

Dave Gagnon, a Windsor, Ontario, native who was signed as a free agent by the Detroit Red Wings on June 11, 1990. In the following season, he played parts of two games, totalling 35 minutes. His first NHL action came when he was inserted in the final period of a game against St. Louis on January 25, 1991. The Red Wings were losing 7–2 and coach Bryan Murray pulled starter Tim Cheveldae. A minute and 50 seconds into the period, Gagnon allowed his first NHL goal. It was scored by none other than Brett Hull. Not only was it Hull's 50th, but it was scored in game number 49, making Hull a member of the select 50-in-50 group discussed in Question 10.

Hull had scored number 49 earlier in the game, against Cheveldae. Gagnon would see 15 more minutes of ice time in the 1990–91 season, allowing four more goals. After his brief NHL stint, Gagnon enjoyed success in the East Coast Hockey League with the Hampton Roads Admirals and the Toledo Storm. His final season of pro hockey was in the ECHL in 2000–01, with the Roanoke Express.

The other goaltenders who made hockey history in their brief NHL careers include Brian Ford, who played 11 games with Quebec and Pittsburgh. As a member of the Penguins, he yielded Mike Gartner's 50th in 1985. Cam Newton, who played 16 career games with Pittsburgh, allowed Rick MacLeish's 50th in 1973. Nick Ricci, whose big-league tenure lasted 19 games with Pittsburgh, gave up Wayne Gretzky's 50th goal in 1983. Harvey Bennett of Boston, who was the goaltender on March 18, 1945, the night Rocket Richard scored number 50, played only 25 NHL games. Ken Broderick, who saw action in 27 games with Minnesota and Boston, gave up Rick Martin's 50th in 1975 while a member of the Boston Bruins. Larry Lozinski, a 30-game man for Detroit, gave up Dennis Maruk's 50th in 1981. In 1985, Dale Hawerchuk scored his 50th of the season against Chicago's Warren Skorodenski, who played a total of 35 games for the Black Hawks and Edmonton Oilers.

David LeNeveu has played 22 NHL games to date for two teams in the NHL. He was with Phoenix when he allowed Jonathan Cheechoo's 50th in 2006. Mike McKenna has 17 NHL games to his credit currently and is on record as being the goalie for one of Alex Ovechkin's 50-goal seasons, his third one in 2009. McKenna was with Tampa Bay at the time.

13) Who is the only player to score his 50th goal of the season on a penalty shot?

Mario Lemieux. This question was really setting up nicely until Mario's comeback. Before his return to active duty against the Toronto Maple Leafs on December 27, 2000, the penalty-shot goal was also the last regular-season goal Lemieux had scored. Only one other player had ever scored his last goal on a penalty shot: King Clancy of Toronto, on November 14, 1936, against Chicago goalie Mike Karakas.

On April 11, 1997, Mario Lemieux scored his 50th goal of the season—the sixth time he had done so. The penalty shot was awarded at 2:28 of the third period against the Florida Panthers, whose goalie was John Vanbiesbrouck. It's very appropriate that the goal was scored on Vanbiesbrouck, whom Lemieux has victimized more than any other in his NHL career. Lemieux scored 32 times on Vanbiesbrouck. No other goalie surrendered nearly so many goals to Lemieux. Glenn Healy and Sean Burke gave up 14 and 13, respectively.

14) How many players have scored their 50th goal of the season into an empty net?

Seven, starting with Reggie Leach of the Philadelphia Flyers in 1980. They were playing Washington. In 1981, the night Wayne Gretzky scored his 50th goal in his 39th game, number 50 was an empty-netter. It was his fifth goal of the game that night against the Flyers. The photo of the goal is a famous one: Gretzky is shooting the puck past a diving Bill Barber, who is wearing Cooperalls. The Cooperall experiment lasted just two seasons in the NHL, and it was not a success. The Hartford Whalers were the only other team to try out the long pants in league play.

In 1991, Boston's Cam Neely was the next to score number 50 into an empty net. The Bruins were playing the Quebec Nordiques that night. Pavel Bure recorded his first of two empty-net 50th goals in 1994. He was with the Vancouver Canucks and they were playing Los Angeles. He pulled off the trick a second time in 2000, as a member of the Florida Panthers, in a game against the New York Islanders. Joe Sakic scored number 50 into an empty net in 1996. He was a member of the Colorado Avalanche and they were playing the Dallas Stars. Five days later, Keith Tkachuk of the Winnipeg Jets guided the puck into an unguarded Los Angeles cage. This was also the last regular-season goal on home ice in Winnipeg Jets history. A year later, the Kings were on the receiving end of another uncontested 50th goal. This time the scorer was Teemu Selanne of the Mighty Ducks of Anaheim.

15) Only twice in NHL history have teammates scored 50th goals in the same game. When did it happen, and who were the players?

On both occasions the Pittsburgh Penguins were involved. On March 21, 1993, Mario Lemieux and Kevin Stevens each scored number 50 of the season against the Edmonton Oilers and goalie Ron Tugnutt. Pittsburgh won the game, 6–4. It's notable that the game was played in neither Pittsburgh nor Edmonton. In 1992–93 and 1993–94, the NHL played an 84-game schedule, adding a couple of games for each team in neutral, non-NHL cities to help raise the league's profile. On this particular night, NHL hockey returned to Cleveland, where it had been for two seasons in the 1970s. Only one other player scored a 50th goal in a neutral-site game. Pavel Bure, also in 1993, scored his 50th for Vancouver against the Buffalo Sabres and goalie Grant Fuhr. The game was played in Hamilton, Ontario.

In 1996, Pittsburgh's Mario Lemieux and Jaromir Jagr scored number 50 in the same game on February 23. The Penguins beat the Hartford Whalers and both men scored on goalie Sean Burke.

To date, there has only been one other occasion when two players recorded number 50 in the same game. In this case, the scorers were on opposing teams. In 1994, Brendan Shanahan of St. Louis and Mike Modano of Dallas each scored number 50 in a 9–5 Dallas win on the Stars' home ice.

16) Who was the last player to score 50 goals in a season and not wear a helmet?

One of my favourites. Al Secord of the Chicago Black Hawks is the answer. The date was March 20, 1983, and Chicago beat the Toronto Maple Leafs 7–3. The goalie that night was Mike Palmateer.

100-POINT SCORERS

Going into the 2012–13 season, 105 NHL players have combined to post 270 100-point seasons. Following are my best trivia questions about these men and their great seasons.

1) Who was the first player to record 100 points in the NHL?

Phil Esposito of the Boston Bruins. The date was March 2, 1969, and Boston beat the Pittsburgh Penguins 4–0. Esposito picked up point number 100 on a goal he scored 17 seconds into the third period. Ken Hodge and Ted Green assisted. Joe Daley was the goaltender. Esposito would go on to record 126 points, breaking the previous NHL high of 97 shared by Stan Mikita and Bobby Hull.

2) How many teenagers have recorded 100 points in an NHL season, and who are they?

Five. Sidney Crosby is the youngest to accomplish this feat. Crosby was eight months past his 18th birthday when he recorded point number 100 for the first time on April 17, 2006. It was Crosby's third assist of the game in a 6–1 win over the New York Islanders. Ryan Malone scored the goal. Dale Hawerchuk is the second youngest .The Winnipeg Jet was a month shy of his 19th birthday when he did it on March 24, 1982. Wayne Gretzky was 19 years 2 months old on February 24, 1980. Mario Lemieux of the Pittsburgh Penguins was 19 years 6 months on April 7, 1985, and Jimmy Carson was 19 years 8 months on March 26, 1988.

A question like this one is a perfect example of how trivia can get extremely intricate. If somebody wanted, he could take this chapter and turn it into a trivia book on its own. Here's a taste of the twists and turns you can end up following. We'll use Hawerchuk's 100th point, which at the time gave him the record for youngest player to reach that many points, and it came on a goal scored against Los Angeles and goaltender Mike Blake. It was one of only two games in which Blake saw action all season. He replaced Doug Keans in that game. Hawerchuk's goal was assisted by Dave Babych. Dave's brother Wayne drew one of the assists on Mario Lemieux's first 100th point on April 7, 1985. Warren Young received the other assist. The Penguins' goalie in that game, a 7–3 loss to Washington, was Brian Ford. On that same night, Mike Gartner recorded his 50th goal and 100th point against Ford.

Gartner is one of only seven players in NHL history to score a 50th goal and 100th point in the same game. Jimmy Carson is another of the seven and he did it on the night in 1988 that he joined the teenage 100-point club. Carson scored three goals in a 9–5 win over Chicago and goalie Darren Pang. His second goal was his 50th of the season, while his third represented his 100th point. The latter goal was assisted by Chris Kontos and goaltender Glenn Healy. Carson was a Los Angeles King at this time, which brings the whole loop back around to Hawerchuk's 100th point, which, of course, he scored against Los Angeles.

3) How many rookies have recorded 100 points in one season?

Seven: Peter Stastny, Dale Hawerchuk, Mario Lemieux, Teemu Selanne, Joe Juneau, Alex Ovechkin and Sidney Crosby. I put this question in to illustrate how the wording of a question can affect the answer. You might think that all four players named in question two would qualify for this answer, but no. Gretzky was not classified as a rookie because of the year he'd spent in the WHA. So while he was a teenager who recorded a 100-point season, he was not a rookie. Although Carson had 100 points as a 19-year-old, he had already played a full NHL season, picking up 79 points, as an 18-year-old.

Among those who do qualify, Stastny was a 24-year-old rookie when he recorded 109 points in 1980–81 for the Quebec Nordiques. At 18, Hawerchuk racked up 103 points for Winnipeg in 1981–82. Lemieux was a 19-year-old rookie with his 100 points in 1984–85. At 22, Winnipeg's Selanne set the rookie point-scoring record with 132 in 1992–93. In the same year, Juneau was a 25-year-old rookie with Boston when he accumulated 102 points.

4) How many players were over the age of 30 when they recorded 100 points for the first time?

Ten. Gordie Howe leads this parade, scoring a goal the night before his 41st birthday, March 30, 1969. This was point number 100 in a season in which he would finish with 103. Four of the remaining nine are also on the list of those who scored their 50th goal of the season for the first time as a 30-year-old: Johnny Bucyk, Vic Hadfield, Jean Pronovost and Joe Mullen. The other five are Bobby Hull, Jean Ratelle, Daniel Alfredsson, Martin St. Louis and Daniel Sedin.

5) How many defencemen have recorded 100 points in a season?

Five. Bobby Orr did it six times, all with Boston. Paul Coffey broke the barrier five times—four with Edmonton and once with Pittsburgh. Denis Potvin of the New York Islanders, Al MacInnis of the Calgary Flames and Brian Leetch of the New York Rangers round out the list. Orr's 139 points in 1970–71 are still tops among blueliners. Coffey came close, finishing with 138 in 1985–86.

6) How many players started a season with one team and finished with another in a year in which they hit the century mark?

Five: Jean Ratelle, John Cullen, Teemu Selanne, Wayne Gretzky and Joe Thornton. Ratelle was traded from the New York Rangers, along with Brad Park and Joe Zanussi, to Boston for Phil Esposito and Carol Vadnais on November 7, 1975. He had 15 points with New York and 90 with Boston for a total of 105. Cullen was next. On March 4, 1991, he was traded from Pittsburgh, along with Jeff Parker and Zarley Zalapski, to Hartford for Ron Francis, Grant Jennings and Ulf Samuelsson. Cullen picked up 94 points with the Penguins and then 16 in the season's final 13 games with Hartford for a total of 110.

Teemu Selanne was traded from the Winnipeg Jets to the Mighty Ducks of Anaheim on February 7, 1996. Accompanying Selanne was a junior player, Marc Chouinard, and a fourth-round pick that would be flipped twice before ending up with the Montreal Canadiens. The Habs selected Kim Staal. Winnipeg acquired Chad Kilger, Oleg Tverdovsky and a third-round pick they used to draft Per-Anton Lundstrom. Selanne had 72 points with the Jets and another 36 with Anaheim for a total of 108.

Wayne Gretzky is on the list in 1995–96. He was traded from the Los Angeles Kings to the St. Louis Blues for Patrice Tardif, Craig Johnson, Roman Vopat and two draft picks—a fifth rounder in 1996, which became Peter Hogan, and a first rounder in 1997, which L.A. used to take Matt Zultek. The date of the deal was February 27. Gretzky had 81 points with L.A. and another 21 with St. Louis for a total of 102. Last on the list is Joe Thornton, who was traded from Boston to San Jose for Brad Stuart, Marco Sturm and Wayne Primeau on November 30, 2005. Thornton not only went on to record 125 points that year but his points total was enough to win him the Art Ross Trophy, making him the first player to have that unique distinction.

7) How many players have accumulated 100 points or more with two different teams?

Seventeen to date. Part of the fun of this question is identifying who was first. It's been reported in many sources that it was Jean Ratelle. It depends on how specific you want to make the question. If you are asking for the first player to score his 100th point of the season for two different teams, then the answer is indeed Ratelle. But if you're asking me who the first player was to accumulate 100 points with two different teams, then the answer is Marcel Dionne. Dionne had a 121-point season with Detroit in 1974–75, and his first of seven 100-point seasons with Los Angeles in 1977. In chronological order, the rest are as follows:

Mike Rogers: Hartford Whalers, New York Rangers
Wayne Gretzky: Edmonton Oilers, Los Angeles Kings
Paul Coffey: Edmonton Oilers, Pittsburgh Penguins
Jimmy Carson: Los Angeles Kings, Edmonton Oilers
Bernie Nicholls: Los Angeles Kings, New York Rangers
Mark Messier: Edmonton Oilers, New York Rangers
Pat LaFontaine: New York Islanders, Buffalo Sabres
Adam Oates: St. Louis Blues, Boston Bruins
Pierre Turgeon: Buffalo Sabres, New York Islanders
Doug Gilmour: St. Louis Blues, Toronto Maple Leafs

Mark Recchi: Pittsburgh Penguins,
Philadelphia Flyers
Ron Francis: Hartford Whalers,
Pittsburgh Penguins
Teemu Selanne: Winnipeg Jets,
Mighty Ducks of Anaheim
Alexander Mogilny: Buffalo Sabres,
Vancouver Canucks
Joe Sakic: Quebec Nordiques,
Colorado Avalanche
Joe Thornton: Boston Bruins, San Jose Sharks

In Sakic's case, Quebec relocated to Colorado, so it's the same franchise but still two different teams. Exactly the same scenario as Keith Tkachuk in his 50-goal seasons with Winnipeg and Phoenix.

8) Who was the fastest player to accumulate 100 points in one season?

Not much doubt here. In 1983–84, Wayne Gretzky took only 34 games to notch 100 points. To put it into the context of the calendar, he scored his 100th point on December 18, 1983—a week before Christmas.

9) Who needed the most games to accumulate 100 points in one season?

Joe Juneau, in 1992–93, required 84 games. Interestingly, of the 270 hundred-point seasons, the player's 100th point was scored on the last night of the regular season only 19 times. In all but six of those cases, the players were playing 80-game schedules. The exceptions were Gordie Howe in 1968–69, in a 76-game schedule; Rick MacLeish in 1972–73, in a 78-game schedule; Paul Kariya in 1998–99, in an 82-game schedule; Marian Hossa and Joe Sakic, also in an 82-game season, the same season, in fact, 2006–07; and Joe Juneau, in one of two seasons that the NHL played an 84-game schedule.

10) Which team has, to date, had the most players score a 100th point?

The answer's the same as it was for Question 8 in the segment on 50-goal scorers: the Pittsburgh Penguins. The Penguins have had 12 players score point number 100 in a season: Pierre Larouche, Jean Pronovost, Mario Lemieux, Rob Brown, Paul Coffey, Mark Recchi, Kevin Stevens, Rick Tocchet, Ron Francis, Jaromir Jagr, Sidney Crosby and Evgeni Malkin.

11) There are five teams that currently have not had a 100-point man in their history. Four of them are expansion franchises that have joined the NHL since 1993. One, however, is a franchise that is over 35 years old. Which one?

Surprisingly, the New Jersey Devils. In fact the Devils, who were originally the Kansas City Scouts, joining the NHL as an expansion franchise in 1974. Two years later they became the Colorado Rockies, and six years after that they moved to New Jersey and became the Devils. The franchise has only had three players break the 90-point barrier: Kirk Muller in 1987–88 scored 94 points, Patrick Elias set a new franchise record with 96 points in 2000–01 and Zach Parise recorded 94 points in 2009. The Florida Panthers, Nashville Predators, Minnesota Wild and Columbus Blue Jackets are the other teams currently without a 100-point man in their history.

12) How many times have teammates scored their 100th point in the same game?

Four: Jacques Richard and Peter Stastny, with Quebec in 1981; Glenn Anderson and Jari Kurri, with Edmonton in 1983; Hakan Loob and Mike Bullard, with Pittsburgh in 1988; and Wayne Gretzky and Bernie Nicholls, with Los Angeles in 1989.

13) Now let's follow up on part of the answer to Question 2 in this section: Besides Mike Gartner and Jimmy Carson, who are the remaining five players to score their 50th goal and 100th point in the same game?

In chronological order, they are Rick MacLeish of Philadelphia on April 1, 1973, in a 5–4 loss to Pittsburgh; Jacques Richard of Quebec on March 29, 1981, in a 4–0 win over Montreal; Gartner—as mentioned—for Washington on April 7, 1985; Carson with Los Angeles, March 26, 1988; Theo Fleury of Calgary on March 26, 1991, helping his Flames beat Vancouver 7–2; Luc Robitaille with Los Angeles on March 15, 1993, as the Kings doubled the Buffalo Sabres, 4–2; and Brendan Shanahan, then with the St. Louis Blues, on April 12, 1994. St. Louis lost to Dallas that night, 9–5.

500-GOAL SCORERS

From 1917–18 until 2011–12, approximately 7,000 players have played in the NHL. To date, only 42 players have scored 500 career goals. The list is widely available, but one of the things you'll find here that you will not see in any other publication are the assists on the 500th goals. One of the many scenes that are indelibly etched in my mind is the night of February 11, 1971. Jean Beliveau scored a hat trick in a 6–2 win over the Minnesota North Stars. His third goal was the 500th of his career. I'll never forget it. The television screen flashed the number 500 with stars all around it as Beliveau was congratulated by his teammates. Frank Mahovlich and Phil Roberto drew the assists.

Twenty-three years later, almost to the day, I hosted an evening in Kars, Ontario, where Jean Beliveau and Yvan Cournoyer were brought in as head-table guests. I talked that night with Beliveau about his historic goal. I told him I remembered who assisted and named the players. "You're right," he said. "Nobody ever remembers Phil Roberto assisting on that play. It's a great trivia question."

That's why you'll see the names of all those who assisted on a 500th goal. Pertinent notes accompany the stats.

MAURICE RICHARD, MONTREAL CANADIENS

Date: October 19, 1957
Assisted by: Henri Richard and Dickie Moore
Goaltender: Glenn Hall of the Chicago Black Hawks
Final Score: 3–1, Montreal

Richard dedicated this goal to the memory of the late Dick Irvin, his long-time coach with the Canadiens, who had passed away on May 16, 1957. To refresh anyone's memory who might have seen this goal, the footage shows a young man wearing number 16 for Chicago skating to the bench after Richard scores. His name was Robert Marvin Hull—better known as Bobby and later the Golden Jet. It was his fifth NHL game. Twelve years, four months and two days later he would join the exclusive 500-goal club.

GORDIE HOWE, DETROIT RED WINGS

Date: March 14, 1962
Assisted by: Alex Delvecchio and Warren Godfrey
Goaltender: Gump Worsley of the New York Rangers
Final Score: 3–2, New York

Howe's goal was scored shorthanded at 17:10 of the second period. It briefly gave Detroit a 2–1 lead. Forty-one seconds later, Earl Ingarfield tied the game and Andy Bathgate scored the winner for New York on a penalty shot in the third period. It took Howe 182 games longer than Richard to get to number 500. However, Howe was like the Energizer bunny in those days: he just kept going and going. He would play over 700 more regular-season games, scoring 300 more goals. (And don't forget what he accomplished in six years in the WHA.)

BOBBY HULL, CHICAGO BLACK HAWKS
Date: February 21, 1970
Assisted by: Lou Angotti and Bill White
Goaltender: Ed Giacomin of the New York Rangers
Final Score: 4–2, Chicago
Hull's milestone goal was scored at 16:51 of the second period. It was his second goal of the game and it proved to be the game winner. Bobby's brother Dennis scored one of the other Chicago goals. Lou Angotti also assisted on Hull's 51st goal of the season on March 12, 1966, making the Golden Jet the first player in NHL history to score more than 50 goals in one season.

JEAN BELIVEAU, MONTREAL CANADIENS
Date: February 11, 1971
Assisted by: Frank Mahovlich and Phil Roberto
Goaltender: Gilles Gilbert of the Minnesota North Stars
Final Score: 6–2, Montreal
The night I remember so well. Beliveau scored the first three Montreal goals. His third of the night was number 500, coming at 6:42 of the second period. He also added an assist for a four-point night. Montreal goaltender Rogie Vachon stopped a penalty shot from the stick of Jude Drouin in the third period.

FRANK MAHOVLICH, MONTREAL CANADIENS
Date: March 21, 1973
Assisted by: Henri Richard and Guy Lapointe
Goaltender: Dunc Wilson of the Vancouver Canucks
Final Score: 3–2, Montreal
Mahovlich's 500th goal was the game winner, scored at 1:27 of the third period. It was somewhat controversial in that Vancouver coach Vic Stasiuk and the Canucks players claimed the play was offside. The goal was also a bit of a fluke in that it skittered off of Mahovlich's stick after the pass from Richard. Jocelyn Guevremont, a Vancouver defenceman at the time, could have cleared the puck but fanned on the attempt.

PHIL ESPOSITO, BOSTON BRUINS
Date: December 22, 1974
Assisted by: Carol Vadnais
Goaltender: Jim Rutherford of the Detroit Red Wings
Final Score: 5–4, Boston
Esposito scored a pair of goals in the second period, two minutes and three seconds apart. The second one was career goal number 500. The time of the goal was 6:49. Esposito became the fastest so far to reach 500, scoring the goal in game number 803—58 games faster than Bobby Hull.

JOHNNY BUCYK, BOSTON BRUINS
Date: October 30, 1975
Assisted by: Ken Hodge and Al Sims
Goaltender: Yves Belanger of the St. Louis Blues
Final Score: 3–2, Boston
Bucyk's 500th goal was scored at 12:52 of the first period. To date, Bucyk remains the oldest player to record his 500th goal—he was almost six months past his 40th birthday. Dave Reece was the winning Bruins goalie in this game. It was his first of seven career wins in the 14 games he played in the NHL. A little more than three months later he would be the victim of Darryl Sittler's six-goal, 10-point outburst in what would be Reece's last game ever in the big leagues.

STAN MIKITA, CHICAGO BLACK HAWKS

Date: February 27, 1977
Assisted by: Phil Russell
Goaltender: Cesare Maniago of the Vancouver Canucks
Final Score: 4–3, Vancouver

Mikita provided quite a charge for the hometown crowd when he scored his 500th goal at 13:56 of the third period. Not only was it a milestone goal, but it was Chicago's third of the period after they entered the third frame trailing 4–0. Mikita's goal was a beauty as well: he took Russell's pass on the fly and split the defence, going in alone to score. Chicago couldn't deliver a victory, however, and the game went into the books a 4–3 win for Vancouver.

MARCEL DIONNE, LOS ANGELES KINGS

Date: December 14, 1982
Assisted by: Ulf Isaksson and Jerry Korab
Goaltender: Al Jensen of the Washington Capitals
Final Score: 7–2, Washington

Dionne scored both goals for L.A. in the 7–2 drubbing at the hands of Washington. His first goal was the historic marker, coming exactly three minutes into the first period. Jean Beliveau made the point about assists on historic goals making for good trivia questions. Well, this is as good as it gets. Many of you, I'm sure, have heard of Jerry Korab—but Ulf Isaksson? I kind of doubt it. Isaksson was a 28-year-old rookie with L.A. that season. He would play only 50 games in the NHL, picking up 7 goals and 15 assists. He saw action in an additional 14 games with New Haven of the American Hockey League, and then it was back to Sweden to finish his career.

GUY LAFLEUR, MONTREAL CANADIENS

Date: December 20, 1983
Assisted by: Pierre Mondou and Bob Gainey
Goaltender: Chico Resch of the New Jersey Devils
Final Score: 6–0, Montreal

Lafleur's 500th was the last goal of the game, scored at 8:34 of the third period. This would turn out to be his last full season with the Montreal Canadiens. Lafleur would retire the following November and not play again until the fall of 1988, when he resumed his career with the New York Rangers.

MIKE BOSSY, NEW YORK ISLANDERS

Date: January 2, 1986
Assisted by: John Tonelli
Goaltender: Empty net. Doug Keans of the Boston Bruins had been pulled for an extra attacker.
Final Score: 7–5, New York

Mike Bossy stole the thunder from teammate Denis Potvin, whom the Islanders organization had honoured earlier in the evening. Potvin had broken Bobby Orr's record for most career points by a defenceman with point number 915 in a 2–2 tie against the New York Rangers on December 20, 1985.

Bossy did little in the game until the dying minutes. With the score tied at five, he scored career goal number 499, which would be the game winner. Then, with Doug Keans pulled, Bossy became the first to join the 500-goal club by popping the milestone goal into an empty net. The time of the goal was 19:43 of the third period. Bossy was also the first player under 30 to reach the plateau. He was 20 days shy of his 30th birthday. To date, only one other player scored 500 goals before turning 30: Wayne Gretzky.

GILBERT PERREAULT, BUFFALO SABRES

Date: March 9, 1986
Assisted by: Mike Foligno and Bill Hajt
Goaltender: Alain Chewier of the New Jersey Devils
Final Score: 4–3, Buffalo

Perreault's goal sparked a three-minute ovation from the home crowd in the Memorial Auditorium. At the conclusion of the game, Foligno and teammate Steven Dykstra hoisted Perreault on their shoulders and carried him around the ice.

WAYNE GRETZKY, EDMONTON OILERS

Date: November 22, 1986
Assisted by: Charlie Huddy and Jari Kurri
Goaltender: Empty net. Troy Gamble of the Vancouver Canucks had been pulled for an extra attacker.
Final Score: 5–2, Edmonton

Gretzky had points on all five Oilers goals in this game, scoring three of them himself. His third goal, into the empty net, was the 500th of his career. The time was 19:42 of the third period. At 25 years 10 months, Gretzky remains the youngest to date to reach the 500-goal mark. Gretzky was also the fastest to reach the milestone, scoring his 500 goals in just 575 games. This was the only game in which Vancouver goalie Troy Gamble appeared during the 1986–87 season.

LANNY MCDONALD, CALGARY FLAMES

Date: March 21, 1989
Assisted by: Jim Peplinski and Joel Otto
Goaltender: Mark Fitzpatrick of the New York Islanders
Final Score: 4–1, Calgary

McDonald's 500th goal was the game winner, scored at 10:54 of the first period. Islanders goalie Mark Fitzpatrick was in his rookie year. Sophomore Joe Nieuwendyk of the Flames scored his 50th of the season, becoming only the second NHL player to score 50 both as a rookie and in his second season. The other was Mike Bossy. Gretzky scored 50 in each of his first two NHL seasons, but was not considered a rookie in 1979–80.

BRYAN TROTTIER, NEW YORK ISLANDERS

Date: February 13, 1990
Assisted by: Gary Nylund and Pat LaFontaine
Goaltender: Rick Wamsley of the Calgary Flames
Final Score: 4–2, Calgary

Trottier opened the scoring in this game at 9:57 of the second period by netting his 500th goal. This would be Trottier's last of 15 years with the Islanders. He was signed as a free agent by Pittsburgh on July 20, 1990.

MIKE GARTNER, NEW YORK RANGERS

Date: October 14, 1991
Assisted by: Mark Messier and James Patrick
Goaltender: Mike Liut of the Washington Capitals
Final Score: 5–3, Washington

Gartner's goal was a power-play marker scored at 3:27 of the first period. The fleet-footed winger would go on to record 40 in the 1991–92 season. Gartner is in the record book as the only player to score 30 goals or more in 15 straight seasons. He's also the only player in NHL history to score 30 or more for five different teams: the Washington Capitals, Minnesota North Stars, New York Rangers, Toronto Maple Leafs and Phoenix Coyotes.

MICHEL GOULET, CHICAGO BLACKHAWKS

Date: February 16, 1992
Assisted by: Steve Larmer and Jeremy Roenick
Goaltender: Jeff Reese of the Calgary Flames
Final Score: 5–5 tie

Goulet scored his big goal on a breakaway at 19:23 of the first period. Goulet was a very consistent goal scorer who recorded 20 goals or more in 14 straight seasons.

JARI KURRI, LOS ANGELES KINGS
Date: October 17, 1992
Assisted by: Unassisted
Goaltender: Empty net. Andy Moog of the Boston Bruins had been pulled for an extra attacker.
Final Score: 8–6, Los Angeles
Jari Kurri had three points on the night, including his 500th goal, which was scored at 19:06 of the third period. Reggie Lemelin had started in goal for Boston but was pulled during the contest for Andy Moog, making Moog the goalie of record when Kurri scored into the empty net.

DINO CICCARELLI, DETROIT RED WINGS
Date: January 8, 1994
Assisted by: Vyacheslav Kozlov and Sergei Fedorov
Goaltender: Kelly Hrudey of the Los Angeles Kings
Final Score: 6–3, Detroit

Ciccarelli scored his milestone goal at 4:20 of the third period. Ciccarelli was once involved in a trade for Mike Gartner. It's the only time in NHL history that two future 500-goal scorers were dealt for each other. The transaction took place on March 7, 1989. Ciccarelli and Bob Rouse went from the Minnesota North Stars to Washington for Mike Gartner and Larry Murphy.

MARIO LEMIEUX, PITTSBURGH PENGUINS
Date: October 26, 1995
Assisted by: Tomas Sandstrom and Dmitri Mironov
Goaltender: Tommy Soderstrom of the New York Islanders
Final Score: 7–5, Pittsburgh
Lemieux scored number 500 three weeks after his 30th birthday. It was game number 605 of Lemieux's career—he reached the milestone in 30 more games than Gretzky, but needed 42 fewer games than the third-fastest, Mike Bossy. Lemieux scored a hat trick in the game. His third goal of the game, at 17:12 of the third period, was number 500.

MARK MESSIER, NEW YORK RANGERS
Date: November 6, 1995
Assisted by: Bruce Driver and Adam Graves
Goaltender: Rick Tabaracci of the Calgary Flames
Final Score: 4–2, New York

Once again the magic of Mark Messier was evident on this historic night. With several relatives in attendance, Messier recorded a hat trick and an assist for a four-point night. His third goal, scored at 12:32 of the third period, was the 500th of his career. It also chased Calgary starter Rick Tabaracci from the game. Trevor Kidd finished up in relief.

STEVE YZERMAN, DETROIT RED WINGS
Date: January 17, 1996
Assisted by: Greg Johnson and Sergei Fedorov
Goaltender: Patrick Roy of the Colorado Avalanche
Final Score: 3–2, Detroit
Yzerman scored Detroit's second goal of the game at 7:52 of the second period. Fedorov's assist on Yzerman's goal meant he joined Henri Richard as the only players to twice assist on 500th career goals. Federov also drew an assist on Dino Ciccarelli's 500th goal.

DALE HAWERCHUK, ST. LOUIS BLUES
Date: January 31, 1996
Assisted by: Rob Pearson and Craig Johnson
Goaltender: Felix Potvin of the Toronto Maple Leafs
Final Score: 4–0, St. Louis

Hawerchuk scored the second goal of the game on a slapshot over Felix Potvin's shoulder. The time was 10:26 of the third period. Standing behind the St. Louis bench was Blues coach Mike Keenan, who'd coached Hawerchuk for a year of Junior B hockey in Oshawa 18 years earlier. Rob Pearson, who drew one of the helpers on the play, also played a year of junior in Oshawa. However, that was at the major junior level.

BRETT HULL, ST. LOUIS BLUES
Date: December 22, 1996
Assisted by: Pierre Turgeon
Goaltender: Stephane Fiset of the Los Angeles Kings
Final Score: 7–4, St. Louis
Hull became the fifth player whose 500th career goal was on the third goal of a hat trick. Hull's third of the night was scored at 10:25 of the third period and it chased Los Angeles goalkeeper Stephane Fiset from the game. Byron Dafoe took his place. This goal made the Hulls, Bobby and Brett, the first father–son combination to reach 500 goals each. Brett's goal came in game number 693, which is the fourth-fastest of all time.

JOE MULLEN, PITTSBURGH PENGUINS
Date: March 14, 1997
Assisted by: Chris Tamer and Alex Hicks
Goaltender: Patrick Roy of the Colorado Avalanche
Final Score: 6–3, Colorado

With this goal, at 16:01 of the second period, Mullen became the first American-born player to score 500. Alex Hicks, who drew one of the assists, is the son of Wayne Hicks, the only American-born player to play on a Cup-winning team in the 1960s. The senior Hicks was with Chicago for their 1961 championship. Mullen also became the second-oldest to record the landmark goal: he was two weeks past his 40th birthday. Johnny Bucyk is the oldest at 40 years 6 months.

DAVE ANDREYCHUK, NEW JERSEY DEVILS
Date: March 15, 1997
Assisted by: Bill Guerin and Lyle Odelein
Goaltender: Bill Ranford of the Washington Capitals
Final Score: 3–2, New Jersey

One of the premier power-play specialists in the modern era, Andreychuk reached 500 with a goal that also gave him 213 scored with the man advantage. The time of that goal was 9:03 of the second period. He retired with 274 power-play goals, still tops in NHL history.

LUC ROBITAILLE, LOS ANGELES KINGS
Date: January 7, 1999
Assisted by: Pavel Rosa and Rob Blake
Goaltender: Dwayne Roloson of the Buffalo Sabres
Final Score: 4–2, Los Angeles

Robitaille's second goal of the game, at 18:14 of the third, was the historic marker. Rosa and Robitaille are both alumni of the Hull Olympiques of the Quebec Major Junior Hockey League.

PAT VERBEEK, DETROIT RED WINGS
Date: March 22, 2000
Assisted by: Steve Yzerman and Nicklas Lidstrom
Goaltender: Fred Brathwaite of the Calgary Flames
Final Score: 2–2 tie

Verbeek's second goal of the game, a power-play marker at 14:48 of the third period, tied the contest at two. He had scored number 499 on the Wings' first shot of the game. Although the well-travelled Verbeek had scored only 22 of those 500 goals for Detroit, the fans still gave him a nice ovation.

RON FRANCIS, CAROLINA HURRICANES
Date: January 2, 2002
Assisted by: Erik Cole and Sami Kapanen
Goaltender: Byron Dafoe
Final Score: 6–3 Boston

The man known as "Ronnie Franchise" gave the hometown fans something to cheer about at 13:12 of the first period on a power play when he banged home a loose puck off a scramble in front of Bruin goalie Byron Dafoe. The Bruins had roared to a 3–0 lead, so the goal was a bit of respite, albeit a brief one. Francis was playing in his 1,000th franchise game with the Hurricanes, and at the time he joined a select group of players, all of whom had recorded 500 goals and 1,000 assists—Gordie Howe, Marcel Dionne, Wayne Gretzky and Mark Messier. Jamie Rivers was in the box for the Bruins, serving a tripping penalty. I state this because I know Jamie personally (just having some fun). Francis would later add an assist for a two-point night. He's also on record, as of this writing, as playing the most games before recording goal number 500—1,533.

BRENDAN SHANAHAN, DETROIT RED WINGS
Date: March 23, 2002
Assisted by: Nicklas Lidstrom and Sergei Fedorov
Goaltender: Patrick Roy
Final Score: 2–0 Detroit
It would be hard to imagine Brendan Shanahan having a better season professionally than 2001–02. He recorded his 1,000th point in January. He helped Canada win its first Gold Medal in hockey in the Winter Olympics in 50 years in Salt Lake City, Utah, in February. A little more than one month later he notched his 500th career goal, and that spring he won his third Stanley Cup. A pretty epic run. His 500th career goal came on a five-on-three power play for Detroit, breaking a scoreless tie at 7:48 of the third period. Check the lineup on the ice: Luc Robitaille, Sergei Fedorov, Shanahan, Nick Lidstrom and Brett Hull. The goal not only stood as the game winner but the victory also locked up the President's Trophy for Detroit. Federov now moved into an exclusive category as the only man to assist three 500-goal scorers.

JOE SAKIC, COLORADO AVALANCHE
Date: December 11, 2002
Assisted by: Derek Morris and Milan Hejduk
Goaltender: Dan Cloutier
Final Score: 3–1 Vancouver
"Burnaby" Joe wasn't far from his roots when he potted number 500 of his career in Vancouver later in 2002. In keeping with the recent trend of 500-goal scorers, his was notched on a power play and it came in a losing effort. Sakic's goal was courtesy of a beautiful pass from Derek Morris to goaltender Cloutier's right, and Sakic made no mistake. The time of the goal was 4:25 of the second period. He became the 13th player in league history to score number 500 with the same franchise.

JOE NIEUWENDYK, NEW JERSEY DEVILS
Date: January 17, 2003
Assisted by: unassisted
Goaltender: Kevin Weekes
Final Score: 2–1 New Jersey
Joe Nieuwendyk scored one of the nicer 500th goals you'll ever see. Stealing the puck from a colleague in the historic-goal club, Nieuwendyk intercepted an errant pass by Ron Francis and flew down the left side of the ice, beating the Carolina defence before sweeping around goaltender Kevin Weekes to tuck in number 500 and become only the second 500-goal scorer to score the goal unassisted (Jari Kurri is the first). The

time of the goal was 11:18 of the first period. The Devils won the contest and surged to 14 games over .500. Interestingly, Nieuwendyk had passed up a chance for number 500 a week earlier on an empty-net opportunity late in another 2–1 New Jersey win, ironically over these same Hurricanes. Later in the season he won the Stanley Cup with the Devils, his third Cup with his third team, permitting him to join a very select group along with eight others who have won Cups with three teams—Frank Foyston, Jack Walker, Mike Keane, Claude Lemieux, Al Arbour, Gord Pettinger, Larry Hillman and Mark Recchi, whose third Cup win with his third team, Boston, was in 2011. Two players, Jack Marshall and Harry Holmes, have won Cups with four teams.

JAROMIR JAGR, WASHINGTON CAPITALS

Date: February 4, 2003
Assisted by: Sergei Gonchar and Robert Lang
Goaltender: Nikolai Khabibulin
Final Score: 5–1 Washington

The Washington Capitals rolled into Tampa for this early February game, and Jaromir Jagr rolled over the Lightning singlehandedly scoring three goals and one assist for four points including his 500th career marker on a power play, and it was the hat trick goal at 7:18 of the second period. It was his 30th goal of the season and his 11th career hat trick; he became the 16th player to score 500 in fewer than 1,000 games, with this game number 928 for him.

PIERRE TURGEON, COLORADO AVALANCHE

Date: November 8, 2005
Assisted by: Marek Svatos and Patrice Brisebois
Goaltender: Vesa Toskala
Final Score: 5–2 Colorado

Pierre Turgeon's milestone goal came on a five-on-three power play for the Avalanche in the third period. His goal was scored at the 9:16 mark, with a beautiful cross-crease pass from Svatos setting up the play. It put the Aves up 4–2 at that time. Turgeon also had an assist on a goal by Svatos earlier in the game.

MATS SUNDIN, TORONTO MAPLE LEAFS

Date: October 14, 2006
Assisted by: unassisted
Goaltender: Miikka Kiprusoff
Final Score: 5–4 Toronto

This was one beauty 500th goal. If not the best play, it certainly represented the most dramatic. Sundin fired a bullet past Miikka Kiprusoff in overtime at the 50-second mark shorthanded. It was his third goal of the night on home ice as the Leafs beat the Calgary Flames, 5–4. Darcy Tucker had taken a penalty late in the third period to put the Leafs a man down. Sundin received a tremendous standing ovation from the fans after the goal.

TEEMU SELANNE, ANAHEIM DUCKS

Date: November 22, 2006
Assisted by: Andy McDonald and Chris Pronger
Goaltender: Jose Theodore
Final Score: 3-2 Colorado

Teemu Selanne became the second Finnish-born player to record 500 goals when he completed an excellent give-and-go on a power play with teammate Andy McDonald. The goal was scored against Jose Theodore, who ironically had received a penalty 18 seconds earlier for tripping. The time of Selanne's goal was 14:54 of the second period, closing the deficit to 2–1, but the Aves prevailed in the contest 3–2 in overtime.

PETER BONDRA, CHICAGO BLACKHAWKS
Date: December 22, 2006
Assisted by: Jassen Cullimore and Michael Holmqvist
Goaltender: Jean-Sebastien Aubin
Final Score: 3–1 Chicago
Pure unbridled emotion is what Peter Bondra exhibited after getting a stick on a point shot from Jassen Cullimore and redirecting it past Jean-Sebastien Aubin for his 500th career goal. He became only the fourth player to record number 500 in a Hawk uniform, joining Bobby Hull, Stan Mikita and Michel Goulet. Michael Holmqvist made great work down low on the goal, stealing the puck from Tomas Kaberle. The goal would stand as the game winner.

MARK RECCHI, PITTSBURGH PENGUINS
Date: January 26, 2007
Assisted by: Ryan Whitney and Sidney Crosby
Goaltender: Marty Turco
Final Score: 4–3 Pittsburgh
Mark Recchi's second goal of the game, at the 11:59 mark of the third period on a power play, was the 500th of his career, and it tied the game 3–3 with the Dallas Stars. I'm not sure what Recchi will remember more—the fact that Sidney Crosby drew the second assist, or that the goal was scored on Wayne Gretzky's 46th birthday. Either way, Recchi became the third Penguin to score the milestone goal, joining Mario Lemieux and Joe Mullen. Erik Christensen scored the eventual game winner in a shootout.

MIKE MODANO, DALLAS STARS
Date: March 13, 2007
Assisted by: Antti Miettinen and Jon Klemm
Goaltender: Antero Nittymaki
Final Score: 3–2 Dallas
Mike Modano became the second Native American to record 500 goals after he knocked home a goal-mouth scramble at 9:36 of the third period. The goal would stand as the game winner. Modano was the 10th player to record number 500 all for one franchise, although he finished his career as a Detroit Red Wing. His final tally of 561 goals is the most of any American-born player to date.

JEREMY ROENICK, SAN JOSE SHARKS
Date: November 10, 2007
Assisted by: unassisted
Goaltender: Alex Auld
Final Score: 4–1 San Jose
There have been beautiful 500th goals, dramatic 500th goals, and then there's Jeremy's Roenick's. As flukey as it was, it was a 500th, and by anybody's standard that's a heck of a career. On the play in question, Roenick picked up the puck in his zone, wheeled out through the neutral zone, cut a bit right and fired a hard wrist shot in toward the right corner. The puck hit a stanchion, and as Alex Auld was coming out to play it behind the net, it caromed right toward the goal. Despite his valiant effort to get back and stop it, it dribbled over the goal line, making 500. The time was 6:35 of the second period, and it turned out to be the game-winning goal.

KEITH TKACHUK, ST. LOUIS BLUES
Date: April 6, 2008
Assisted by: Ryan Johnson and Barret Jackman
Goaltender: empty net
Final Score: 4–1 St. Louis
Keith Tkachuk scored three goals in his final two games to accomplish his milestone in the final game of the 2007–08 regular season. What he needed was more games against Columbus, and both of the final two games were against the Jackets. After a wild scramble in front of the St.

Louis goal, the play moved over toward the side-boards, where a couple of Blues tried to move it out of the zone. The Columbus net was empty, and Tkachuk found himself with an opportunity to clear the puck, so he did, shooting it the length of the ice from his own zone. It found the back of the net vacated by Columbus goalie Frederik Norrena. Tkachuk joined Wayne Gretzky as the only other player to date to record number 500 into an empty net. The time of the goal was 18:26 of the third period, and it was a short-handed goal also.

JAROME IGINLA, CALGARY FLAMES

Date: January 7, 2012
Assisted by: Curtis Glencross and Olli Jokinen
Goaltender: Niklas Backstrom
Final Score: 3–1 Calgary

Not quite in the Jeremy Roenick stratosphere of flukes, but this 500th ranks right up there (though I'm sure Iginla will take it). In a standard break-out play, Iginla took the puck through the neutral zone, over to the right sideboards and in deep as Curtis Glencross and Jay Bouwmeester went hard to the net, taking two Wild players with them on the back check. Iginla threw the puck toward the front of the net, and it hit not one skate but two, the last being that of Wild captain Mikko Koivu, who inadvertently directed it by his own goalie. The goal was scored even strength at 8:35 of the third period, and it stood as the game winner.

1,000-POINT SCORERS

Going into the 2012–13 season there have been 79 players representing 26 teams who have accumulated 1,000 points in their NHL career. Wayne Gretzky is the fastest to reach the mark, recording point number 1,000 in his 424th game. Mario Lemieux, who comes closest to Gretzky's record, took 513 games—nearly 100 games more. Nicklas Lidstrom, a defenceman, holds the record for taking the longest. He needed 1,336 games, 28 more than Dale Hunter, who needed 1,308, and 61 more than Pat Verbeek, who played 1,275 games before recording point number 1,000.

Following are all 79 players, listed according to the team they were with when they reached the milestone.

DETROIT RED WINGS

GORDIE HOWE

Date: November 27, 1960

Howe assisted on a goal scored by Howie Glover at 6:36 of the first period. Warren Godfrey also drew an assist. Detroit beat Toronto 2–0. It took Howe 938 games to score 1,000 points. Later in the game, Howe drew another assist on a Norm Ullman goal. That gave him a combined total of 1,091 in the regular season and playoffs, tying him with Rocket Richard for the most total career points in NHL history. Wings goaltender Terry Sawchuk also recorded an assist on the Ullman goal.

ALEX DELVECCHIO

Date: February 16, 1969

Delvecchio assisted a goal scored by Gordie Howe at 15:01 of the third period. Detroit beat Los Angeles, 6–3.

STEVE YZERMAN

Date: February 24, 1993

Stevie Y assisted on a goal scored by Keith Primeau. Dino Ciccarelli also had an assist. The time of the goal was 11:22 of the first period of a real shoot-out—Buffalo won, 10–7. Yzerman had four points that night. Alex Mogilny of the Sabres scored four goals.

DINO CICCARELLI

Date: March 9, 1994

Ciccarelli's 1,000th point was a goal against Mike Vernon of the Calgary Flames in a 5–1 Detroit victory. Coincidentally, Yzerman recorded the only assist, meaning that they figured in each other's 1,000th point. Time of the goal was 7:29 of the second period.

PAT VERBEEK

Date: February 27, 2000

Verbeek assisted on a goal scored by, who else, Steve Yzerman. The goal came 40 seconds into a 3–1 Detroit victory over Tampa Bay. Nicklas Lidstrom also drew an assist.

BRENDAN SHANAHAN

Date: January 12, 2002

Shanahan ripped point number 1,000 right through Marty Turco's five hole to give Detroit a 1–0 lead in a game in which he would record two goals and an assist in a 5–2 win. The big point came 2:39 into the contest, and as mentioned in the 500-goal section, this feat was part of the best year of Shanahan's professional career.

NICKLAS LIDSTROM

Date: October 15, 2009

On October 5, 1991, Nicklas Lidstrom recorded his first two NHL points in his second NHL game, both assists against Toronto on goals by Jimmy Carson and Steve Yzerman. Eighteen years later almost to the day, he recorded point numbers 999 and 1000, each with an assist on a goal by a long-time Swedish teammate, Tomas Holmstrom and then Henrik Zetterberg. Detroit beat L.A. 5–2, with Lidstrom's historic point coming on a power play at 3:24 of the third period.

MONTREAL CANADIENS

JEAN BELIVEAU

Date: March 3, 1968

Beliveau's 1,000th point came when he opened the scoring at 4:56 of the first period in a 5–2 Habs loss to Detroit. Bobby Rousseau and Dick Duff assisted. It was career game number 911 for Beliveau.

FRANK MAHOVLICH

Date: February 17, 1973

The Big M assisted on a goal scored by Serge Savard at 2:38 of the second period. Guy Lapointe also assisted. Montreal lost 7–6 to the Philadelphia Flyers.

HENRI RICHARD

Date: December 20, 1973

At 1:38 of the second period, Richard assisted a goal scored by Jim Roberts. The goal gave Montreal a 2–0 lead, but Buffalo would come back to tie the game, which ended in a 2–2 deadlock.

GUY LAFLEUR

Date: March 4, 1981

Lafleur scored point number 1,000 in his 720th NHL game. It came on a goal he scored against Winnipeg goaltender Michel Dion. Dion was with the Jets for only 14 games, but it was long enough for him to be part of this historic night. Lafleur scored 54 seconds into the third period of a 9–3 Montreal win. Keith Acton and Larry Robinson assisted.

CHICAGO BLACKHAWKS

BOBBY HULL

Date: December 12, 1970

Hull assisted on a goal scored by his brother, Dennis, at 15:11 of the second period. Stan Mikita also earned an assist. Chicago beat the Minnesota North Stars, 5–3.

STAN MIKITA

Date: October 15, 1972

Mikita assisted on a Cliff Koroll goal at 13:45 of the first period. Chicago lost to St. Louis, 3–1. Jerry Korab drew the second assist.

DENIS SAVARD

Date: March 11, 1990

Chicago lost 6–4 to St. Louis, but at 3:02 of the second period Savard assisted on a goal scored by Al Secord. Steve Larmer also drew an assist.

MICHEL GOULET

Date: February 23, 1991

Goulet scored all three Chicago goals in a 3–3 tie with the North Stars. His third of the night was also his 1,000th point. Jon Casey was the goaltender. Dirk Graham and Greg Gilbert assisted on the marker, scored at 7:31 of the third period.

TORONTO MAPLE LEAFS

NORM ULLMAN

Date: October 16, 1971

Ullman assisted on a Paul Henderson goal scored at 14:55 of the first period. Jim Dorey also drew an assist. The Leafs lost 5–3 to the New York Rangers.

GLENN ANDERSON

Date: February 22, 1993

Anderson scored on Vancouver goalie Kirk McLean at 11:30 of the third period in an 8–1 win for the Leafs. He was assisted by Mike Krushelnyski.

DOUG GILMOUR

Date: December 23, 1995

At 8:55 of the first period, Gilmour assisted on a goal scored by Mats Sundin in a 6–1 victory over the Edmonton Oilers. It had originally been thought that Gilmour had picked up point number 1,000 with an assist on a Mike Craig goal moments earlier. But a look at the replay resulted in that goal being disallowed. Next shift, Sundin scored; the goal—and the historic point—stood.

LARRY MURPHY

Date: March 27, 1996

Murphy became the fourth defenceman to register 1,000 points when he scored a goal against Vancouver goalie Kirk McLean in a 6–2 Leaf victory. The time was 9:40 of the first period. Mats Sundin and Doug Gilmour assisted. I'm not going to say a word about the connections between these last three events.

MATS SUNDIN

Date: March 10, 2003

Sundin's 31st goal of the season was point number 1,000 for him, and despite the game being in Edmonton, the many Leaf fans in attendance made sure the goal was saluted. Alex Ponikarovsky drew the only assist, but it was really a cursory one as Sundin did yeoman's work behind the net and scored on his own rebound off a wraparound on countryman Tommy Salo.

ALEXANDER MOGILNY

Date: March 15, 2004

This night exemplifies why hockey can be such an electrifying sport. Playing in Buffalo, which is like a second home for the Leafs anyway, Toronto spotted the Sabres a 5–2 lead after two periods. Mogilny had assisted on both Leaf goals for points number 998 and 999. Toronto roared back with three straight goals to tie the game at 5 in the third period, with the tying marker coming off a draw with 41 seconds to go, deep in the Buffalo end. Joe Nieuwendyk won it clean to Bryan McCabe, who fed a pass to Mogilny. He one-timed a hard wrist shot that was deflected by Gary Roberts, with Mats Sundin sitting right on goaltender Martin Biron's doorstep. Point number 1,000 with 38 seconds to play! The Leaf fans in the building went crazy. And that wasn't even the final chapter. Mogilny took an obstruction penalty in OT, the Leafs killed it, he stayed on the ice and set up Tomas Kaberle for the game winner in overtime for point number 1,001. He was the second Russian-born player to record 1,000 points, coming one month and one day after his long-time friend and former World Juniors teammate Sergei Fedorov. Classic.

BOSTON BRUINS

JOHN BUCYK

Date: November 9, 1972

Bucyk's 1,000th point was a goal scored on Detroit goaltender Denis DeJordy at 9:35 of the second period. DeJordy had been a Red Wing a little over a month at this time. Assists went to Ken Hodge and Phil Esposito. Boston won the game, 8–3.

PHIL ESPOSITO

Date: February 15, 1974

The same trio that figured in Bucyk's 1,000th point was involved in Esposito's: Bucyk scored, assisted by Hodge and Esposito. Time of the goal: 5:27 of the first period. Boston beat Vancouver 4–2.

JEAN RATELLE

Date: April 3, 1977

Ratelle assisted on Gregg Sheppard's goal at 18:31 of the second period of a 7–4 Boston win over Toronto. Matti Hagman also assisted.

RAY BOURQUE

Date: February 29, 1992

Bourque was the third defenceman to score 1,000 points. He drew an assist on Bobby Carpenter's goal at 18:22 of the third period. It was the tying goal in a 5–5 draw with the Washington Capitals. Jim Wiemer also assisted.

BRIAN LEETCH

Date: October 18, 2005

The man Mark Messier referred to as the greatest New York Ranger ever, regrettably for Ranger fans did not score point number 1,000 in Ranger blue. No matter, he became the seventh defenceman in league history to record the number. Leetch was playing in what would be his final NHL campaign. The Bruins' opponents were their arch-rival Canadiens in Montreal on this October night, and Leetch had helped stake them to a 2–0 lead with point number 999 in the first period. Montreal battled back from that deficit and a 3–2 Boston lead to win the contest 4-3, but not before Leetch set up fellow defenceman Nick Boynton on a power play at 15:43 of the second period five seconds after Mike Riberio was whistled off for tripping. Dave Scatchard also drew an assist on the play.

NEW YORK RANGERS

ROD GILBERT

Date: February 19, 1977

Rod Gilbert's 1,000th point came in a 5–2 loss to the New York Islanders. At 12:01 of the second period he scored on Islanders goalie Glenn "Chico" Resch. Walt Tkaczuk and Dave Farrish drew the assists.

MIKE GARTNER

Date: January 4, 1992

Gartner scored against New Jersey goaltender Craig Billington at 4:17 of the third period. Sergei Nemchinov drew the only assist. The Rangers lost to the Devils, 6–4.

STEVE LARMER

Date: March 8, 1995

Larmer's historic point was one of four on the night as he helped the Rangers beat New Jersey, 6–4. Number 1,000 was an assist on a goal scored by Brian Noonan at 4:50 of the third period. Petr Nedved also drew an assist on the goal.

PAT LAFONTAINE

Date: January 22, 1998

LaFontaine became the third U.S.-born player to record 1,000 career points when he scored against the Philadelphia Flyers and goaltender Garth Snow at 8:53 of the third period. The Rangers lost 4–3 to the Flyers. Alexei Kovalev and Wayne Gretzky drew assists.

THEO FLEURY

Date: October 29, 2001

Fleury picked up point number 1,000 with an assist on a goal scored by Michael York. It was his second assist in the game, both on goals by York. The milestone point was scored at 12:49 of the second period, and it turned out to be the game-winning goal as the Rangers beat Dallas, 4–2.

LOS ANGELES KINGS

MARCEL DIONNE

Date: January 7, 1981

At 10:35 of the third period in a 5–3 Kings win, Dionne scored against Hartford Whalers goalie John Garrett. Dionne's Triple Crown linemates Charlie Simmer and Dave Taylor assisted. It took Dionne 740 games to reach the 1,000-point mark.

DAVE TAYLOR

Date: February 5, 1991

Taylor assisted on Steve Duchesne's goal at 10:09 of the second period. Todd Elik drew the other assist. Los Angeles beat the Philadelphia Flyers, 3–2.

LUC ROBITAILLE

Date: January 29, 1998

Robitaille got an assist on a goal scored by Craig Johnson at 15:13 of the third period. Los Angeles beat Calgary 5–3. Ray Ferraro drew the other assist.

PHILADELPHIA FLYERS

BOBBY CLARKE

Date: March 19, 1981

Clarke's 1,000th point was a goal scored against Boston goaltender Marco Baron 31 seconds into the third period. Reggie Leach drew the only assist. In the game, which the Flyers won 5–3; Tim Kerr recorded his first career hat trick.

DARRYL SITTLER

Date: January 20, 1983

One year to the day after the Maple Leafs dealt him to Philadelphia; Sittler logged his 1,000th point, scoring a goal against the Calgary Flames and goaltender Don Edwards. Bill Barber and Brad Marsh drew the assists. The Flyers won, 5–2. The Sittler trade was a controversial and emotionally charged move. In return for Number 27, the Leafs got Rich Costello, Ken Strong and a second-round draft pick with which they selected Peter Ihnacak.

MARK RECCHI

Date: March 13, 2001

Mark Recchi scored at the 6:54 mark of the first period in a 5–2 victory over the St. Louis Blues. Roman Turek was the Blues goalie. Chris Therien and Keith Primeau assisted. Recchi became the 60th player to record point number 1,000 in the NHL. The goal was one of three points for the speedy forward on the night. Despite missing 13 games due to injury, Recchi maintained one of the highest points-per-game-ratios all season long.

JEREMY ROENICK

Date: January 30, 2002

Roenick's 1,000th point was a goal scored at 17:52 of the first period in Ottawa against goaltender Patrick Lalime. I was at this game, and he was given a very nice hand by the Ottawa faithful on that Wednesday night in 2002. The goal gave the Flyers a 1–0 lead, but the Senators erased that with three straight, including Todd White's empty-net tally, to win the contest 3–1. Simon Gagne drew the only assist on Roenick's big goal.

BUFFALO SABRES

GILBERT PERREAULT

Date: April 3, 1982

Perreault's third point of the night was the 1,000th of his career. At 19:40 of the third period, he assisted on Andre Savard's game-winning goal in a 5–4 Sabres victory over the Montreal Canadiens. That's the same Andre Savard who replaced Rejean Houle as general manager of the Habs in 2001.

DALE HAWERCHUK

Date: March 8, 1991

Dale Hawerchuk's milestone point was a goal against Chicago Blackhawks goalie—and future Sabres star—Dominik Hasek in a 5–3 Buffalo loss. The goal was scored at 6:27 of the second period and it was assisted by Dave Andreychuk and Grant Ledyard.

EDMONTON OILERS

WAYNE GRETZKY

Date: December 19, 1984

Gretzky took the drama out of this one early by recording point number 1,000—an assist on Mike Krushelnyski's goal—at 1:41 of the first period. He put his usual exclamation mark on the rest of the night, adding five more points for a total of six in the 7–3 Oilers win over Los Angeles. Jari Kurri also drew an assist.

JARI KURRI

Date: January 2, 1990

Kurri assisted on a goal scored by Esa Tikkanen at 5:35 of the third period. It would prove to be the game-winning goal in a 6–4 Edmonton win over the St. Louis Blues. Adam Graves also assisted.

MARK MESSIER

Date: January 13, 1991

Messier's 1,000th point came when he assisted on the 400th goal of Glenn Anderson's career in a 5–3 Edmonton victory over the Philadelphia Flyers. The time of the goal was—and I kid you not—5:35 of the third period. Earlier in the same game, Esa Tikkanen picked up his 200th assist on a goal scored by Anatoli Semenov.

NEW YORK ISLANDERS

BRYAN TROTTIER

Date: January 29, 1985

Trottier's historic point was a shorthanded goal, scored at 15:16 of the second period against goaltender Rollie Melanson in a 4–4 tie with the Minnesota North Stars. Melanson was a former Islander, having been traded to Minnesota two and a half months prior to this game.

MIKE BOSSY

Date: January 24, 1986

In his 656th career game, Bossy recorded point number 1,000. The historic point was an assist on a goal scored by Bryan Trottier at the 19:01 mark of the third period cementing a 7–5 New York victory over the Washington Capitals. Brent Sutter also drew an assist. It was Bossy's fourth point of the night.

DENIS POTVIN

Date: April 4, 1987

With his goal against Buffalo Sabres goalie Jacques Cloutier—his second of the game—Potvin became the first NHL defenceman to score 1,000 points. The goal, which tied the score at six, was scored at 19:43 of the third period and was assisted by Mikko Makela and Bryan Trottier.

DOUG WEIGHT

Date: January 2, 2009

It's not often a goaltender gets to share the spotlight in a positive way for a player's milestone achievement. New York Islander Rick Dipietro did on this date, late in the third period of the Isles contest versus the Phoenix Coyotes. With the Islanders trailing by three goals and less than four minutes to play, Dipietro passed the puck up to Doug Weight, who, seconds later, fed Richard Park for the goal at 16:54 of the third period. Only 2:38 later, Weight recorded point number 1,001 with another assist, this time the secondary one again, on a Richard Park goal, making the score 5–4. Unfortunately for Isles fans, that's as close as they got, and the Coyotes and goaltender Michael Tellqvist hung on to preserve the win.

ST. LOUIS BLUES

BERNIE FEDERKO

Date: March 19, 1988

Federko was the first player in league history to record 50 or more assists in 10 consecutive seasons, so it's only fitting that his 1,000th point was an assist. He and Tony Hrkac drew the helpers on a goal scored by Mark Hunter at 11:17 of the third period. St. Louis lost to the Hartford Whalers, 5–3.

AL MACINNIS

Date: April 7, 1998

MacInnis was the sixth NHL defenceman to score 1,000 points. He joined this elite club by assisting on Pierre Turgeon's goal at 14:58 of the third period. Brett Hull also assisted on the historic marker, which was recorded in the Blues' 5–3 loss to the Detroit Red Wings.

PIERRE TURGEON

Date: October 9, 1999

At 13:23 off the third period, Turgeon scored against the Edmonton Oilers and goaltender Tommy Salo. The Blues won, 4–3. Scott Young and Ricard Persson drew the assists.

KEITH TKACHUK

Date: November 30, 2008

Tkachuk became the eighth American to record the historic total of 1,000 points. He tipped home a point shot from Eric Brewer on a power play at 15:03 of the second period past Atlanta Thrasher goaltender Ondrej Pavelec. His goal tied the game 2–2, and the Blues went on to win the contest 4–2.

CALGARY FLAMES

LANNY MCDONALD

Date: March 7, 1989

McDonald's 1,000th point was a goal against Winnipeg Jets goaltender Bob Essensa at 2:46 of the first period. Jiri Hrdina and Dana Murzyn assisted. It was the first of two in the game for McDonald. Calgary won the game 9–5.

JAROME IGINLA

Date: April 1, 2011

The Flame franchise waited a long time for another player to record point number 1,000, but it was worth the wait, given who it was and how the game unfolded. Calgary was trailing 2–0 with less than five minutes to play in the second period against the St. Louis Blues when Iginla scored to cut the lead in half. That was point 998. In the third period, he assisted a goal by Alex Tanguay at the eight-minute mark for point number 999 to tie the game. Six minutes later, at 14:47 of the third, Iginla took a breakaway pass from Tanguay and fired a wrist shot past Jaroslav Halak for the game winner and point number 1,000.

QUEBEC NORDIQUES

PETER STASTNY

Date: October 19, 1989

Stastny was the first player to earn his 1,000th point by scoring into an empty net. The time of the goal was 19:52 of the third period and Mike Hough assisted. Quebec beat Chicago 5–3. The Hawks' goalie of record was Alain Chevrier.

PITTSBURGH PENGUINS

PAUL COFFEY

Date: December 22, 1990

At the six-minute mark of the second period, Coffey assisted on a goal scored by Kevin Stevens. John Cullen also drew an assist. Coffey became only the second defenceman to record 1,000 points. Pittsburgh beat the New York Islanders, 4–3.

MARIO LEMIEUX

Date: March 24, 1992

At 10:04 of the second period, Kevin Stevens scored his 50th goal of the season against Detroit's Tim Cheveldae. Lemieux assisted, giving him 1,000 points in his career. The assist was one of three points Lemieux registered on the night in a 4–3 loss to the Detroit Red Wings.

RON FRANCIS

Date: October 28, 1993

Francis scored a goal against Quebec Nordiques goalie Jocelyn Thibault at 5:39 of the second period. Larry Murphy and Martin Straka assisted. Pittsburgh lost 7–3 to Quebec.

JOE MULLEN

Date: February 7, 1995

Point number 1,000 was one of four that Mullen recorded on the night. He assisted on John Cullen's goal, scored 28 seconds into the second period of a 7–3 Pittsburgh win over the Florida Panthers. Grant Jennings also drew an assist.

JAROMIR JAGR

Date: December 30, 2000

Jagr became the fourth European-born player to record 1,000 career points, with a goal scored against the Ottawa Senators at the 5:55 mark of the second period. The goal was one of three points Jagr scored in a 5–3 Pittsburgh victory. The milestone was somewhat overshadowed as this was the second game of Mario Lemieux's comeback, and he picked up four points, including the 1,500th of his career with an assist on Jagr's second goal of the game, which made Lemieux one of only 13 players to accomplish this in the NHL. Lemieux's assist on Jagr's first goal was point number 1,499. Hans Jonsson drew the second assist on Jagr's milestone goal.

MINNESOTA NORTH STARS

BOBBY SMITH

Date: November 30, 1991

Smith assisted on a goal scored by Mike Craig at 17:29 of the second period. Ulf Dahlen also drew an assist. The North Stars beat Toronto, 4–3.

NEW JERSEY DEVILS

BERNIE NICHOLLS

Date: February 13, 1994

Nicholls tipped Scott Stevens' point shot past Tampa Bay goalie Pat Jablonski for point number 1,000. John MacLean also assisted on the goal. Nicholls scored point number 1,001 later in the game when he tied the score at three and that's how the game ended.

DAVE ANDREYCHUK

Date: April 7, 1996

Andreychuk scored against New York Rangers goaltender Mike Richter at 14:16 of the first period. Scott Stevens drew the only assist.

JOE NIEUWENDYK

Date: February 23, 2003

Nieuwendyk's 1,000th point came via a goal that tied the game at 3–3 versus the Pittsburgh Penguins and goaltender Sebastien Caron. Jeff Friesen drew the only assist, and the time of the goal was 9:04 of the third period. New Jersey went on to win the game 4–3.

HARTFORD WHALERS

BRIAN PROPP

Date: March 19, 1994

With 1.7 seconds left in the game, Propp scored into an empty net, becoming only the second player to reach 1,000 points by scoring an empty-net goal. Robert Kron and Chris Pronger got the assists. The historic point was recorded in a 5–3 Hartford win over the Philadelphia Flyers at the Spectrum—the same building in which Propp had scored his first NHL point 15 years earlier. And both points—number 1 and number 1,000—were announced by the same public-address announcer, Lou Nolan. The Flyers' goalie of record was Dominic Roussel. Propp had scored point number 999 earlier in the game on an 80-foot wrist shot that Roussel whiffed on.

This marked the second time that a delay-of-game penalty was called against a team for clearing the bench to congratulate a significant goal scorer. A rule had been passed calling for this penalty to be assessed, although it could be circumvented if prior authorization was sought from the league, as Boston had done the night Ray Bourque passed Johnny Bucyk to become the all-time leading scorer in Bruins history.

WASHINGTON CAPITALS

ADAM OATES

Date: October 8, 1997

Oates had a five-point night in a 6–3 Capitals win over the Islanders. His 1,000th point came early in the game, as he scored his first of three goals against Islanders goalie Tommy Salo. It was a shorthanded effort. Mark Tinordi drew the only assist.

PHIL HOUSLEY

Date: November 8, 1997

Housley become the second American-born player, and the fifth defenceman, to record 1,000 points when he assisted on a goal scored by Calle Johansson at 4:48 of the first period. Adam Oates also drew an assist. Washington won the game against the Edmonton Oilers, 2–1.

DALE HUNTER

Date: January 9, 1998

Hunter's third point on the night, an assist on a Craig Berube goal at 18:21 of the second period, was the 1,000th of his career. Kelly Miller drew the second assist. Berube also had three points on the night—for the first time in his career—as the Caps beat the Philadelphia Flyers, 4–1.

BRIAN BELLOWS

Date: January 2, 1999

Bellows assisted on a goal scored by Jeff Toms at 3:34 of the third period. The marker helped Washington beat the Toronto Maple Leafs, 5–2.

DALLAS STARS

BRETT HULL

Date: November 14, 1998

Hull had two goals on this night, but his 1,000th point came on an assist, as he helped on a goal scored by Jere Lehtinen at 19:26 of the third period. Mike Modano drew the other assist. Dallas beat the Boston Bruins, 3–1.

MIKE MODANO

Date: November 15, 2002

Modano's historic point came via an assist on a goal scored by Ulf Dahlen at the 10:50 mark of the first period. Bill Guerin also drew an assist. The goal gave Dallas a 2–1 lead at the time, and they would go on to win the contest over the Colorado Avalanche, 4–2. The game featured another milestone, as Colorado goalie Patrick Roy became the NHL career leader in minutes played midway through the third period, breaking the mark held by Terry Sawchuk. Roy finished the night with 57,202 minutes. Sawchuk had 57,194 in his 21-season NHL career.

COLORADO AVALANCHE

JOE SAKIC

Date: December 27, 1999

Sakic recorded his 1,000th point in his 810th NHL game, making him the fastest to reach the plateau since Mario Lemieux did it in his 513th game in 1992. Sakic's historic point was an assist on Chris Dingman's goal at 12:03 of the third period. Colorado beat the St. Louis Blues, 5–1.

SAN JOSE SHARKS

VINCENT DAMPHOUSSE

Date: October 14, 2000

Damphousse became the first player in a San Jose uniform to record number 1,000. The milestone was an assist recorded on a shorthanded goal by Marco Sturm at 13:43 of the first period in a 5–2 Shark victory over the Boston Bruins. Marcus Ragnarsson drew the other assist. A sellout crowd of 17,496 was on hand and the game featured two rookie goaltenders, Boston's Andrew Raycroft and San Jose's Evgeni Nabokov, who picked up his first NHL win. Nabokov won the 2001 Calder Trophy.

JOE THORNTON

Date: April 8, 2011

The San Jose Sharks were making a furious comeback against the Phoenix Coyotes led in part by Joe Thornton's 1,000th point, which was a goal scored at 9:27 of the third period. Logan Couture and Doug Murray assisted, and the goal came a little more than a minute after Shane Doan had made it 4–1 Phoenix. The Sharks would add another but not fully close the gap, thanks to some solid saves from goaltender Ilya Bryzgalov. Thornton and Mats Sundin both took 994 games to record point number 1,000, which represents the closest to a point-a-game pace of all the 1,000-point scorers to date.

PHOENIX COYOTES

RAY WHITNEY

Date: March 31, 2012

The man known as the Wizard, Ray Whitney notched point number 1,000 with an assist on a goal scored by Radim Vrbata. The Whitney pass was classic, a cross-seam beauty through traffic that found Vrbata's stick, and he fired it home past Jeff Drouin-Deslauriers, a rookie goalie for the Anaheim Ducks. The goal was scored at 16:14 of the second period, and it came on an extended five-on-three for the Coyotes, which they stayed on due to the penalties from an earlier fight. Forty seconds later, Whitney scored point 1,001 with a goal on the same power play. The Coyotes won the game 4–0, and it was a big two points in their playoff push.

MIGHTY DUCKS OF ANAHEIM

SERGEI FEDOROV

Date: February 14, 2004

History was made on this date as Sergei Fedorov became the first Russian-born player and the first Anaheim player to accumulate 1,000 points. After starring for Detroit for years, Fedorov joined the Ducks in 2003–04. He won a draw in the offensive zone as clean as you can imagine, back to the point where defenceman Keith Carney was waiting. Carney ripped a shot that seemed to fool goaltender Johan Hedberg of the Vancouver Canucks. The time of the goal was 3:00 of the second period. Fedorov picked up point 1,001 in the third period on the game-winning goal scored by Peter Schastlivy.

TEEMU SELANNE

Date: January 30, 2006

Selanne's 1,000th point came on his second goal of the night, and for all the drama that many of these historic moments have provided, this one has to be noted for the pass that sprang Selanne on his breakaway coming in from the right-wing position as he so often has in his NHL career. Andy McDonald threw a backhand pass to Selanne on the fly that was as good as you'll see in hockey anywhere, anytime. Keith Carney also drew an assist, meaning he was in on both the Anaheim 1,000th-point plays to date. The time of the goal was 8:33 of the third period, and the Ducks beat the L.A. Kings and goaltender Mathieu Garon in overtime, 4–3.

CAROLINA HURRICANES

ROD BRIND'AMOUR

Date: November 4, 2006

Brind'Amour became the first Hurricane to record 1,000 points, with an assist on an Erik Cole goal scored on a power play at 15:03 of the second period that put the Hurricanes up 2–1 against the Ottawa Senators in a game they would win 3–2. Ray Whitney also drew an assist on the marker. The Hurricanes were the defending Cup champs that season, and Brind'Amour recorded one of his best seasons ever, finishing with 82 points. I was at this game in Ottawa, 18 years after I first saw him play as a member of the Notre Dame Hounds in a playoff game against the Pembroke Lumber Kings in the 1988 Centennial Cup playoffs. That game went into triple overtime before ending on a goal scored by the Lumber Kings' Brian Downey, but Brind'Amour and the Hounds won the rematch, advanced to the finals and won the national championship.

OTTAWA SENATORS

DANIEL ALFREDSSON

Date: October 22, 2010

Cue the drama, as we've so often seen on these historic occasions. No exception here. With Buffalo goaltender Ryan Miller on the bench for an extra attacker, Daniel Alfredsson corralled a puck by the sideboards and flipped a backhand into the unguarded net for his third goal of the night, his eighth hat trick and his 1,000th career point. Mike Fisher and Sergei Gonchar picked up assists on the goal scored at 19:38 of the third period. It was a year and a week after Nick Lidstrom had become the second Swede to notch 1,000 points. Alfredsson is the first Ottawa Senator to record 1,000 points.

ALEX KOVALEV

Date: November 22, 2010

Kovalev scored point number 1,000 with a power-play goal at the 10-minute mark of the first period of a 3–2 Ottawa win over the L.A. Kings, exactly one month to the day after Daniel Alfredsson had become the first player in a Senator sweater to record point number 1,000. Once again Sergei Gonchar found himself on the score-sheet of a historic marker, drawing the first assist as his point shot was blocked, and the rebound came right to Kovalev, who ripped a shot past Jonathan Quick. In fact Kovalev's stick broke on the shot. Chris Phillips drew the other assist, and for good measure Kovalev added point number 1,001 on the game-winning goal scored by Jason Spezza in the third period. He is just the third Russian-born player to reach this milestone.

Bruce Bennett Studios/Getty Images

BOBBY ORR recorded six straight 100+ point seasons; he was the first player with 100+ assists in one season, 1970–71; and he won the James Norris Trophy eight straight times as the league's top defenceman, revolutionizing the position. In 1970–71, he was a stunning plus-124. He won two Stanley Cups and was MVP of the inaugural Canada Cup in 1976. Shown here in his second NHL season, 1967–68, Orr is speeding around Chicago's Hubert "Pit" Martin. In a lopsided trade, Martin went from Boston to Chicago on May 15, 1967, along with Gilles Marotte and minor-league goaltender Jack Norris for Fred Stanfield, Ken Hodge and the great Phil Esposito.

7

MY TOP QUESTIONS

I'M OFTEN ASKED FOR MY number-one question of all time—or a list of some of my best questions of all time. Many of those appear in this publication under a specific heading—defunct teams, existing teams, Hall of Fame players and the like. This chapter contains a range of questions that are just a tad different. Oddities, unusual circumstances, obscure number references—if you can name it, you'll probably find it in this chapter. Following are a list of 50 questions that I feel rank as some of the best.

1) How many players in NHL history have worn number 99?

Five—or six, depending on which publication you read. There's Gretzky, of course. Wilf Paiement wore the number with Toronto between 1980 and 1982, while Rick Dudley wore number 99 with Winnipeg in 1981. Those are the three modern players. There are three other names associated with the number, all of who played with the Montreal Canadiens in the 1934–35 season.

At that time, the NHL was in dire straits, as was most of North America, because of the Great Depression. A number of teams had folded, and fans were staying away in droves. In an unusual marketing ploy, the Canadiens decided to steal a page from the NFL. The Habs felt that part of the league's success in stimulating fan interest was the high sweater numbers worn by its players, so they had players suiting up in number 75, 88, 55, 64—you name it.

It had long been thought that three players on that Canadiens team wore the number 99: Leo Bourgeault, Des Roche and Joe Lamb. Research done by hockey historian Gerry Rochon of Trois-Rivieres, Quebec, indicates that Roche did not wear 99 but instead number 75. So take your pick, depending on what you've read. For the record, I'll go with Mr. Rochon.

Following are a couple of items on the three Habs, and I've included Roche because the little gem I unearthed on him is one of the all-time best. Joe Lamb led the NHL in penalty minutes in 1929–30 with 119 in 44 games. He was a member of the Ottawa Senators at that time. Des Roche and his brother Earl are the only brother combination to play together on four different NHL teams—the Montreal Maroons, Ottawa Senators, St. Louis Eagles and Detroit Red Wings. In my opinion, this is one of the most amazing facts that I have ever discovered. Leo

Bourgeault was on a Stanley Cup winner with the New York Rangers in 1927–28.

2) How many different goaltenders did Wayne Gretzky score against in his NHL career?

It's a staggering number: 155. Gretzky's five most frequent victims combined to allow 115 of his 894 regular-season goals. Richard Brodeur led the way, with 29; Mike Liut gave up 23; and Don Beaupre, Kirk McLean and Greg Millen each surrendered 21.

Brodeur is the only goalie Gretzky ever beat on a penalty shot. Of his five career attempts, only one was a goal. It happened on January 19, 1983, against Vancouver. Those who successfully stopped him included Winnipeg's Pierre Hamel, in 1981; Michel "Bunny" Larocque, then with Toronto, in 1982; Pat Riggin of Washington, also in 1982; and Peter Ing of Toronto in 1991. Gretzky was a member of the Los Angeles Kings at that time.

3) Wayne Gretzky scored at least one point in 48 of the 49 NHL arenas he played in. Which was the only rink in which he did not score a point during his NHL career?

The Springfield Civic Center. This rink was the temporary home of the Hartford Whalers for the last year and a half of their WHA existence and the first five months of their NHL residency. Their permanent home, the Hartford Civic Center, was being repaired during that time after its roof collapsed during a blizzard on January 18, 1978. Actually, this is a bit of a trick question because, while Gretzky did not record a point in Springfield during his NHL career, he did score a goal there during his first visit—in the one season he played in the WHA—on November 9, 1978.

4) A very strong argument can be made that Bobby Orr was, and still is, the greatest player in the history of the game. I've covered some of this territory in Chapter 3, but there is some additional information with regard to Bobby Orr and the number four that I think you may find interesting. On May 10, 1970, Bobby Orr scored what has been voted the greatest goal ever in the history of the National Hockey League. For some unknown yet fascinating reason, there are a number of unusual connections between this goal and the number four. In fact, I've compiled 10 different correlations between the two. Of all the statistics and all the trivia questions I've seen, none comes remotely close to this strange, yet true, series of coincidences. Consider the following:

1) Bobby Orr wore number 4 for Boston.
2) Noel Picard, who tripped Orr just as he scored the goal, wore number 4 for St. Louis.
3) It was Picard's fourth playoff year.
4) It was Picard's 44th career playoff game.
5) It was the fourth game of the series.
6) It was the fourth period of the fourth game.
7) The goal was scored at the 40-second mark of overtime.
8) Derek Sanderson assisted on the goal. His sweater number was 16. (I admit it's a stretch, but four times four is 16.)
9) It was Sanderson's fourth assist of the playoffs.
10) Sanderson registered points against four different goalies that playoff year: Eddie Giacomin, Tony Esposito, Ernie Wakely and Glenn Hall.
11) Sanderson was one of four Boston Bruins in that game born in the month of June. Rick Smith, Ken Hodge and Wayne Cashman were the other three.
12) Sanderson was one of four members of that Boston team born in 1946. Gary Doak, Wayne Carleton and Bill Lesuk were the others.
13) Sanderson was one of four players on the team who had played Junior A hockey with

the Niagara Falls Flyers. Eddie Westfall, Don Awrey and Don Marcotte were the others.

14) Sanderson was one of four Bruins players to draw an assist in the final game. Ken Hodge, Rick Smith and Johnny McKenzie were the others.

15) Sanderson finished fourth on the Bruins in playoff goal scoring that year with five goals. Phil Esposito, Johnny Bucyk and Bobby Orr were ahead of him.

16) Sanderson was one of four Boston players that playoff year listed as six feet tall. Jim Lorentz, Johnny Bucyk and Don Awrey were the other three.

17) It was Boston's fourth goal of the Cup-winning game.

18) The win gave Boston its fourth Stanley Cup title. The Bruins also won in 1929, 1939 and 1941.

19) Boston general manager Milt Schmidt was the fourth GM in Bruins history. Art Ross, Lynn Patrick and Hap Emms were the others.

20) Boston had beaten four different opponents in the Stanley Cup finals: the New York Rangers in 1929, the Toronto Maple Leafs in 1939, the Detroit Red Wings in 1941 and the St. Louis Blues in 1970.

21) It was Blues goalie Glenn Hall's fourth defeat on the road in overtime in his playoff career. The others happened on March 26, 1960, at Montreal; April 22, 1968, at Minnesota; and May 9, 1968, at Montreal.

22) The 1969–70 season was Harry Sinden's fourth as coach of the Bruins.

23) It was the fourth consecutive game in which St. Louis had given up four goals or more.

24) It was the fourth series in the 1970 playoffs that had ended in a four-game sweep.

25) The goal marked the conclusion of Orr's fourth season in the NHL.

26) By winning the Conn Smythe Trophy after the playoffs, Bobby Orr became the first player to win four major trophies in one season. Besides the Smythe, he won the Art Ross Trophy as scoring leader, the Hart Trophy as league MVP and the James Norris Trophy as the best defenceman.

27) Orr was the fourth non-goalie to win the Conn Smythe Trophy since its inception in 1965. Jean Beliveau, Dave Keon and Serge Savard were the other three.

28) Orr was the fourth defenceman to score a Cup-winning goal. The others were Babe Pratt in 1945, Bill Barilko in 1951 and J.C. Tremblay in 1968.

29) Orr was the fourth player in NHL history to record 20 or more points in one playoff year. Gordie Howe, Stan Mikita and Phil Esposito were the others.

30) Orr had two points in a game four times that playoff year.

31) Orr established or tied four Stanley Cup records that year: most points by a defenceman (20), most goals by a defenceman (9), most consecutive games with at least one point (14) and, the record he tied, most shorthanded goals in one period (one).

32) Orr's goal gave him at least one goal in four different periods that playoff year. He had two goals in the first period, three in the second, three in the third and the overtime winner in the "fourth" period.

33) Orr was one of four Bruins to score a goal in the Stanley Cup–deciding game. Rick Smith, Phil Esposito and Johnny Bucyk were the other three.

34) Orr's Cup-winning goal was the fourth fastest from the start of a period that playoff year. Bill Goldsworthy and Larry Keenan were fastest on the draw, at 19 seconds. Jean-Guy

Talbot scored 31 seconds into a period. Then came Orr, at 40 seconds.

35) Orr had four game-winning assists that playoff year, on April 14 versus the New York Rangers, April 19 against Chicago, and May 5 and May 7 versus St. Louis.
36) Orr finished fourth overall in total playoff assists that year with 11.
37) Orr had four power-play assists that playoff year.
38) Orr had four assists in the Stanley Cup finals that year.
39) Orr scored goals in four road games that playoff year.
40) Orr surpassed the previous record for goals in one playoff year by four. His nine goals in 1970 were four better than Earl Seibert's five with Chicago in 1938.
41) Orr surpassed the previous record for points in one playoff year by a defenceman by four points. His 20 points in 1970 eclipsed Tim Horton's mark of 16 with Toronto in 1962.
42) Orr was the fourth defenceman to score on Glenn Hall that playoff year. Barry Gibbs, Duane Rupp and Rick Smith were the others.
43) Four different Bruins scored game-winning goals in the finals: Bucyk in game one, Westfall in game two, McKenzie in game three and Orr in game four.
44) Esposito had two playoff hat tricks that year, giving him a career total of four.
45) The Boston Bruins scored goals in all four periods in the Cup-deciding game.
46) Boston outshot St. Louis in all four games: 35–29 in game one, 35–19 in game two, 46–21 in game three and 32–31 in game four.
47) It was the fourth time that playoff year that Boston had scored exactly four goals in a game. The other three occasions were April 16, against the Rangers; April 21, against Chicago; and May 7, against St. Louis.
48) It was the fourth game played in the month of May that year.
49) It was the fourth time, in playoff series featuring two American teams, that one of the teams swept. Coincidentally, all four of these sweeps involved the Bruins. The first was in 1929, when Boston defeated the New York Rangers; in 1941, Boston prevailed over Detroit; and in 1943, the Red Wings eliminated Boston.
50) It was the fourth time that playoff year that the Bruins and their opponents combined for seven goals. It had also happened in game three of the quarterfinals against New York (the Rangers won, 4–3); game three of the semifinals against Chicago (Boston won, 5–2); and game one of the finals against St. Louis (a 6–1 Bruins victory).
51) Boston defenceman Bill Speer finished the playoffs with four penalty minutes.
52) Boston forward Eddie Westfall also finished the playoffs with four penalty minutes.
53) Boston forward Jim Lorentz finished the playoffs with four penalty minutes.
54) St. Louis forward Terry Gray finished the playoffs with four penalty minutes.
55) St. Louis forward Andre Boudrias also finished the playoffs with four penalty minutes.
56) Boudrias finished the playoffs with four assists.
57) St. Louis forward Tim Ecclestone finished the playoffs with four assists.
58) Boston forward Wayne Carleton finished the playoffs with four assists.
59) Boston forward Wayne Cashman finished the playoffs with four assists.
60) Boston forward Fred Stanfield finished the playoffs with four goals.
61) Boston goalie Eddie Johnston finished the playoffs with a goals-against average of 4.00.
62) Johnston allowed four goals in the only game he played in the playoffs.

63) St. Louis goalie Glenn Hall finished the playoffs with four wins.
64) St. Louis goalie Jacques Plante also finished the playoffs with four wins.
65) St. Louis goalie Ernie Wakely finished the playoffs with four losses.
66) Boston goalie Gerry Cheevers chalked up four wins in the finals.
67) St. Louis finished with four power-play goals in the finals.
68) With the loss, St. Louis had lost four consecutive games in the playoffs.
69) Four Boston defencemen finished the playoffs with 14 games played.
70) Jean-Guy Talbot, who retired following the series, ended his career with four playoff goals.

5) What are the two biggest trades in NHL history in terms of the number of players involved—including draft picks?

There were two deals that totalled 11 players in all.

- On July 3, 1981, Philadelphia traded Rick MacLeish, Blake Wesley, Don Gillen and three draft choices to Hartford. The draft picks were used to select Paul Lawless, Mark Paterson and Kevin Dineen. Coming from Hartford to Philadelphia were Ray Allison, Fred Arthur and three draft choices. The Flyers used one of the picks to take Ron Sutter and another to take Miroslav Dvorak. The third draft pick was later traded to Toronto, who used it to select Peter Ihnacak.
- On June 15, 1985, Montreal traded Mark Hunter, Michael Dark and four picks to St. Louis for five draft picks. With the four picks, St. Louis drafted Herb Raglan, Nelson Emerson, Dan Brooks and Rick Burchill. The five picks for Montreal translated into Donald Dufresne, Jose Charbonneau, Todd Richard, Martin Desjardins and Tom Sagissor.

6) Herb Raglan's father played in the NHL, and he was involved in a very unusual and noteworthy deal himself. What was his name and what was the transaction?

Clare "Rags" Raglan has the distinction of being involved in the trade that included the most players being exchanged for the least amount of cash. Raglan was a member of the Detroit Red Wings, and he was dealt to Chicago along with George Gee, Jimmy Peters Sr., Clare Martin, Max McNab and Jimmy McFadden for $75,000 and a player named Hugh Coflin. The date was August 20, 1951.

Coflin was a career minor-leaguer whose only NHL experience came in the 1950–51 season when he played 31 games for Chicago. He never suited up for Detroit. The elder Raglan's NHL career encompassed 100 games for Detroit and Chicago. George Gee was a runner-up to Edgar Laprade for the 1946 Calder Trophy. He assisted on the second and third goals of Bill Mosienko's record-setting hat trick (scored in 21 seconds) on March 23, 1952. Jimmy Peters Sr. played on Cup winners in Montreal and Detroit. He's one of only two players who played with Gordie Howe and then saw their sons later play with Howe. Jimmy Peters Jr. was a Red Wing call-up on four occasions during Howe's career in Detroit. Sid Abel was the other player with that interesting distinction. His son, Gerry Abel, played one game in the NHL in 1966–67.

Clare Martin played 237 games spread out over four teams in his NHL career: Boston, Detroit, Chicago and New York. Max McNab was on a Cup winner as a player with Detroit in 1950, and he would go on to become the second general manager in the history of both the Washington

Capitals and New Jersey Devils. His son Peter also played in the NHL and another son, David McNab, is the senior vice president of hockey operations, Anaheim Ducks. Jimmy McFadden, born in Northern Ireland, won the Calder Trophy as a Red Wing in 1948. He was 28, making him the oldest winner of the rookie of the year to that date. That record stood for 42 years until 1990, when Sergei Makarov won the trophy shortly before his 32nd birthday. This, of course, was a joke, and the NHL finally got with the program and changed the criteria for the award. The way it stands now, for a player to be eligible he cannot have reached his 26th birthday by September 15 of the season for which he is being considered.

7) Who are the highest-scoring brothers in NHL history?

At the beginning of the 2000–01 season, Ron Sutter was released by the San Jose Sharks, where his brother Darryl was coach. For the first time since 1975, there was not a single Sutter brother playing in the NHL. When the Calgary Flames signed the 37-year-old Ron in February 2001, it meant that the race was on again for total points by a brother combination, but by the end of his playing days his scoring impact was negligible. The family name continues to live on with various offspring playing pro and in the NHL, details on them below.

The question, if phrased as above, can cause a problem. Am I talking about goals or points? Regular-season only, or including playoffs?

There are many who still believe that the Howes, Gordie and Vic, are the top-scoring brothers of all time. In the early 1950s, Vic played 33 games for the New York Rangers over three seasons, picking up 7 points. But the Howes haven't held the record for more than 40 years. Others are adamant that the Gretzkys are the correct answer, and if you phrase the question a certain way, those fans are correct.

It's in the category of total points, including playoffs, that you'll find the most amazing stat. The Gretzkys—or, if you like, Wayne—lead all other brother acts, including all six Sutters. On October 17, 1998, Gretzky scored his first goal of the final season he would ever play in the NHL. It was a power-play goal scored at 4:50 of the second period, assisted by Adam Graves and Brian Leetch. It was scored against Pittsburgh goalie Peter Skudra. Added to the 4 points Brent Gretzky scored for the Tampa Bay Lightning, Wayne's goal gave the Gretzky family 3,185 points—one more than the Sutter brothers, who had amassed 3,184. Wayne picked up 58 more points that season, bringing his family total to 3,243. Ron Sutter had yet to record a point that season, but he did eventually rack up 9 regular-season points in 1998–99 and followed that with 17 more points before his career ended, bringing the total number of points by the Sutter brothers to 3,210. The following table shows the highest-scoring two-brother combinations.

NAME	REG SEA PTS	TOTAL PTS	REG SEA G	TOTAL G
Wayne/Brent Gretzky	2,861	3,243	895	1,017
Maurice/Henri Richard	2,011	2,266	902	1,033
Frank/Peter Mahovlich	1,876	2,066	821	902
Bobby/Dennis Hull	1,824	2,020	913	1,008
Gordie/Vic Howe	1,857	2,017	804	872

Here are the numbers for the top three-brother combination, the Stastnys—Peter, Anton and Marian:

NAME	REG SEA PTS	TOTAL PTS	REG SEA G	TOTAL G
Peter/Marian/ Anton Stastny	2,169	2,348	823	881

Finally, here are the stats for the six Sutter brothers:

NAME	REG SEA PTS	TOTAL PTS	REG SEA G	TOTAL G
Brian/Duane/ Darryl/Brent/ Rich/Ron Sutter	2,935	3,210	1,320	1,442

If you change the question to ask for the top-scoring family, you'll get a different answer. With the addition of Mark and Marty's stats, the Howes' totals increase to 2,854 (again, total points including playoffs). However, when you add Brett's numbers, the Hulls get the top spot with 3,601. Interestingly, the next generation of Sutters has arrived in the NHL, and between Brandon and Brett Sutter they have accumulated 112 points to date. But when the points are added to the Sutter family stats, their total of 3,322 still leaves them far behind the Hulls, for now.

8) How many players to date have taken part in only one game in their entire NHL career—when that one game was a playoff game for a team that won the Cup that season?

To date there have been 27 players whose only NHL action has come in the playoffs. Four of them appeared in only one game and had the good fortune to be on a Cup winner. First was Lester Patrick with the NY Rangers in 1928. As the Rangers coach and general manager, he was famously pushed into emergency duty as a goaltender when his starter, Lorne Chabot, was injured in game two of the Cup finals against the Montreal Maroons. Patrick hung on in the net, allowed only one goal and the Rangers won the game in overtime. Joe Miller replaced the injured Chabot for the remaining three games, and the Rangers went on to win their first Stanley Cup. The others were Doug McKay and Gord Haidy, who each played his one game with Detroit in 1950, and Chris Hayes with the 1972 Boston Bruins.

McKay and Haidy were members of Detroit's farm team, the Indianapolis Capitals, when injuries made it necessary to call them up. On April 4, 1950, Haidy played in game four of Detroit's seven-game semifinal win over Toronto. Detroit won the game, 2–1, in overtime and Haidy, a defenceman, did not figure in the scoring. McKay got his shot at glory in game three of the finals, on April 15, 1950. Like Haidy, he scored no points and drew no penalties. Detroit won that game 4–0 over the New York Rangers.

Hayes played one game for Boston in the 1972 semifinals against St. Louis and did not figure in the scoring. He was called up from the Oklahoma City Blazers, Boston's affiliate in the Central Hockey League. Honourable mention goes to Steve Brule, who played in game three of New Jersey's semifinal series against Philadelphia on May 18, 2000. The Flyers won the game, 4–2, and Brule played without making a mark in the scoring summary. The Devils would go on to win their second Stanley Cup. It was the only playoff game of his career to go along with two regular season NHL games with the Colorado Avalanche.

While all of these players had their brief taste of the big time, making contributions to Cup championships, Steve Brule and Lester Patrick were the only ones to have their name etched on Lord Stanley's mug. Patrick's would have been engraved regardless as the coach and GM. There have been a number of other oddities regarding the names on the Stanley Cup, but the current rule states that a player must appear in half of the team's regular-season games or at least one game in the finals to be immortalized on the Stanley Cup's silver bands. The NHL changed its rule after the name of defenceman Don Awrey, who had played 72 regular-season games for the 1975–76 Montreal Canadiens but did not dress for a single playoff game, was left off the Cup.

Before Brule, the only two exceptions both played with the New York Rangers in 1994. Eddie Olczyk and Mike Hartman's names appear on the Cup. Olczyk played in 37 regular-season games, less than half the Rangers' 84-game schedule, and one playoff game—not in the finals. Mike Hartman played in 35 regular-season games and did not dress for a single playoff game. Olczyk told me in an interview that he and Hartman owe a great deal of thanks to Mike Gartner, a former Ranger and president of the NHL Players Association. He was instrumental in having the rule waived on their behalf. (Gartner, who played 71 games for the Rangers that season before a last-minute trade to the Maple Leafs, is not on the Cup.) Most recently, the 2010-11 Bruins went one-for-three in applications for exceptions. Marc Savard was granted the special status and had his name engraved on the Cup despite playing only 25 regular season games. Shane Hnidy and Steve Kampfer were denied, although the Bruins presented both of them with Cup rings and they were included in the official team photo.

Considering Olczyk and Hartman's names appear on the Cup, I've often wondered why not have Don Awrey's name engraved for his contribution to the 1976 win or Mike Gartner's for the regular season games he played with New York in 1994? Fortunately, Awrey also played for Boston's championship teams of 1970 and '72, wins for which his name does appear, and his stats show him as being on three winners despite the 1976 oversight.

9) Here's one of the more popular questions of all time: Who scored the fastest hat trick in NHL history? The answer is Bill Mosienko of Chicago on March 23, 1952. He scored three goals in 21 seconds. But whose record did Mosienko break?
Carl Liscombe, from Perth, Ontario. On March 13, 1938, as a rookie with the Detroit Red Wings, Liscombe scored three goals in 1:52, or 112 seconds. The goals were scored at 16:02, 17:31 and 17:54 of the first period. They helped cement a 5–1 Detroit win over Chicago and goalie Mike Karakas. Liscombe broke the record of 2:57 set by Alfred "Pit" Lepine of the Montreal Canadiens on March 3, 1927, in a 7–1 win, also over the Chicago Black Hawks.

10) November 10, 1963, will forever remain one of the most memorable nights in NHL history. What happened on that night?
Gordie Howe scored career regular-season goal number 545, passing Rocket Richard for top spot on the all-time list of goal scorers. The goal was scored shorthanded at 15:06 of the second period in Detroit. Billy McNeill assisted. It was his only NHL assist that season. The Detroit player in the penalty box was Alex Faulkner, the first Newfoundlander to play in the NHL. He was born in Bishop Falls. He was serving a major penalty for high sticking. It was the only major penalty of his NHL career. The Red Wings beat Montreal, 3–0.

Faulkner scored the third goal of the game. Bruce MacGregor scored the other Red Wings goal.

We're not done yet. Charlie Hodge was the Canadiens goalie Howe scored against, while Terry Sawchuk was in the Detroit net. The shutout Sawchuk recorded was number 94 in his career, tying the record set by George Hainsworth, a former Montreal Canadien and Toronto Maple Leaf. Sawchuk would retire with 103 regular-season shutouts, which is still the second-best career mark behind Martin Brodeur's 119 to date. There were 15,027 people in attendance that night, including two of Gordie's sons, Mark and Marty, who would both play in the NHL one day. Quite the historic night.

11) There's an unusual connection between Wayne Gretzky and the number 1,851. What is it?

Wayne Gretzky scored his first NHL goal on October 14, 1979, against Vancouver goalie Glen Hanlon. The time of the goal, which tied the score at four, was 18:51 of the third period. Brett Callighen and Blair MacDonald assisted. How many points did Gretzky have to score to surpass Gordie Howe on the all-time list? You guessed it: 1,851. He scored point number 1,851 on October 15, 1989, 10 years and one day after his first goal. The record-breaking point was also a goal, scored at 19:03 of the third period against Edmonton goalie Bill Ranford. Like his first-ever NHL goal, it tied the game at four. Steve Duchesne and Dave Taylor drew the historic assists. L.A. won the game in overtime on a goal by, who else, Wayne Gretzky.

For some reason, anomalies like that dot the careers of many of the game's superstars. For instance, Maurice Richard scored his first goal in the NHL on November 8, 1942. He became the league's all-time goal-scoring king on November 8, 1952, exactly 10 years later.

12) Who was the youngest player to score a Stanley Cup–winning goal?

Ted "Teeder" Kennedy of the 1947 Toronto Maple Leafs was four months past his 21st birthday when he scored in game six of the Cup finals against Montreal. Alex Tanguay of the Colorado Avalanche was six months past his 21st birthday when he scored his Cup-winning goal against New Jersey in 2001. Mario Tremblay was eight months past his 21st when he scored the Cup winner in game six of the 1978 finals against Boston. Howie Morenz was nine months past his 21st birthday when he scored his first of two Cup winners for Montreal. The year was 1924 and the opposition was the Calgary Tigers. Bobby Orr was one month and 20 days past his 22nd birthday when he scored his first of two Cup winners for Boston. The year was 1970 and the opposition was the St. Louis Blues.

13) Who was the first American-born player to record five goals in an NHL regular-season game?

Another beauty that's been tripping people up for years—including yours truly, twice. On February 23, 1983, Mark Pavelich of the New York Rangers scored five goals in a game against Hartford and goalie Greg Millen. It was reported at the time that he was the first American-born player to score five goals in a game. That would be correct.

On March 6, 1920, a player named Mickey Roach fired five goals, helping his Toronto St. Pats beat the Quebec Bulldogs 11–2. The Quebec goalie was Frank Brophy. Roach played 211 games in his NHL career, scoring 77 goals and 34 assists for 111 points. He played for the Toronto St. Pats, Hamilton Tigers and New York Americans. It was later reported that Roach was born in Boston, but further research shows that he was actually born in Halifax, Nova Scotia, Canada, and moved to Boston at a very young age. So Pavelich is in fact the right answer.

14) Who are the four players in NHL history who have won the Stanley Cup, then won the Calder Trophy as rookie of the year in the following season?

Ken Dryden, Tony Esposito, Danny Grant and Gaye Stewart all share that unique distinction. Stewart was with the Toronto Maple Leafs when they won the Cup in 1942. He played three playoff games for them that year. In 1943, still with the Leafs, he won the Calder.

Grant played one regular-season game with the Montreal Canadiens in 1965–66, the same year he led the Ontario Hockey Association in goals, with 44. Grant was a Peterborough Pete at the time. Two years later, in 1967–68, he was called up for 22 regular-season games and 10 playoff games as Montreal won its 16th Cup title against St. Louis. That summer, he was traded to Minnesota. Because he hadn't played 25 games in the previous season, he was still considered a rookie. He played a full season for the North Stars in 1968–69, scoring 34 goals and winning the Calder Trophy.

Tony Esposito was in a similar position to Grant. He played 13 games with the Canadiens in 1968–69 and was the number three goalie on their roster that spring as Montreal went on to win championship number 17. He did not get any playing time in the playoffs. Chicago claimed him in the intra-league draft that summer and he was the rookie of the year in 1969–70 after posting a modern-day record of 15 shutouts.

Dryden rounds out this quartet. He played in six games of the regular season in 1971 before appearing in all 20 of Montreal's playoff games, helping them win the Cup for the 18th time. He was rewarded with the Conn Smythe Trophy as playoff MVP, then won the Calder Trophy in 1972.

15) Who was the oldest rookie in NHL history?

The question regarding oldest rookies is always a good one because the names are not well known. Connie "Mad Dog" Madigan leads the way. When he finally made it to The Show with St. Louis in 1973, he was 38 years old. He debuted on February 6, 1973, as St. Louis beat the Vancouver Canucks, 5–1.

Why would a guy almost 40 finally get a chance, you ask. There were two reasons. First of all, he was involved in a type of transaction that was fast disappearing: a trade between an NHL team and a minor-league club. Madigan was traded from the Portland Buckaroos, a team in the long-defunct Western Hockey League, to the St. Louis Blues in exchange for the loan of a player named Andre Aubry in January 1973. That's reason number one. Reason number two is that, even at his advanced age, he was one of the most feared men in hockey. Madigan played 20 games in St. Louis (picking up three assists), plus another five games in the playoffs. This was to be his only taste of life in the NHL. In the minors, he was an eight-time all-star, and was the Western League's top defenceman in 1966 with Portland. He picked up 3,308 penalty minutes in his 20-year pro career.

Two players, Jim Anderson and Helmut Balderis, were 37. Balderis actually owns the distinction of being the oldest player ever drafted in NHL history. He was taken 238th overall by the Minnesota North Stars in 1989, and he played 26 games for the Stars that season. As noted in Question 4, the 1989–90 season was the last one in which anyone over the age of 25 would be eligible for the Calder Trophy. You could still be referred to as a rookie, but would not be in the running for rookie of the year.

Jim Anderson's story is similar to Madigan's. A career minor-leaguer, primarily with Eddie Shore's

Springfield Indians of the American Hockey League, Anderson finally got a shot at the big time with the Los Angeles Kings in their inaugural season, 1967–68. He played seven games, picking up a goal and two assists. This came 13 seasons after he was the American League's rookie of the year in Springfield in 1955.

16) Who are the only three players in NHL history to score in their only NHL game?

Rolly Huard, with the 1930–31 Toronto Maple Leafs, Dean Morton with the 1989–90 Detroit Red Wings and Brad Fast with the 2003–04 Carolina Hurricanes.

Morton, who played his major junior hockey with the Oshawa Generals, was drafted by the Wings in 1986. He wore sweater number 5 in his lone NHL game. He retired from pro hockey as a player after spending 1992–93 with the Brantford Smoke of the Colonial Hockey League (now the United League). These days he's back in the NHL as a referee, following in the footsteps of Kevin Maguire and Paul Stewart, both former NHL players who also worked as officials.

Rolly Huard was an injury replacement whom the Leafs borrowed from the Buffalo Bisons of the International-American League. The date of his game was December 13, 1930, and the undermanned Leafs were trounced 7–3 by the visiting Boston Bruins. Huard retired from pro hockey in 1934 with the St. Louis Flyers in the American Hockey Association.

Brad Fast's lone game and goal is significant in hockey history. It's now noted as the last goal scored in the last tie game ever in the NHL: the implementation of the shootout rule after the lockout of 2005 meant no more tie games, so the conclusion of the 2003–04 regular season was the last with ties. On the final day of the regular season, April 4, 2004, there were two games that ended in a tie—Philadelphia and the NY Islanders, a 3–3 game that started at 1 p.m. EST, and a 6–6 tie between the Florida Panthers and the Carolina Hurricanes in a game that started at 3 p.m. EST. Brad Fast, playing in his first and only NHL game, scored his one NHL goal at 17:34 of the third period against Florida goalie Roberto Luongo. The game went to overtime, but there was no goal scored, meaning that this was the last tie game in NHL history. Luongo also set the NHL record for facing the most shots in one season with 2,475, a mark he would break in 2006 with a total of 2,488 shots faced.

17) Who are the only two players to wear number 00 in an NHL regular-season game?

John Davidson of the New York Rangers was the only player in NHL history to wear number 00 until December 26, 1995. Rookie Martin Biron of the Buffalo Sabres played the first and third periods of a game against the Pittsburgh Penguins that night, wearing number 00. Biron allowed four first-period goals, but none in the third. Buffalo lost 6–3. Steve Shields, appearing in only his second NHL game, played the second period for Buffalo. He wore number 31.

18) Who were "Les Trois Denis," and what was their connection to hockey?

Les Trois Denis (the three Denis) were three hockey players who grew up together in Verdun, a suburb of Montreal, Quebec. They were Denis Savard, a Hall of Fame player known to many hockey fans, Denis Cyr, who was also an NHL player, and Denis Tremblay. They ended up on the same hockey team as early as eight years of age, when it was discovered that they not only had the same first name but also the same birth year, 1961, the same birth month, February, and unbelievably the same birthday, the fourth. This might constitute the greatest coincidence in the history of hockey. The line would play two full seasons of Junior A hockey together for the Montreal Canadien Juniors from 1977 to 1979. The line combined for 299 points in its first season and 366 in its second. Tremblay was traded after 24 games in 1979–80; however, Savard and Cyr both demolished their previous career highs, scoring 181 and 146 points respectively. While Tremblay would never be drafted, Cyr and Savard both got drafted in the first round of the 1980 NHL entry draft. Savard would be drafted third overall by the Chicago Black Hawks, and Cyr was drafted 13th overall by the Calgary Flames. Cyr would play one more season in junior, but he did finish the season playing 10 games for the Flames. Cyr wasn't able to continue his scoring prowess with the Flames, and as a result he was traded to the Chicago Black Hawks in 1982 for Carey Wilson. The Hawks were hoping for Cyr to rekindle his chemistry with Denis Savard, who had already established himself as an elite NHLer by this time. However, Cyr could still not secure a permanent NHL position and after a couple of seasons moved on to the St. Louis Blues, then retired after three seasons in their organization, most of which were spent playing for their minor-league affiliate, the Peoria Rivermen of the International Hockey League. Cyr finished his NHL career with 193 games played, scoring 41 goals and 43 assists for 84 points. He currently works on behalf of the Chicago Blackhawk Alumni Association.

19) Who was the first winner of the Calder Award as rookie of the year, and what unusual distinction does he share with only one other honouree in the 69-season history of the award?

Carl Voss. You read about him in Chapter 5, where I identified him as the man who scored the final goal in St. Louis Eagles history. Prior to that, he was named rookie of the year with Detroit in 1933.

Voss is the answer to some of the best trivia questions from that era. He was the first player signed to a contract by Conn Smythe and the Toronto Maple Leafs. The date was February 16, 1927, and because Voss was not yet 21, his mother had to sign the deal with him. Voss played 12 games for the Leafs that season, and two more for them two years later, but none of that experience was enough for him to lose his rookie status. After four years of minor-pro hockey, Voss began the 1932–33 season with the New York Rangers. The Blueshirts sold Voss to Detroit 10 games into the season and he finished the year as a Red Wing. His performance of 8 goals and 15 assists for 23 points earned him top-rookie honours. Voss remains one of only two players in NHL history to be traded in the season in which they were the rookie of the year. Eddie Litzenberger was the other. He was originally a Montreal Canadien, but was dealt to Chicago during the 1954–55 season.

20) What are the details about the night that Bobby Orr became the record holder for most goals in a season by a defenceman?

Orr set numerous records in his brief career, but the one I've always liked came on his 21st birthday, March 20, 1969. That night, Orr scored goal number 21 of the season, breaking the existing mark for most goals in a season by a defenceman set by William "Flash" Hollett in 1945. Hollett was a former Bruin, but was with Detroit at the time he set the record.

Orr scored the goal at 19:59 of the third period—just one second to go in the game—tying the score at 5–5. The goalie was Chicago's Denis DeJordy. Johnny Bucyk and Fred Stanfield assisted. Also of note: in the same game, Chicago's Bobby Hull scored two goals, both on the same power play. His second goal was number 55 of the season, breaking his own single-season mark by one.

I know what you're thinking. "How did Hull score two goals on the same power play? After all, wasn't the rule changed in 1957 to allow the penalized man to come out of the box?" Yes, quite correct, unless that penalized man is serving a major penalty. The Hawks were on the extra-long power play because of a wild stick-swinging incident involving Johnny McKenzie, Phil Esposito, Doug Mohns and Bobby Orr. Obviously, Orr atoned for his penalty with the game-tying, and NHL record–setting, goal.

21) One of the fun things you can do with hockey history is try to find connections through time from players in today's game to those in the first year of the NHL. A case in point is the recently retired Nick Lidstrom. Follow along to see what I mean.

Nick Lidstrom's first season was 1991–92. Goaltender Greg Millen was a teammate of Lidstrom's that season. Millen began his NHL career in 1979 with the Pittsburgh Penguins. Coaching the Penguins that season was former Red Wing great Johnny Wilson, who was a teammate of Gordie Howe's on the four Red Wing Cup championships of the early 1950s. Another teammate of Wilson's was Sid Abel, who played on the Production Line with Howe and Ted Lindsay. Abel's first season in the NHL was 1938–39, and his coach was the legendary Jack Adams. Adams was the GM of the Wings when they won the Stanley Cup four times in the 1950s, but prior to that he was a long-time coach and before that a very solid NHL player. He was on the last team to win a Cup in the City of Ottawa with the Senators in 1927, and he was a member of the Toronto Arenas in the first year of the NHL, also a Cup-winning campaign for Mr. Adams. That's a three-person connection between Jack Adams and Nick Lidstrom, not to mention the obvious Detroit association.

22) Who were the first three Soviet/Russian-born players in NHL history?

This question has different answers if you add the criterion of being raised and trained in Russia before joining the NHL. Back in the early days of the NHL, many players were born outside Canada and later found their way to the big league, surprisingly even Russian-born players. Vic Hoffinger holds the distinction of being the first player in the NHL born in Russia. He was from a Russian town called Seltz, and he played parts of two seasons for the Chicago Black Hawks, from 1927 to 1929. That second season, 1928–29, Hoffinger was joined on the Hawks roster by Johnny Gotselig, born in Odessa, Russia. Gotselig enjoyed a tremendous career in Chicago, helping them to their first two Stanley Cup victories in 1934 and 1938, the latter as captain. That gave the Hawks two Russian-born players on their roster in 1928–29, which was the most until the 1989–90 New Jersey Devils, who employed Viacheslav Fetisov, Alexei Kasatonov and Sergei Starikov. The third Russian-born player is in the Hall of Fame. His name is Dave "Sweeney" Schriner. Though born in Kraft, Russia, Schriner listed his new hometown of Calgary as his place of birth to alleviate the constant harassment from border officials as he crossed from Canada to the States and back to play hockey. Schriner was a rookie of the year in the NHL in 1935 with the New York Americans, when it was still known as the Calder Award. He later won back-to-back scoring championships in the NHL in 1936 and 1937 with the Americans, and he was a two-time Stanley Cup champion with the Toronto Maple Leafs in 1942 and 1945.

23) Who was the first player in NHL history to score against his brother?

Paul Thompson of Chicago scored on his brother, Cecil "Tiny" Thompson of Boston, on February 14, 1937. Earl Seibert assisted the goal scored at 4:32 of the second period. Boston would go on to win the game, 2–1. Scoring for the Bruins were Aubrey "Dit" Clapper and Charlie Sands. Milt Schmidt assisted the Clapper goal, while Ray Getliffe helped out on the Sands goal. Clarence Campbell and Cecil "Babe" Dye were the officials.

May I digress for just a moment? I'm sorry, but this has to be said. Aren't those names just screaming out, "Look at the Rocket Richard connections!" First of all, Clapper was the first man that the Rocket ever fought in an NHL game. Charlie Sands wore number 9 for Montreal before Richard. Ray Getliffe was the man responsible for hanging the "Rocket" nickname on Richard. During practice one day, he remarked that Richard, who'd been known as the Comet prior to his NHL career, skated like a rocket.

Clarence Campbell, the referee, would become president of the NHL and would suspend Richard in 1955, triggering the Richard Riot.

Number two in the brother-versus-brother category was the late Brian Smith, who scored on his brother Gary on December 19, 1967. The time of the goal was 10:02 of the second period. Brian was a Los Angeles King, while the well-travelled Gary was a goalie for the Oakland Seals. Brian also scored an empty-net goal as Los Angeles won the game, 3–1.

24) There have been two occasions in NHL history when a team did not participate in an amateur draft. Who are the teams and what were the circumstances?

The St. Louis Blues and Toronto Maple Leafs. In 1983, the Blues were going through an ownership change and some financial woes, so the franchise opted not to participate in the draft. They got some mileage out of their fourth pick from the 1982 draft, Doug Gilmour, before trading him to Calgary in 1988.

In 1965, the Leafs were the only other NHL team to pass on all rounds in the draft. At that time, the pool of draft-eligible players consisted only of those who were not already on a sponsored junior team. The crop of available players in '65 was judged to be the weakest ever, so Toronto opted not to make any selections. In fact, none of the other five NHL teams used its full complement of four draft picks, and only 10 players were chosen in all by NHL clubs.

Here's an interesting fact about those early drafts. The order in which teams made their picks rotated from year to year. It didn't matter where they finished in the standings.

25) There have been two years in which the amateur draft produced more first-round selections than there were teams. What were those years, and what were the reasons for this oddity?

The two years were 1969 and 1978. The 1969 draft saw the end of an old practice that dated back to the late 1930s. In those days, the Montreal Canadiens franchise was sinking in the standings and at the box office. It was thought that boosting the French-Canadian content on the Habs' roster would make the product more attractive to the paying customers in Montreal. So they were given first crack at Québécois talent. The policy was rescinded a few years later, but a version of it was introduced in 1963, when the NHL launched the amateur draft. The Habs were given the option of selecting up to two players from the province of Quebec before any of the other teams could draft. In 1969, the Canadiens exercised their option for the last time, claiming Rejean Houle and Marc

Tardif. The selections were registered as the first and second picks in the draft. The remaining 11 picks were then made, thereby creating a situation in which 13 players were drafted in the first round by members of a 12-team league.

It's a falsehood perpetuated by some—most of them anti-Montreal fans or those who have not done their homework—that Montreal's priority selections are the reason they won all, if not most, of their 24 Stanley Cup championships to date. Nothing could be further from the truth. Besides Houle and Tardif, the only other time the Habs exercised their "cultural" option was in the 1968 draft, when they took goalie Michel Plasse. All three have their names on the Cup, but none was a front-line player for the Habs. Houle and Tardif would have better luck with Quebec in the WHA. As for the protected players from the late 1930s, I have not come across a single one who even played a game on an NHL roster. Perhaps an astute reader may be able to offer up a name or two.

The 1978 draft was a very special one—and an unusual one. If you look at the list of names, you'll see that 18 players were taken in the first round. Yet the NHL was a 17-team league at the time.

During the summer, the Cleveland Barons had folded operations and merged with the Minnesota North Stars. The NHL held a special dispersal draft of Cleveland's players, as well as its first- and second-round draft picks. It was open to the teams that had missed the 1978 playoffs, plus the relatively weak Colorado Rockies, who'd just completed their second season in Denver after moving from Kansas City. If a team opted to take over Cleveland's amateur draft picks, it would be entitled to use the first-round selection at the end of the round, rather than in the fifth-overall slot where the Barons would have drafted. There was no way the league would let one team have two picks in the top five!

Only two ex-Barons were selected in the dispersal draft—the St. Louis Blues took Mike Crombeen, while Vancouver took Randy Holt. The Washington Capitals, who owned the league's second-worst record, opted for the Cleveland draft choices. That meant they had four of the top 23 choices. And so, in addition to their second-overall pick, Ryan Walter, they chose Tim Coulis as the 18th player taken in the first round. With Cleveland's second-round pick, the 23rd overall, they chose Paul MacKinnon. Coulis played 47 games in the NHL, while MacKinnon's career spanned 147 matches. Walter fared better, playing in 1,003 games and scoring 264 career goals.

26) What was the first year in which a player was drafted for the second time?

In 1977, the NHL made a rule that any drafted player who had not signed a contract within a year less two days could re-enter the draft pool to be selected again. Six unsigned players from the 1977 draft were selected again in 1978: Randy Ireland, Dan Eastman, Richard Sirois, Dan Clark, Mark Toffolo and Harald Luckner. All were chosen lower in the draft the second time around, except for Luckner, who moved up from 121st in 1977 to 56th in '78. Of the six, only two played in the NHL. Ireland and Clark played in two and four games respectively.

27) What brother combinations were chosen in back-to-back drafts, in the exact same position?

In 1979, the New York Islanders selected Duane Sutter 17th overall from the Lethbridge Broncos. That year's draft is often regarded as the greatest in NHL history because for the first time in the modern draft system teams could select not just 20-year-olds, but 18- and 19-year-olds as well. That was also the year that the draft was reclassified from amateur draft to the entry draft. There were a number of professionals drafted from various WHA teams, including the first overall selection, Rob Ramage, from the Birmingham Bulls. In 1980, the Islanders selected 17th overall again, and they drafted Duane's brother Brent from the Red Deer Rustlers. Brent would play on two of the Islanders' four Stanley Cup winners, Duane on all four of them. In 1984, the Montreal Canadiens cemented their future by selecting Patrick Roy from Granby of the Quebec Major Junior league with the 51st-overall pick. Coincidentally, with the 51st pick in the '85 draft, the Minnesota North Stars took Stephane Roy, a centreman, also from Granby. Unfortunately, he did not enjoy anywhere near the success of his brother, appearing in only 12 NHL games. He spent a considerable time with the Canadian National Team and has played for several teams in the minors. In 2008, the Toronto Maple Leafs selected Luke Schenn fifth overall from the Kelowna Rockets. In 2009, Los Angeles selected his brother Brayden Schenn fifth from the Brandon Wheat Kings.

28) What former head coach in the NHL was the last player chosen in the 1985 amateur draft?

Paul Maurice. Maurice became the head coach of the Carolina Hurricanes 12 games into the 1995–96 season. He is the franchise's winningest coach. Maurice was indeed the last player chosen in the 1985 draft. He was taken 252nd overall by the Philadelphia Flyers. In all fairness, it should be mentioned that he had suffered an eye injury, so to draft him in any position would have been a gamble. He never did play in the NHL, but he did play four seasons of major junior hockey with the Windsor Compuware Spitfires of the Ontario Hockey League.

29) To date, who has played the most NHL games after being selected with the last-overall pick in the NHL amateur draft?

Technically, Gerry Meehan is the correct answer. He played 670 games for six NHL teams after being selected 21st overall by Toronto in the first draft, held in 1963. Credit should also go to Andy Brickley, who played 385 games in the NHL for five teams—including the Philadelphia Flyers, who drafted him with the 210th and final pick in the 1980 draft. Jonathan Ericsson and Brian Elliott are the two lowest-drafted players to make the NHL. They were both selected 291st overall in back-to-back years, Ericsson by Detroit in 2002 and Elliott by Ottawa in 2003. In Ericsson's case, he was the last selection. Elliott was the second-last pick in 2003. Ericsson has played in one Cup final to date with Detroit in 2009. Brian Elliott completed a season and made a comeback for the ages with the St. Louis Blues in 2011–12, when he finished first not only in GAA with a stellar mark of 1.56 but also recorded the second best single-season save percentage that we know of in NHL history with a .940. That number eclipsed Dominik Hasek's .937, and as of this writing it is second only to Jacques Plante's .942 with the 1971 Toronto Maple Leafs.

30) What NHL team once drafted a player who did not exist?

The Buffalo Sabres. In 1974, the Sabres had one of the league's most creative public-relations people on their staff. Paul Weiland was his name, and he was the impetus behind one of the best practical jokes of all time on draft day. Weiland came up with fake stats for a player named Taro Tsujimoto from the Tokyo Katanas in the Japanese league. With the Sabres' second-last pick, 183rd overall, Taro was selected. Judging by the bogus stats being circulated around the room, it was thought that Punch Imlach and company had just made the steal of the draft.

When the prank was uncovered, NHL president Clarence Campbell was not amused. He ruled the pick invalid and denied Buffalo permission to choose a real player in Tsujimoto's place. The Sabres had one more selection in the draft, 196th overall, and they did take a real player with that one: Bob Geoffrion from the Cornwall Royals. Like the fictitious Taro Tsujimoto, Geoffrion never played in the NHL.

31) Who was the first player chosen in an amateur draft whose father had played in the NHL?

Syl Apps Jr. In 1964, Apps was selected 21st overall by the New York Rangers from the Kingston Midgets. He went on to play more than 700 games in the NHL. Apps was named MVP of the 1975 All-Star Game, played at the Montreal Forum, and as a member of the Pittsburgh Penguins he played on a line known as the MAP Line. His linemates were Lowell MacDonald, and Jean Pronovost, and the line took its name from the first letter in their last names. Apps's father was, of course, Syl Apps Sr., a star for the Toronto Maple Leafs in the late 1930s and '40s.

32) Terry Sawchuk's final NHL shutout and Martin Brodeur's record-breaking 104th career shutout were both accomplished against the same NHL team. Which one?

The Pittsburgh Penguins. Sawchuk's final whitewash occurred on February 1, 1970, in a 6–0 win for his New York Rangers over the Penguins. Dave Balon, with his first of three goals of the night, scored the game winner in this historic contest. Brodeur passed Sawchuk's mark in Pittsburgh on December 21, 2009, almost 40 years later. Bryce Salvadore scored the winner for the Devils in this epic event.

33) Who is the only player in NHL history to have a penalty-shot goal disallowed?

Calgary's Joe Mullen. On March 28, 1987, in a game that Calgary led, 4–3, Mullen was awarded a penalty shot with 35 seconds to play after Los Angeles Kings goaltender Al Jensen threw his stick. Just before Mullen took the shot, L.A.'s Bernie Nicholls, at the direction of Kings coach Mike Murphy, told referee Kerry Fraser that the Kings were protesting under Rule 20(e) and calling for a stick measurement. The rule at the time stated that there would be a measurement, but only after the shooter had taken his shot—and only if he scored. The penalty shot went ahead and Mullen scored. The stick was measured. It was found to be illegal and the goal was disallowed.

The rule has since been changed. As it currently stands, if a team calls for a measurement prior to the penalty shot, it will result in a penalty against the team lodging the protest if the shooter's stick turns out to be legal. If the stick is illegal, the shooter will be assessed a minor penalty, but he still is able to take the shot—with a different stick, of course.

34) Who are the four players in NHL history to take penalty shots in consecutive games?

Mike Walton, Brent Peterson, Esa Pirnes and Erik Cole. Walton took his two shots on March 9 and March 10, 1968. He scored on Detroit's Roger Crozier in a 7–5 shootout win for the Leafs on home ice. The next night, Walton was stopped by Jack Norris of the Black Hawks in a 4–0 loss in Chicago.

Brent Peterson took his two shots on January 13 and January 14, 1984. Peterson was stopped by Edmonton Oilers goalie Grant Fuhr in a game the Sabres won, 3–1, on home ice. The next night, in Detroit, Peterson scored against Red Wings goalie Greg Stefan in a 2–1 Buffalo victory.

Peterson is the answer to another great question. On October 11, 1987, Doug Jarvis's iron-man streak, an NHL record 964 games, came to an end when Jarvis was scratched from the lineup by Hartford Whalers coach Jack "Tex" Evans. In his place, Evans dressed Peterson. It was the first time in Jarvis's career, dating back to 1975, that he did not dress for a regular-season game.

Esa Pirnes was with the Los Angeles Kings in 2003–04, and he had his first of two successive shots on October 10, 2003. He was stopped by Pittsburgh's Marc-Andre Fleury in a 3–0 L.A. victory. Two nights later, Pirnes's Kings won again, this time over Chicago, 4–2. Again he was thwarted on a penalty shot, this time by Hawks goalie Jocelyn Thibault.

Erik Cole's penalty shot story is arguably the most interesting. On November 9, 2005, Cole, then with the Carolina Hurricanes, was awarded not one but two shots in the same game, the only player in NHL history with this distinction to date. Carolina was playing the Buffalo Sabres. Cole was successful in his first attempt but was stopped in the second. Martin Biron, one of only two goalies in NHL history to wear 00, was the goalie of record in this contest. Carolina won the game 5–3, setting a new club record in the process with their eighth straight franchise victory. Cole's penalty shot, which was awarded while his team was shorthanded, was the game winner, and with his two assists he was voted the second star of the game. Two nights later, Cole joined the exclusive group named above with yet another penalty shot, this time against the Florida Panthers and goalie Roberto Luongo. His attempt was stopped by Luongo, but Cole did manage an assist on the game's only goal, by Eric Staal, as Florida extended their club winning streak to nine games.

35) What player holds the distinction for the most time elapsed between penalty-shot goals?

Even by my standards, this is an obscure question. On February 18, 2001, Joe Nieuwendyk broke the mark held by Bob Nevin for the longest time between penalty-shot goals. Nieuwendyk scored on a penalty shot against the Detroit Red Wings in a 2–1 loss. It was 12 years, two months and two days since he'd scored on a penalty shot for the Calgary Flames against the Vancouver Canucks and goaltender Steve Weeks. Four days prior to that attempt, Nieuwendyk was awarded his first-ever penalty shot, against Allan Bester and the Toronto Maple Leafs. He missed.

On November 5, 1966, Nevin scored on a penalty shot against Leaf goalie Terry Sawchuk. It was the only Rangers goal in a 3–1 loss. Nine years, three months and six days later, Nevin, then a Los Angeles King, scored against Chicago goaltender Tony Esposito in a 7–4 L.A. victory.

Third on this obscure list is Tomas Sandstrom. He scored goals nine years, five days apart—first for Los Angeles, then for Anaheim. Gordie Howe scored on penalty shots eight years, nine months and 26 days apart for the Detroit Red Wings.

36) Every single number in NHL history has been worn in a regular season game, from 00 and 0 right through 99. What was the last number to be put in circulation and for which player?

Number 84. Guillaume Latendresse was the first NHL player to ever wear 84, when he started the 2006–07 season with the Montreal Canadiens. Latendresse had worn number 22 in junior with Drummondville, but that number was being worn in Montreal by Steve Begin. Incidentally, Latendresse was the second player drafted in the 2003 QMJHL midget draft, behind Sidney Crosby. After three-plus seasons with Montreal, he was traded to the Minnesota Wild for Benoit Pouliot. With the Wild, Latendresse wears number 48.

37) In the history of Stanley Cup play—in other words, since 1894—only once did three brothers play on a Stanley Cup–winning team. Who were the brothers and the team, and in what year did this happen?

Dave, Suddy and Billy Gilmour were all members of the 1903 Ottawa Senators, a team better known as the Ottawa Silver Seven. Dave Gilmour was with Ottawa only for this one championship. Suddy was on this team and the one that followed, in 1904. Billy played on four Ottawa Cup winners, in 1903, 1904, 1905 and 1911.

All three brothers contributed in the two Stanley Cup series played by Ottawa in 1903. The first was a two-game, total-goals series against the Montreal Victorias. The first game ended in a 1–1 draw, while Ottawa took game two, 8–0. The Gilmours combined for six of the nine Ottawa goals. A second challenge match, another two-game, total-goals series, was set up against the Rat Portage Thistles. Ottawa prevailed by an aggregate score of 10–4. The Gilmours scored six of the 10 goals.

38) Sam Gagner of the Edmonton Oilers had an amazing couple of nights during the month of February in the 2011–12 season. He had the Twitterverse on fire as people tried to find out where his consecutive point streak and his points in two successive games stood on the all-time lists. Do you know which player holds the NHL record for recording a point on the most consecutive goals and which player has recorded the most points in two successive NHL games?

Gagner's big game of eight points, four goals and four assists in the Oilers 8–4 victory over the Chicago Blackhawks on February 2, 2012, tied the Edmonton Oilers' record for points in a game set by the legendary Wayne Gretzky (he did it twice) and defenceman Paul Coffey. In the Oilers' next contest two nights later, on February 4, Gagner picked up where he'd left off and recorded a point on the first three Oiler goals, two scored by him, before finally being kept off the score-sheet on the game-tying marker scored by Jordan Eberle. That sent the game into OT and eventually a shootout, during which, unbelievably, Gagner scored again. His tally of points on 11 straight goals was phenomenal, but it's not an NHL record for consecutive points or a two-game total for points. Peter and Anton Stastny each recorded 14 points in two successive games for the Quebec Nordiques during the 1980–81 season (see Chapter 5 for more information about how the Stastny brothers achieved their most unusual record). The mark for points on consecutive goals is 15, held by Jaromir Jagr with the Pittsburgh Penguins in 1999–2000. That's an amazing number, but even more so when you consider that it was accomplished during a seven-game stretch in which the Penguins did not win a game, going 0–5–2 from October 16 to November 4.

39) Who is the only player to play an NHL game before being drafted by an NHL team?

Anatoli Fedotov. In 1991, the Winnipeg Jets signed the 25-year-old Fedotov, who was playing for Moscow Dynamo, to an American Hockey League contract. In 1992–93, the Jets convinced him to come to North America, where he played almost the entire season with the Moncton Hawks of the AHL. The Jets brought him up for one game, against Edmonton, and he recorded two assists. The NHL deemed that he had been promoted improperly because the Jets didn't own his NHL rights, and his contract was voided. Fedotov had to enter the entry draft of 1993, where he was selected 238th overall by the Mighty Ducks of Anaheim. He played three games with the Ducks in 1993–94 before being sent back to the minors. He returned overseas in 1995.

40) One of the greatest traditions in recent NHL memory has been that of players having an opportunity to invite their fathers on a road trip with the team. Which team is believed to have been the first to start this tradition?

The Nashville Predators continue to make history by way of having only one general manager, David Poile, and one coach, Barry Trotz, manage and coach the team since its inception in 1998. Another interesting move on the franchise's part was to invite its players' fathers on a road trip during that inaugural season, something that has spread to most, if not all, the other NHL teams at this point. Poile's name is synonymous with certain moments in the league's history, whether they were his own doing, such as when as Washington GM he was instrumental in getting the NHL to use video replay of goals, or whether they were his father's accomplishments as a player, winning a Stanley Cup in 1947 with Toronto and later being part of one of the trades with the most impact in NHL history. Poile, Gaye Stewart, Gus Bodnar, Bob Goldham and Ernie Dickens were traded to Chicago for Max Bentley and Cy Thomas on November 2, 1947. In addition to his father, Norman "Bud" Poile," David Poile also had an uncle play in the NHL, Don Poile.

41) Which goaltenders are on record as having the shortest NHL careers of any retired goalie?

Robbie Irons of the St. Louis Blues and Christian Soucy of the Chicago Blackhawks. Irons played three minutes in a game on November 13, 1968. Soucy played three minutes and 21 seconds of a game on March 31, 1994.

On November 13, 1968, Glenn Hall started the game for the Blues against the New York Rangers at Madison Square Garden. It was the first game in which Hall wore a mask. Irons was backing up because either Hall or Jacques Plante, the other regular St. Louis goaltender, took the occasional night off—not only from playing, but also from sitting on the bench. Given that Hall had once played in 502 consecutive regular-season games and it was early in the season, Blues coach Scotty Bowman didn't feel the need to have Plante dress. That was until all hell broke loose at 2:01 of the first period.

Hall had just been scored on by the Rangers' Vic Hadfield. He did not think the goal should have counted, and he let referee Vern Buffy know as much in no uncertain terms. Buffy gave Hall a misconduct penalty. Had Hall quieted down, play could have resumed with him in the net and a St. Louis skater serving the 10-minute penalty. No such luck. Hall continued to badger Buffy and was thrown out of the game. Enter Irons.

Bowman instructed Irons to stall as much as possible while Plante, who was watching the game in his hotel room, raced to the rink to dress. Irons did so, but there was a limit to how much he could dawdle, so it was inevitable that he'd have to play a bit. He recorded three uneventful minutes in the Blues' net before Plante arrived and entered the game at 5:01 of the first period. He shut the Rangers down the rest of the way while Bill McCreary, Ron Schock and Frank St. Marseille scored for the Blues. They won, 3–1. Irons retired from pro hockey in 1981 with the Fort Wayne Komets of the IHL.

Soucy's story was much simpler and less eventful. On March 31, 1994, the Blackhawks were at home to the Washington Capitals. Despite a couple of late goals by Jeremy Roenick, the Hawks were still losing 6–3 when head coach Darryl

Sutter pulled starter Jeff Hackett so that Soucy, a 23-year-old rookie, could get some game action. Soucy played the last 3:21 of the game, facing no shots. That was it for his NHL career. Soucy played in the minors until 2003.

42) There has only been one regular-season doubleheader in NHL history. What was the date, which teams were involved and what was the reason?

The date was March 3, 1968. The Philadelphia Flyers were one of six expansion teams that had joined the league that season, and a freak storm had blown the roof off of their home arena, the Spectrum, two nights earlier. That catastrophe would force the Flyers to play a number of "home" games at other locations. The Colisée in Quebec City, home of the Flyers' farm team, was the venue for many of them. Maple Leaf Gardens was also the Flyers' home rink on occasion. But on this date, March 3, they moved into the brand new Madison Square Garden, home of the New York Rangers.

The Flyers played a matinee against the Oakland Seals. Larry Cahan scored for Oakland, while Don Blackburn scored for Philadelphia in the 1–1 tie. The second game of the doubleheader was a regularly scheduled tilt between the Rangers and Chicago. Vic Hadfield paced the Blueshirts to a 4–0 win with two goals. Reggie Fleming and Don Marshall added singles.

It was an eventful day in hockey history. There was this doubleheader, of course, which had never happened before or since. Elsewhere, there was a blockbuster seven-player trade. Frank Mahovlich was sent from Toronto to Detroit, along with Pete Stemkowski, Garry Unger and the NHL rights to Carl Brewer, for Paul Henderson, Floyd Smith and Norm Ullman. Then there was Jean Beliveau recording his 1,000th point against Detroit. Finally, Eddie Shack had a hat trick for the Boston Bruins in a 9–3 win over the St. Louis Blues and goaltender Glenn Hall. All on the same day. Amazing.

43) Which two teams played against each other 10 times in one season—but in five different rinks?

The Philadelphia Flyers and Los Angeles Kings. Few people know that the Kings played in three different arenas in their first year: the Long Beach Arena, the Los Angeles Sports Arena and the Forum—or, as it was often called, the "Fabulous Forum." L.A. hosted the Flyers in their first-ever game, played at the Long Beach Arena. The Kings won, 4–2. On December 8, 1967, the Kings lost to the Flyers, 3–0, at the L.A. Sports Arena. On December 30, 1967, the Kings lost to the Flyers, 2–0, in the first game played at the Fabulous Forum.

The Kings and Flyers met four times at the Spectrum in Philadelphia that season, including the last one before the roof blew off. The date of that game was February 29, 1968, and L.A. won, 3–1. On March 14, 1968, the Kings met the "homeless" Flyers at the Colisée in Quebec City. The game ended in a scoreless draw. Recording career shutout number 102 for L.A. was Terry Sawchuk. It was the fifth career shutout for Philadelphia's goalie, Bernie Parent. Both men are in the Hockey Hall of Fame.

44) Comebacks in the NHL have been prevalent for many years. Mario Lemieux's in 2000–01 caused quite a stir, as well it should. However, what would you say about a player who went almost 19 years between NHL appearances? Or how about 14 seasons between NHL goals? Any idea who holds these records?

Moe Roberts and Fred Hucul. Roberts was a goaltender who played a handful of games in the

NHL over a nine-year period, the last of those coming in December 1933. He then had a fine career in the minors before his playing days were interrupted for three years of military service during World War II. He returned for one final year with the Washington Lions of the Eastern Amateur Hockey League in 1945–46. By the early '50s, Roberts had become an assistant trainer for Chicago. In the second game of a home-and-home series against the Detroit Red Wings, Hawks starter Harry Lumley went down with a knee injury and the call went out to the goalie-turned-trainer. The date was November 25, 1951. Roberts was 45 years old. He played the third period and did not allow a goal.

Fred Hucul was a defenceman with Chicago in the early '50s. He had played 121 regular-season games for the Hawks by the conclusion of the 1953–54 season. Then he was traded to Calgary of the Western Hockey League, and like many players in the six-team days, it would prove difficult for Hucul to regain his NHL job. In fact, Hucul did not get another shot at the big league until the modern expansion era in 1967–68, with the St. Louis Blues.

The 13 seasons between NHL games was a dubious mark that was equalled by Larry Zeidel, a teammate of Hucul's on Chicago in 1953–54. Zeidel played parts of two seasons with the Philadelphia Flyers, beginning in their first year, 1967–68. The difference between the two was that Zeidel scored a goal in that final season with Chicago, while Hucul did not. They both scored for their respective teams in 1967–68, so that meant that Hucul is the player who went the longest between NHL goals. He'd scored five times for Chicago in 1952–53. An interesting note about Zeidel: he got his second chance at the NHL after he sent out resumés to every NHL team. The Flyers were the only ones interested.

45) Here's a similar type of question. Which player holds the record for the longest gap between goals for the same team?

Randy Cunneyworth scored two goals for the Buffalo Sabres in 1981–82 as a call-up from their farm team, the Rochester Americans. The second goal was scored on November 15, 1981. Some 830 games later, having played with five NHL teams over the course of 17 years, two months and 27 days, Cunneyworth found himself in the exact same position. The Sabres called him up from the Rochester Americans and on February 11, 1999, he scored a goal. No player has gone longer between goals for the same team.

Cunneyworth broke the mark held by Detroit's Billy Dea, who went 11 years, 11 months and 11 days between goals for the Red Wings. The dates were November 28, 1957, and November 8, 1969. Did he wear number 11, you may well ask. No; he wore numbers 15 and 21 in his two stints with Detroit.

46) Who is the only NHL goaltender to face penalty shots as a member of five different NHL teams?

Sean Burke. Burke's first penalty shot came when he was a member of the New Jersey Devils, and it was a save against the Los Angeles Kings' Luc Robitaille in 1989, in overtime. Two more attempts were stopped when he was a member of the Hartford Whalers: one in 1995 against Washington's Michal Pivonka and the other in 1996 against Wayne Presley of the Toronto Maple Leafs.

In 1998, he made it four for four, stopping Kevin Stevens of the New York Rangers. This time Burke was a member of the Philadelphia Flyers. In 1999, Burke kept the hot hand rolling in the most exciting play in hockey, stopping Terry Yake of the St. Louis Blues on November 18. Burke this time was a member of the Florida

Panthers. Not for long. Despite the save, Florida lost the game 3–0 to the Blues and Burke was on his way to his newest destination that night: the Phoenix Coyotes. Finally, on January 10, 2000, Sean Burke gave up a goal on a penalty shot. The scorer was the New York Islanders' Brad Isbister. The Phoenix Coyotes were Burke's seventh NHL team and the fifth for which he had faced a penalty shot. Vancouver and Carolina were the two other teams that he played for.

47) Which teams were involved in the game that saw the most empty-net goals scored in history?
The Chicago Black Hawks and the Montreal Canadiens on April 5, 1970. The Hawks scored five empty-net goals in what still has to be regarded as one of the more bizarre games in NHL history. Because of the rules of the day, the Habs were desperately trying to score five goals in their final game in Chicago. Aside from winning or tying the contest, which would have automatically seen them make the playoffs because they would have moved ahead of the New York Rangers in the standings, they could still participate in the post-season despite a loss by scoring one more goal than the Rangers. With Montreal trailing 3–2 entering the third period, anything was still possible; however, two goals by Chicago's Pit Martin in three and a half minutes completed his hat trick and put the Hawks up 5–2 with only half a period to go in what was the final regular-season game for both teams. It called for desperate measures, so Montreal coach Claude Ruel began pulling goalie Rogie Vachon whenever they had puck possession in the Hawks' end. The move backfired big time, and the Hawks reeled off five straight empty-net goals en route to a 10–2 win that eliminated Montreal from the playoffs for the first time since 1948. Scoring the uncontested goals were Cliff Koroll, Eric Nesterenko, Dennis Hull, Bobby Hull and Gerry Pinder. Montreal goalie Rogie Vachon could only sit and watch from his team's bench. During the off-season, the rule was changed so that the first criterion was wins followed by success in head-to-head competition. Montreal and New York were tied with identical records of 38–22–16 that season, but Montreal won the season series 4–3–1. But that wouldn't matter until the rule changed for next year, so history was made, likely never to be repeated.

48) What goaltender played against the same NHL team three times in one year—for a different team each time?
Sean Burke. During the 1997–98 season, Burke played the Florida Panthers three times—once each as a member of the Carolina Hurricanes, Vancouver Canucks and Philadelphia Flyers. The Panthers must have liked what they saw because they signed Burke as a free agent on September 12, 1998.

49) Who are the only two goaltenders to share a shutout with their netminding partners in their NHL debuts?
Michel Dumas of the Chicago Black Hawks and Goran Hogosta of the New York Islanders. Dumas was called up from Chicago's farm team in Dallas of the Central League on February 16, 1975. At the time, Tony Esposito was Chicago's regular goaltender and Mike Veisor was the backup. Veisor had been bombed 12–3 by the Montreal Canadiens the day before. Yvan Cournoyer did much of the damage, scoring five goals.

Dumas had been Chicago's property since signing with the Hawks as a free agent in 1971, but he had never seen a single minute of NHL action. In February 1975 he signed with Cincinnati of the WHA, but the contract wasn't to take effect until the start of the 1975–76 season. Chicago promoted Dumas and told him he would back up Esposito but probably not see any action. On February 23, 1975, the Hawks were beating the Atlanta Flames, 4–0, when Tony Esposito's catching glove developed a rip. Rules dictated in those days that when a goalie needed equipment repairs, the backup would play until the repairs were complete. It took only a minute, literally, to mend the glove, but Dumas's name went onto the scoresheet. Esposito returned and shut out the Flames the rest of the way, so the game is in the books as a shared shutout. Michel Dumas played in a total of eight games in his NHL career.

Goran Hogosta was born on April 15, 1954, in Appelbo, Sweden. After success in the Swedish junior ranks, he rose to prominence with the Swedish National Team that competed in the inaugural Canada Cup in 1976. In the summer of 1977, after the World Championships in Vienna, Austria, he signed as a free agent with the New York Islanders and ended up on their farm team in Hershey. A call up to the parent club came in late October, and finally he had an opportunity to dress as a backup to Billy Smith on November 1, 1977. With nine minutes to go in a blowout win for the Islanders, Hogosta was pressed into service because of an injury to Smith. He faced four shots in the nine minutes of his NHL debut, going on record as sharing a shutout in his first ever NHL action and becoming the first European-born and -trained goalie to play in the NHL. Of note, Bryan Trottier recorded four goals and one assist in the Islanders' 9–0 victory.

50) On October 28, 2000, two New Jersey Devils scored four goals each in the same game. It was the first time this had happened in the NHL in almost 80 years. Who were the Devils players, and whose record did they tie?

John Madden and Randy McKay each had four goals in a 9–0 New Jersey victory over the Pittsburgh Penguins. The last time two teammates each had four-goal games was on January 14, 1922, when the Cleghorn brothers, Sprague and Odie, each scored four times in a 10–6 Montreal victory over the Hamilton Tigers.

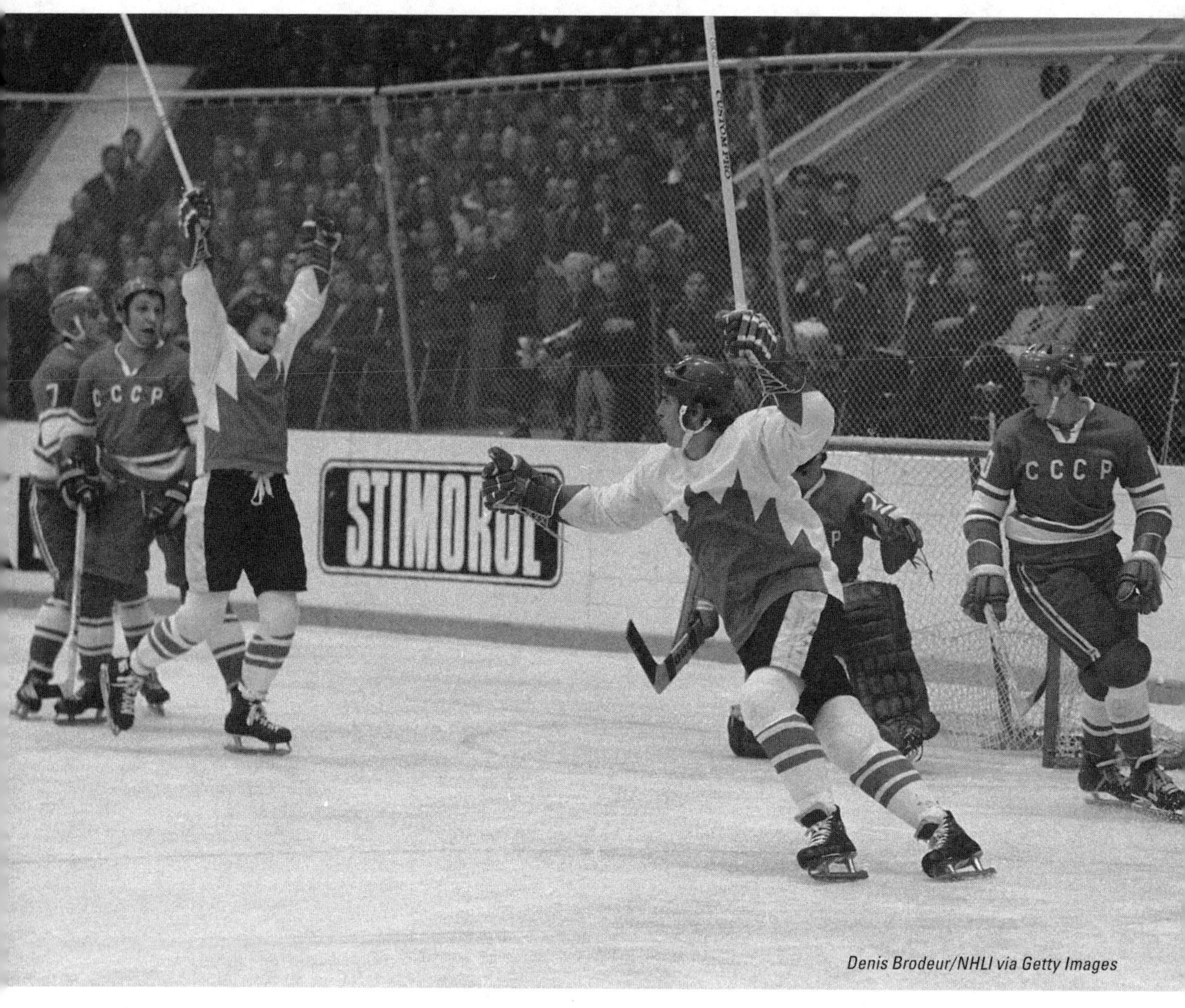

Denis Brodeur/NHLI via Getty Images

PAUL HENDERSON celebrates his first goal in game five of the Summit Series on September 22, 1972. Henderson scored a second after a slash behind the knee sent him into the boards and he was concussed. He would score the winners in games six and seven, and in the epic game eight, with thirty-four seconds to go. In the background is his linemate Bobby Clarke. They and Ron Ellis formed the only line kept intact right from training camp. Henderson remains outside the Hockey Hall of Fame looking in, despite an excellent career and seven goals in the Summit Series, including in game eight the goal with the biggest impact in the history of hockey.

8

PAUL HENDERSON

ON THURSDAY, SEPTEMBER 28, 1972, at approximately 2:30 p.m. Eastern Standard Time, at 19:26 of the third period in the eighth game of the Summit Series between the Soviet National Team and Team Canada, Paul Henderson scored what many in hockey circles call "the goal heard around the world."

This goal has become the single most significant moment in Canadian sports history. To recognize this, Team Canada 1972 was acknowledged by the Canadian Press as the "Team of the Century." CP has a long and distinguished annual tradition of naming the teams and individual athletes who elevated themselves or their team above all others in any sport during a particular year. The arrival of the new millennium prompted the news service to go this one step further. And even though teams of Canada's best hockey players have since won Olympic gold medals in Salt Lake City in 2002 and Vancouver in 2010, neither team nor their victories, dramatic as they might have been, changed Canadians or their game the way the Summit Series did.

Among the candidates CP considered for its Team of the Century honour were the great Montreal Canadiens of the 1950s and '70s, the Toronto Maple Leafs dynasties of the 1940s and '60s, the Edmonton Eskimos of the Canadian Football League in the 1980s and the back-to-back World Series champion Toronto Blue Jays of 1992 and '93. But the team that stood out was Team Canada 1972. And this for playing an eight-game series. That speaks volumes about the impact of that series on Canadian hockey fans and the importance of the one goal that decided it. Yet the man who scored this goal is not in the Hockey Hall of Fame, while Vladislav Tretiak, the goaltender who let it in, was inducted in 1989.

It's a great bone of contention among Canadians that the losing goaltender from that series is in and the player who scored seven goals on him in eight games is not. Many hockey fans have a hard time swallowing Tretiak's induction, chiefly because he never played in the NHL.

An examination of his numbers reveals that they might be on to something.

Tretiak played no more than 42 games in one regular season. To put that into perspective, since 1982—the year the Vezina Trophy was first awarded to a single goaltender judged to be the league's best, rather than to the goaltender(s) on the team with the fewest goals against—only one goaltender has played as few as 42 games and won the award: Tom Barrasso, in 1984. And winning a single Vezina Trophy is a far cry from being considered Hall of Fame material. My point is this: Hall of Fame goaltenders who played in the NHL have had to play 50, 60 and, on numerous occasions, 70 games per season. I will grant you that the Soviet regular season was much shorter than the NHL's, but I just don't feel it's fair to elevate Tretiak's achievements year in and year out when he played roughly two-thirds the number of games that the best goaltenders in the NHL played. Tretiak did not have a goals-against average under 3.00 in the entire decade of the 1970s. Not only was he the losing goalie in 1972, but he was also the losing goalie for the Soviets in the semifinals of the 1976 Canada Cup. He was pulled in the Challenge Cup of 1979 and pulled again in the Olympics in 1980. His resumé of World Championships and Olympic gold medals was built against inferior teams dotted with only a few bona fide players. He played on a stacked club team in Russia that had the country's best players funnelled onto its roster so that it was effectively the Soviet national team. He's known primarily in this country for two things: he was the goalie for the Soviets in 1972, and he had an outstanding game against the Montreal Canadiens on New Year's Eve 1975 as part of the "Super Series," when a pair of Soviet club teams played a series of exhibition games against NHL teams.

I think Tretiak was a very good goaltender. But he never had to endure the travel and other rigours of the NHL. When playing the best in the world—which was clearly Canada in those days—he had a losing record and a less-than-stellar goals-against average. Tretiak's contribution to the game of hockey has been outstanding. As an ambassador, a teacher and a player on the international scene, he is revered. His name conjures up tremendous memories, and they definitely have some value when discussing the merits of his inclusion among the Hall's honoured members. But I'm of the opinion that his statistical record, the quality of his opposition—which I feel was vastly inferior game in and game out to what his North American counterparts faced—his performance against Canada and the fact that he did not play in the NHL are reasons enough to exclude him. That is my opinion. The fact that he is in and Paul Henderson is not raises some serious questions in my mind about the induction process.

Paul Henderson is regarded as a national treasure, and so he should be. Yes, he had his finest moment as an athlete in the most emotionally charged hockey series ever played. But what frustrates fans who feel as I do about him is that it's been almost forgotten that he scored seven goals and 10 points in those eight games. And another thing: after the Soviets won game five, the first one played in Russia, the series stood at three wins for the Soviets, one for Canada, and one tie. That left three games to play, all of them in a hostile Moscow arena, and Team Canada needed to win all three to take the series.

The Canadians won all three games, each by one goal—and Paul Henderson scored the winner each time. In game seven, his winning goal was scored with 2:06 to play. All he did on that goal was beat four Soviet defenders and then, while falling, put it high into the net behind Tretiak. If Henderson hadn't scored that winning goal in game seven, game eight would have been superfluous—a Russian win. Hollywood's best screenwriters could never have created a better scene than what played out in real life in those eight games—especially on that final Thursday in September 1972. Thirty-four seconds to go in the final game, and the series, and Henderson jams home his own rebound for the game- and series-winning goal. The picture is worth a million words. It will stand the test of time.

So why isn't Paul Henderson in the Hall of Fame? Here, in the Hall's own words, are the criteria used to judge whether a player should be inducted: playing ability, sportsmanship, character and his contribution to the team or teams and to the game of hockey in general. Notice that there's nothing about scoring 500 goals. Nothing about winning a Stanley Cup, which is a good thing because there are currently 41 players in the Hall who didn't win a championship. Let's check off the criteria point by point and see how Henderson fares.

Playing ability. Henderson was a Memorial Cup winner with Hamilton in 1962. He played in two Stanley Cup finals and two NHL All-Star Games. He scored 20 goals seven times, scored 30 twice, played in more than 750 NHL games and racked up 247 career goals. Henderson was the last man in the Original Six era to record a four-goal game; he scored four goals for Detroit against the New York Rangers on October 27, 1966. On top of his NHL career, he played another 365 games in the WHA, scoring 141 goals. These numbers are better than those of more than three dozen current inductees, and when you combine what was a very solid pro career with his incredible accomplishments in the Summit Series, how can there be any doubt about the man's playing ability? After all, would it not have been his playing ability that earned him a spot on Team Canada?

Sportsmanship. In an era when the attitude seemed to be "an eye for an eye, a tooth for a tooth," Henderson drew but one fighting major during his entire pro career. He played hard but within the rules; he was never suspended, yet never backed down from confrontation.

Character. As a fan, how do you measure character? How about three game winners in a row in the greatest series ever played? How about returning to the ice against doctor's advice, after suffering a slight concussion, to score your second goal of the game—as Henderson did in game five of the Summit Series? Think about this next one, now: could a player who was devoid of character possibly have played for notorious taskmasters Sid Abel or Punch Imlach?

Contribution to his team. During the 1962 Memorial Cup playoffs, Henderson contributed 10 points in 10 games. In 1962–63, he scored 49 goals in 48 games, which by the way led the Ontario Hockey Association. Henderson scored 21 goals in 46 games with Detroit in 1966–67. Bruce MacGregor led the Wings that year with 28. Norm Ullman was next with 26, Gordie Howe had 25 and Dean Prentice scored 23. They played in 70, 68, 69 and 68 games respectively. Henderson was third on the Toronto Maple Leafs in goals and points in 1970–71. In 1971–72, the season he was picked for Team Canada, he scored 38 goals—15 more than the next two highest-scoring players, Norm Ullman and Ron Ellis. Is that not contributing? Keep in mind that this is all aside from what he did for Team Canada. He should have been handed his ticket into the Hall the minute he got off the plane from Moscow.

Contribution to the game of hockey in general. Quite simply Henderson's contribution to the game can be defined in one word: impact. As we roll through the 40th calendar year since the Summit Series and the goal Henderson scored to decide that incredible event, the impact of his goal is still being felt, on fans and the game itself.

If you're 45 or under as of 2012, what you know about the Summit Series probably comes from DVDs, interviews and old footage on YouTube or television. Maybe you've had the chance to meet or talk to some of the players from Team Canada; maybe you've even met Paul

Henderson. Family, friends or colleagues you've spoken to about it remember exactly where they were when Henderson scored *the* goal, just as surely as others remember the first moon landing or the assassination of JFK. You can sense in their stories just what an impact those players had on them that September—and more important what Henderson's goal represented to millions of Canadians and for millions of hockey fans the world over.

If you're older than 45, you need no such prompting. The Summit Series likely resonates as the greatest sporting event you ever witnessed. Watching the grainy footage, listening to the iconic Foster Hewitt as he calls the most significant goal in the history of the sport of hockey: it's a permanent time machine that transports you to another part of your life, a time that for many is cherished. Whether you were in school, perhaps early years on the job, or at home with your family, it didn't matter. For one afternoon, in September of 1972, Canada simply shut down. It was as if the world stopped spinning on its axis, and time stood still. What a goal, can't believe we won, how did he do it again, how did we come from behind, again—you just couldn't believe it. As we look back 40 years and measure what we've become as a nation, and not just as a *hockey* nation, we again have to measure the goal with one word—impact.

Consider this. Every single solitary instance of a non–North American player skating in the NHL, every single hockey tournament at any age level that features a Canadian team, owes its existence to the Summit Series. The drama, the comeback, the phenomenal photo taken by the late Frank Lennon, the two solitudes of Paul Henderson from Ontario and Yvan Cournoyer from Quebec in front of the fallen Tretiak: this moment is the genesis of the global sport hockey has become today.

The Summit Series begat Canadian participation in the World Juniors, then the inaugural Canada Cup (later known as the World Cup), the Challenge Cup of 1979 and a smattering of pros being allowed in Olympic competition. Then in the 1970s and '80s came the Swedes and Finns, players from the Czech Republic and Slovakia, complementing the rosters of NHL teams, and in some cases leading them. Our appetite was whetted by a seemingly endless series of phenomenal games and exhibition series against the Soviets, and then came the final instalments of this great change, the Eastern Bloc players admitted to play in the NHL and the full-on participation of NHLers in the greatest tournament of all, the Winter Olympics. All these developments can be traced back to the Summit Series, not just because it established an international rivalry but because of *how* it was played and the drama with which it ended. And because the volumes of material that have been spoken, written and broadcast about it since can point to only one conclusion: that series and that goal scored by Paul Henderson represent the greatest impact any single event has had on its sport in the history of sports.

As I write this, campaigns have sprung up again in support of Paul Henderson's induction into the Hockey Hall of Fame. He is embroiled in a fight that makes those old wars on the ice seem trivial, at least for the moment; after his initial two-year battle with leukemia, he has learned that the cancer has spread, and he will soon begin a more aggressive fight against the disease. I hope that the medical measures will allow him to continue some quality of life and reasonable health. (If you feel like supporting a petition for Paul Henderson's place in the Hockey Hall of Fame, please visit www.putpaulinthehall.ca and cast your vote. You too can have an impact.)

If the Summit Series taught us anything, it's that Canada might frequently be the best hockey nation in the world, but we've never been as dominant as we like to think. In any given year, somewhere on the international scene, Canada will lose a tournament or a game, maybe finish second or third instead of winning. And the next day, without fail, someone, somewhere in the media will warn, "The rest of the world is catching up (or has caught up) to Canada."

Let's see. We needed a series-winning goal with 34 seconds to play in the deciding game to beat the Russians in 1972. We needed overtime in game two of a best-of-three series to beat Czechoslovakia in the inaugural Canada Cup in 1976. (That Czech team, by the way, beat Canada 1–0 in the round-robin portion of the tournament.) A team made up primarily of Canadians was smoked 6–0 in the third game of a three-game series for the 1979 Challenge Cup. Canada was hammered 8–1 by Russia in the final of the 1981 Canada Cup. Canada sent a junior team to compete in the World Junior Championships every year from 1974 on, but did not win a gold medal until 1982. In fact, after taking two bronze and two silver medals in its first four years of competition, Canada slumped to finishes of fifth, fifth and seventh in 1979, 1980 and 1981. Factor in Team USA's Miracle on Ice in 1980, as well as Sweden's emergence as an international power (a gold-medal win at the 1981 World Juniors and a trip to the finals of the 1984 Canada Cup). And since NHL players have been permitted in the Winter Olympics, Canada has twice won gold but also twice failed even to reach the podium. At exactly what point over the past 40 years would you say that Canada exhibited complete dominance in the sport of hockey?

On March 3, 1875, the earliest recorded hockey game was played at the Victoria Rink in Montreal, between McGill and the Victoria Skating Club. The teams played with nine men a side. Eighteen years later, the governor general of Canada, Sir Frederick Arthur Stanley—Lord Stanley of Preston, soon to become the Earl of Derby—commissioned the Dominion Challenge Cup of Canada, which would eventually become known as the Stanley Cup. Hundreds of thousands of lives have been altered because of these humble beginnings. This great game, now enjoyed worldwide, had its origins in Canada, was developed in Canada, was excelled at by Canadians and continues to be excelled at by Canadians. Let's not be a close-minded nation of fanatics that expects some sort of perpetual lock on hockey supremacy. Let's enjoy the sport for what it is. A tremendously entertaining, fast and furious game, played at such a pace and level of skill in so many places that on any day the question of who's best can perhaps be most accurately answered with that old road-hockey decider: "Next goal wins!"

Following are some Team Canada 72 trivia questions regarding the players and the games of the greatest hockey series ever played.

TEAM CANADA TRIVIA

1) Who was the only member of Team Canada 1972 not to play in a losing game?

Serge Savard of the Montreal Canadiens. Savard played in all four wins and the tie in game three in Winnipeg. He suffered a cracked ankle bone in the Winnipeg game and probably should have sat out the rest of the series, but he rejoined the team on the ice for game six in Russia.

2) Who was Canada's third goaltender?

Eddie Johnston. Johnston did not play in any of the eight games against Russia although he dressed as a backup on several occasions. He saw action in one of the exhibition games against

Sweden. That game ended 4–4. It was the second of a two-game set played in Sweden between game four in Vancouver and the last four games of the series in Russia. Canada won the first game against Sweden, 4–1. In the 4–4 tie, Canada tied the game with 47 seconds to play courtesy of a shorthanded goal by Phil Esposito.

If you can believe it, Team Canada played an exhibition game the day after game eight against the Soviets. After being up until approximately 6 a.m., the players had to pack up and fly to Prague for a game against Czechoslovakia. Incredible as it may seem, the game ended in a 3–3 tie. Canada's Serge Savard scored the tying goal with four seconds to play. It seems as if they just were not destined to lose.

3) Who were the only two right-handed shots on the Soviet team in 1972?

Vladimir Petrov and Yuri Liapkin. All of the other players shot left.

4) What were the final penalty totals for the two teams?

Russia ended up with 84 penalty minutes. Canada had 147.

5) What were the total shots on goal in the eight games?

Canada 267, Russia 227. Phil Esposito led all shooters with 52 shots. Alexander Maltsev was the highest on Russia with 32.

6) What were the power-play statistics in the eight games?

Russia's power play went 9-for-38 for a 23.7 percent success rate. Canada scored just two power-play goals in 23 chances over the eight games. That's 8.7 percent. Can you believe that? Yvan Cournoyer in game two and Phil Esposito in game eight scored Canada's only power-play goals.

Russia scored three shorthanded goals to Canada's one. And what a goal that one was. Pete Mahovlich scored the insurance goal in game two with Pat Stapleton in the box. From an aesthetic point of view, this goal and Paul Henderson's winner in game seven were the two nicest goals of the 31 Canada scored.

7) How many players on both teams played in all eight games?

The Soviet team had eight players play all eight, Team Canada had seven. For Russia, it was Vladislav Tretiak, Alexander Yakushev, Vladimir Shadrin, Vladimir Petrov, Boris Mikhailov, Alexander Maltsev, Vladimir Lutchenko and Alexei Tsygankov. For Canada, it was Phil Esposito, Paul Henderson, Yvan Cournoyer, Brad Park, Bobby Clarke, Ron Ellis and Gary Bergman.

INDEX

Liam Maguire is regarded as the world's number-one NHL historian. *Next Goal Wins!* is his third book. Liam is the president of Liam Maguire's Ultimate Hockey, a new online hockey portal that will ultimately be the go-to spot for hockey audio, video, blogs, contests and exclusive interviews. In addition, he travels Canada and the United States speaking at numerous events and fundraisers as an entertainer with his encyclopedia knowledge of Canada's national sport. To date, his appearances number more than 2,500 coast to coast. Along the way, he has worked with Gordie Howe, Bobby Orr, Bobby Hull, Jean Beliveau and Wayne Gretzky, who has written the foreword to *Next Goal Wins!* Ultimate Hockey can be found on Facebook, and you can follow Liam on Twitter at Liams_Hockey.